On Message

On Message:

Communicating the Campaign

by
Pippa Norris, John Curtice, David Sanders,
Margaret Scammell and Holli A. Semetko

SAGE Publications
London • Thousand Oaks • New Delhi

A SAGE Publications Ltd
6 Bonhill Street
London EC2A 4PU

SAGE Publications Inc.
2455 Teller Road
Thousand Oaks, California 91320

SAGE Publications India Pvt Ltd
32, M-Block Market
Greater Kailash-I
New Delhi 110 048

British Cataloguing in Publication Data

A catalogue record for this book is available from the British Library

ISBN 0 7619 6073 2
ISBN 0 7619 6074 0 (pbk)

Library of Congress catalog card number

Typeset by Anneset, Weston-super-Mare, Somerset
Printed and bound in Great Britain by Athenaeum Press, Gateshead

Contents

List of tables   vi
List of figures   ix
Preface   xi
Notes about the authors   xiii

Part I: Context   1
1. Theories of Political Communications   1
2. The Campaign Context   22
3. Understanding Media Effects   43

Part II: Process   53
4. The Party Strategy   53
5. The News Agenda   69
6. The Public's Reaction   85

Part III: Impact   97
7. The Impact on Civic Engagement   97
8. The Impact on the Public's Agenda   114
9. The Effects of Television News on Party Preferences   130
10. The Effects of Newspapers   152

11. Conclusions: The Impact of Political Communications   170

Technical Appendix   187
Bibliography   198
Name Index   210
Subject Index   213

List of Tables

2.1   National Daily Press: Ownership, Circulation and Partisanship   25

2.2   Favourability of the Press, 1997 Campaign   27

2.3   Favourability of the Press, 1992 Campaign   28

2.4   Ratio of Election Broadcasts and Proportion of Election News, Major Parties 1964–1997   30

2.5   Favourability of Television News Coverage, 1997 Campaign   32

2.6   General Election Expenditure, 1983–97   39

2.7   General Election Expenditure at Constant Prices, 1983–97   39

2.8   Type of Campaign Expenditure, 1997   40

4.1   Issues in the Major Party Manifestos, 1997   63

4.2   Comparison of Party Agendas: Manifestos, Press Releases and Party Election Broadcasts, 1997   64

4.3   The Internal Coherence of Party Campaigns, 1997   65

4.4   Tone of Press Releases and Party Election Broadcasts by Party, 1997   66

5.1   Change in the Main Subject of Political TV News Stories, 1992 and 1997   73

5.2   Main Subject of Front-Page Broadsheet Newspaper Stories, 1997   76

5.3   Main Subject of Front-Page Tabloid Newspaper Stories, 1997   77

5.4   Main Subject of Front-Page Newspaper Stories, 1992–97   78

5.5   Party Press Releases and News Agendas, 1997   81

5.6   Correlations between Party Press Releases and News Agendas, 1997   82

5.7   Correlations between Party Press Releases and Newspaper Agendas, 1997   83

6.1   The Audience for Party Election Broadcasts, 1997   89

6.2   Social Characteristics of the News Audience, 1997   91

6.3   Political Characteristics of the News Audience, 1997   92

6.4   The Audience for Party Election Broadcasts by Vote, 1997   93

6.5   Public Evaluation of Television Coverage, 1997   94

6.6   Public Evaluation of Standards of Television News, 1997   95

7.1   Changes in Knowledge of Party Policies   103

7.2	Changes in Knowledge of Party Policies by Patterns of Media Use and Attention	104
7.3	Regression Models of Knowledge of Party Policy Scale by Patterns of Media Use, with Social Controls	105
7.4	Knowledge of Civics by Patterns of Media Use and Attention	106
7.5	Knowledge of Candidates by Patterns of Media Use and Attention	107
7.6	Changes in Political Efficacy by Patterns of Media Use and Attention	108
7.7	Changes in Political Participation by Patterns of Media Use and Attention	110
7.8	Trends in Reported Patterns of Media Use	111
7.9	Changes in Knowledge, Efficacy and Probability of Voting by Change in TV News Use	112
7.10	Who Turned Off?	113
8.1	Agenda-Setting Effects by Type of Issue	119
8.2	Issue Salience (Open-Ended Measures)	120
8.3	Effects of Exposure to Taxation Video on Issue Salience	121
8.4	Effects of Video Exposure on Issue Salience	122
8.5	Difference of Mean Change in Issue Priority: Corrected Measures	123
8.6	Effects of Video Exposure on Issue Salience: Corrected Measures	124
8.7	The Public's Campaign Agenda	127
9.1	Average Ratings on Party Preferences	137
9.2	Mean Changes in Party Preferences by Positive/Negative News	138
9.3	Direct Effects of Positive and Negative News on Party Preferences	139
9.4	Mean Changes in Party Preferences by Stop-Watch Balance	141
9.5	Direct Effects of Stop-Watch News on Party Preferences	142
9.6	Mean Changes in Party Preferences by Agenda-Setting News	143
9.7	Summary Model of the Effects of News Videos on Party Preferences	144
10.1	Newspaper Partisanship and Vote in 1997	156
10.2	Perceived Partisanship of Newspapers, 1992–97	157
10.3	Change in Conservative and Labour Support during 1997 Campaign by Readership	158
10.4	Logistic Model of Vote Switching in 1997 Campaign by Readership	161
10.5	Change in Conservative and Labour Support by Readership, 1992–97	163
10.6	Logistic Regression of Party Support, 1992–97	165

10.7	Logistic Regression of Newspaper Buying, 1992–97	167
11.1	Change in the Share of the UK Vote, 1992–97	173
11.2	Changes in Voting Intentions during the Long and Short Campaigns, 1996–97	174
11.3	Flow of the Vote Between General Elections, 1992–97	176
11.4	Flow of the Vote During the Long Campaign, May 1996–97	177
11.5	Reported Timing of Voting Decision, 1964–97	179
11.6	Changes in Party Leadership Ratings, Official Campaign	180
11.7	Changes in Party Images, Official Campaign	180
A.1	Response Rate	190
A.2	Weighting Procedure	192
A.3	Timing of 30-Minute Video Experimental Stimuli	195

List of Figures

1.1	The Schematic Model of Political Communications	10
2.1	Partisan Balance of the Press, 1945-97	24
2.2	Audience for Television News	33
2.3	Party Popularity, 1992-97	36
3.1	The 1997 British Election Study	45
5.1	The Main Components of the Agenda-Setting Process	70
6.1	Audience for Evening News (31 March–1 May 1997)	86
6.2	Audience for Current Affairs (March–April 1997)	87
6.3	Election Night Audience, 1997	90
7.1	Core Hypotheses about Civic Engagement	101
8.1	The British Campaign Agenda, 1997	125
9.1	BES Campaign Panel Estimates of Variations in Party Support, 1–30 April 1997	145
9.2	Poll of Poll Estimates of Variations in Party Support, 1–30 April 1997	145
9.3	Conservative Support and Balance of Conservative TV Coverage, April 1997	146
9.4	Labour Support and Balance of Labour TV Coverage, April 1997	146
9.5	Liberal Democrat Support and Balance of Liberal Democrat TV Coverage, April 1997	147
11.1	Campaign Polls 17 March–1 May 1997	175

Preface

In common with most large-scale projects this book has incurred many debts upon the way. The British General Election Study Campaign Panel 1997 was conducted by the Centre for Research into Elections and Social Trends (CREST). CREST is an ESRC Research Centre linking Social and Community Planning Research (SCPR) and Nuffield College, Oxford, in conjunction with Pippa Norris (Harvard University). In the Campaign Panel Waves B to D and the Election Study module on wave A were funded by the ESRC (grant no. H552/255/003). The survey was directed by Anthony Heath, Roger Jowell, John Curtice and Pippa Norris and it would not have been possible without the help of Geoffrey Evans and Bridget Taylor at Nuffield College, Katarina Thomson and Alison Park at SCPR, and Ann Mair at Strathclyde University. We would also like to thank all the fieldwork interviewers and all the respondents who cooperated with the 1997 survey.

The experimental studies in television news were directed by David Sanders and Pippa Norris, and were organized at the University of Essex. The project was also generously funded by the ESRC (grant no. R000236756). The fieldwork depended upon the invaluable assistance of many graduate students at the University of Essex and the University of Westminster, who were ably organized by Deborah Harris. We would also like to thank the University of Westminster for fieldwork facilities. We greatly benefited from the help of Steven Barnett in the Department of Communications, University of Westminster, and also from Stephen Ansolabehere (MIT) and Shanto Iyengar (UCLA) who advised us on the research design.

The content analysis of Television and Press News during the 1997 British general election campaign was directed by Maggie Scammell (University of Liverpool) and Holli Semetko (University of Amsterdam). It was funded by the ESRC (grant no. R000236802) and the Amsterdam School of Communications Research. The coding was conducted by Peter Goddard and Katy Parry at the University of Liverpool and we are also grateful for the research assistance of Suzan van der Post.

The data on television audiences from the Broadcasters Audience Research Board (BARB) was generously supplied by Bill Meredith and we would also like to acknowledge the assistance of Jane Sancho-Aldrich and Bob Towler at the Independent Television Commission who provided data from the ITC survey *Television: The Public's View*. We would also like to thank Peter Christopherson at CARMA International Ltd. for additional content analysis data.

This book is a companion volume to three closely related studies focusing on different aspects of electoral change: *Critical Elections: British Parties and Voters in Long-term Perspective* edited by Geoffrey Evans and Pippa Norris (Sage 1999), Alice Brown *et al. The Scottish Electorate* (Macmillan 1998), and *New Labour and the Future of the Left* by Anthony Heath *et al.* (forthcoming). This book is the product of collaboration between all the authors who worked together on this project in the United States, Britain and The Netherlands, with opportunities to come together mainly in conjunction with professional conferences. In terms of the division of labour, Margaret Scammell had the primary responsibility for Chapter 4 on party strategy, Holli Semetko for Chapter 5 on the news agendas, David Sanders for Chapter 9 on the impact of television and John Curtice for Chapter 10 on the influence of the press. We thank Katarina Thomson for material in the Technical Appendix. Pippa Norris contributed the remainder with invaluable help from all colleagues. As a results of our collaboration we hope that the overall book is more than the sum of its parts.

Our intellectual debts are many and varied. We would particularly like to acknowledge Jean Blondel and the members of ESRC's Election Study Management Advisory Committee (ESMAC) for supporting the research. We also appreciate comments from colleagues and discussants when draft papers were presented at a series of professional meetings in 1997 and 1998, including annual conventions of the Political Studies Association of the UK, the Elections, Parties and Public Opinion section of the PSA (EPOP), the European Consortium of Political Research, the Midwest Political Science Association, the American Political Science Association and the International Communication Association. Lastly the book would not have been possible without the constant encouragement, stimulus and critical advice from Marvin Kalb, Marion Just, Tim Cook, Fred Schauer, Richard Parker, Anna Greenberg, Edie Holway, Nancy Palmer and all colleagues at the Shorenstein Center on the Press, Politics and Public Policy at the Kennedy School of Government.

Harvard University, Cambridge, November 1998

Notes About the Authors

John Curtice is Deputy Director of CREST, and Professor of Politics and Director of the Social Statistics Laboratory at the University of Strathclyde. His publications include *How Britain Votes* (1985, with Roger Jowell and Anthony Heath); *Understanding Political Change* (1991, with Anthony Heath and others); and *Labour's Last Chance?* (1994, co-edited). He has been a co-editor of SCPR's British Social Attitudes series since 1994 and is a regular consultant and commentator on electoral matters for the media.

Pippa Norris is Associate Director (Research) at the Shorenstein Center on the Press, Politics and Public Policy at the Kennedy School of Government, Harvard University. Recent books include, among others, *Critical Elections* (1999, with Geoffrey Evans); *Critical Citizens* (1999); *Elections and Voting Behaviour* (1998); *Britain Votes 1997* (1997); and *Electoral Change Since 1945* (1997). She was co-director of the 1997 British Election Study and co-edits *The Harvard International Journal of Press/Politics*.

David Sanders is Professor of Government and Pro-Vice-Chancellor (Research) at the University of Essex. His books include *Patterns of Political Instability (1981), Lawmaking and Cooperation in International Politics* (1986) and *Losing an Empire, Finding a Role* (1990). His recent publications include articles on electoral forecasting and outcomes in *Political Studies, Electoral Studies, Political Quarterly, Parliamentary Affairs*, and contributions to numerous edited volumes. He is co-editor of the *British Journal of Political Science*.

Margaret Scammell is Senior Lecturer in Social Psychology at the London School of Economics, and she has previously taught at the University of Liverpool and been a freelance journalist. As well as articles on political communications for journals such as *Media, Culture and Society*, the *European Journal of Marketing* and *Political Studies*, her books include *Designer Politics* (1995) and *The Press and Democracy* (co-edited with Holli A. Semetko, 1999).

Holli A. Semetko is Professor of Audience and Public Opinion Research and Chair of the Department of Communication Science, and directs the

International Ph.D. Program at the Amsterdam School of Communication Research at the University of Amsterdam. Her publications include journal articles and book chapters on US and European news media, elections, and public opinion, as well as three books, *The Formation of Campaign Agendas* (1991 with Jay Blumler, Michael Gurevitch and David Weaver); *Germany's 'Unity Election'* (1994 with Klaus Schoenbach); and *The Press and Democracy* (1999, co-edited with Margaret Scammell). She is currently writing *Campaigning on Television: News and Elections in Comparative Perspective.*

PART I

CONTEXT

---

1   Theories of Political Communications

On 1 May 1997 the sheer size of the Labour landslide victory surprised almost everyone, even Tony Blair. In the immediate aftermath, a common consensus quickly emerged to explain Labour's historic success after eighteen years in the wilderness. The conventional account of the election stressed that Blair won as a result of a radical re-branding of the image of New Labour. Peter Mandelson, chief Labour strategist, was credited as the primary architect of victory. The creation of New Labour started in the mid-1980s and continued under the leadership of Neil Kinnock, John Smith and Tony Blair. The project involved three major components: the modernization of the party organization, by-passing activists so that internal power flowed upwards towards the central leadership and downwards towards ordinary party members; revision of traditional party policies with the abandonment of socialist nostrums and the adoption of a 'third way' straddling the middle ground of British politics; and last, but not least, the deployment of strategic communications to convey the image of New Labour.

The techniques of professional political communications were commonly regarded as so effective that Labour managed to stay 'on message' throughout the period of the 'long' campaign in the year before the election, and the six-week official campaign from mid-March to 1 May 1997. Moreover, in this view Labour's assiduous wooing of the press paid off in reversing their historical disadvantage: during the 1997 election twice as many people were reading a newspaper which backed Labour than were reading one backing the Conservatives. *The Sun*'s defection into the Labour camp is often regarded as particularly important. In contrast, Conservative defeat has often been attributed to their failure to project a consistently positive image, with their election campaign derailed by leadership splits over Europe and dogged by news headlines dominated by sleaze. The lessons of strategic communications apparently embodied in Labour's remarkable victory have been noted by many other parties, in the United States and Europe, not least by the Conservative Party in Britain.

But is the conventional view of the importance of strategic political communications correct? Often popular interpretations are based on *post hoc* explanations. The party which wins an election, especially with a landslide, is usually assumed to have run the most effective campaign. In this view the proof of a campaign is in the votes. Party consultants, strategists and journalists who frame our view of the outcome have a natural tendency and self-interest to believe that their role was important, indeed decisive. But if we look more closely and critically, is there systematic evidence to support this interpretation? The 1997 British general election campaign provides a case-study for testing two central claims: are strategic communications by parties important for electoral success? And do the news media have a powerful impact upon the electorate in election campaigns?

One of the most striking developments in recent years is the widespread adoption of the techniques of strategic communications by political parties. This process involves a coordinated plan which sets out party objectives, identifies target voters, establishes the battleground issues, orchestrates consistent key themes and images, prioritizes organizational and financial resources, and lays out the framework within which campaign communications operate. This development is part of the 'professionalization' or 'modernization' of campaigning, giving a greater role to technical experts in public relations, news management, advertising, speech-writing and market research. Many observers assume that the use of these techniques has become critical for the outcome of modern elections in many countries (Swanson and Mancini 1996).

New Labour's victory in 1997 was widely regarded as a textbook triumph of packaging over politics, spin over substance, and image-building over ideology. This conventional explanation accords with an expanding literature which emphasizes the growing importance of political marketing, spin doctors and sound-bites, and the rise in the power of the news media as 'king-makers' in Britain (Franklin 1994; Kavanagh 1995; Scammell 1995; Jones 1995). The first concern of this book is therefore to establish how far strategic communications are important today for electoral success. In particular, did Labour's communication strategy prove the most effective, as widely assumed, in the 1997 British general election? Were Labour most successful in influencing the news agenda? And as a result did they boost their party fortunes during the long and short campaign? Our answers, contrary to the conventional wisdom, are no, no and no. Insights into this issue help us to understand the process of strategic communications and its limitations in the modern campaign.

Equally important, many observers have emphasized the rise in the power of the mass media and their growing influence, for good or ill, in election campaigns. Some hope that television and the press can help to mobilize and energize voters, generate effective public deliberation which informs citizens, and produce 'enlightened preferences' (Gelman and King 1993; Lupia and McCubbins 1998). Others fear that predominant news values and journalistic practices lead to campaign coverage focusing on the strategic election game, tabloid scandal and down-market sensationalism rather than serious policy debate. Such practices are believed to encourage public cynicism, to alienate voters, and to lead to civic disengagement (Fallows 1996; Patterson 1993; Putnam 1995; Cappella and Jamieson 1997).

The second major concern of this book is to establish how far political coverage on television and in the national press has the capacity to influence the electorate, in particular their levels of civic engagement, issue priorities, and party preferences. We argue that the more exaggerated hopes and fears overestimate the power of newspapers and television to change the electorate within the limited period of an election campaign. Nevertheless we demonstrate that there is systematic and plausible evidence for consistent long-term learning, mobilization and persuasion effects associated with patterns of media use. Moreover, in contrast to previous British studies, we show that newspapers have only limited ability to change party support during the campaign but nevertheless positive television news has the capacity to boost a party's fortunes significantly in the short term.

These issues are important in analyzing the specific reasons for the outcome of the 1997 British general election, but also more generally for understanding the impact of party communications and the news media in a modern democracy. While there are many other books about the 1997 election, including a companion study focusing on long-term social and ideological dealignment in the electorate (Evans and Norris 1999), there has been little examination of the systematic evidence about the effects of political communications in Britain. Since the structure of the information environment and the political system is important for electoral choice, we need to test whether we can generalize to the British context from the extensive literature on political communications in the United States and Europe. This book presents the first results of a research design combining three major elements: content analysis of party and news messages during April 1997; the 1997 British Election Study (BES) campaign panel survey; and an experimental study of the effects of television news (see Chapter 3 for details). To consider the central issues this introduction lays out alternative theories about the influence of political communications, describes the core conceptual framework, and outlines the plan of this book.

Theories of Mass Propaganda

We can identify three main schools of thought which have developed to account for the influence of political communications: pre-war theories of mass propaganda, post-war theories of partisan reinforcement, and recent theories of cognitive, agenda-setting and persuasion effects which form the framework for this book.

The earliest accounts of mass communications, popular in the 1920s and 1930s, were greatly impressed by the rapid growth and potential reach of mass communications, and stressed that the public could easily be swayed by propaganda on the radio and in newspapers. In *Public Opinion*, first published in 1922, Walter Lippmann emphasized that the 'manufacture of consent' and the 'arts of persuasion' were nothing new, since there had always been popular demagogues. Nevertheless he believed that the growth in circulation of the popular press, developments in advertising, and the new media of moving pictures and the wireless, had decisively changed the ability of leaders to manipulate public opinion:

> Within the life of the generation now in control of affairs, persuasion has become a self-conscious art and a regular organ of government. None of us begins to understand the consequences, but it is no daring prophecy to say that the knowledge of how to create consent will alter every political calculation and modify every political premise. (Lippmann 1997)

Not only were the effects of mass communication pervasive, they were also seen as generally harmful for democracies. Lippmann's premonitions seemed to be confirmed by the use of the media by authoritarian regimes in the inter-war years, and the development of more sophisticated and self-conscious psychological techniques of mass persuasion by the Allies in wartime. In the 1930s the Payne Fund Studies in the United States looked at the impact of movies on delinquency, aggression and prejudice, while early experimental studies by Hovland *et al.* (1949, 1953) examined the impact of the media for planned persuasion (McQuail 1992; Lowery and DeFleur 1995). Popular accounts in the inter-war years reinforced the notion that the mass media could have a direct and decisive impact upon shaping public opinion, and ultimately voting choices.

Theories of Partisan Reinforcement

Yet propaganda theories came under strong challenge from the first systematic research using the modern techniques of sample surveys to examine public opinion. Paul Lazarsfeld, Bernard Berelson and Hazel Gaudet at Columbia University used panel surveys in their classic study of Erie County during the 1940–44 American elections, in *The People's Choice* (Lazarsfeld *et al.* 1944; Berelson *et al.* 1954). The Erie County study concluded that the main impact of the campaign was 'reinforcement not change', since partisans were strengthened in their voting choice. In this account elections went through four stages. First, as the campaign gathered momentum the rising volume of political news meant that people who had not been interested began to pay attention. As citizens woke up to the campaign, many increased their exposure to political information, thereby increasing their interest, in an interactive 'virtuous circle'. To cope with the rising tide of political propaganda that became available, people brought selective attention into play. Partisans tuned into the information most congruent with their prior predispositions: in 1940 more Democrats listened to speeches by Roosevelt while more Republicans tuned into Wilkie. Political propaganda thereby served mainly to reinforce party support, reducing defections from the ranks. Once sufficient information had been acquired from the campaign, Lazarsfeld suggested, for many people uncertainty evaporated and the voting decision crystallized.

Nevertheless Lazarsfeld suggested that there were clear socioeconomic biases in 'the attentive public' so that the more educated became most informed as the campaign progressed. There was a small but politically important group of waverers who tended to be less attentive to the campaign, and (by implication) less informed than average (1944: 95–100). The conclusions undermined the assumptions of liberal democratic theory that elections should involve a process of rational deliberation about issues, candidates and parties by well-informed citizens. The overall message from the Lazarsfeld study was that theories of propaganda had largely exaggerated the effect of political communications on the mass public.

> In summary, then, the people who did most of the reading and listening not only read and heard most of their own partisan propaganda but were also most resistant to conversion because of strong predispositions. And the people most open to conversion – the ones the campaign manager most wanted to reach – read and listened least. . . . The real doubters – the open-minded voters who make a sincere attempt to weigh the issues and the candidates dispassionately for the good of the country as a whole – exist mainly in deferential campaign propaganda, in textbooks on civics, in the movies, and in the minds of some political idealists. In real life, they are few indeed. (Lazarsfeld *et al.* 1944: 95–100)

Following in Lazarsfeld's footsteps, the new orthodoxy in post-war American studies stressed theories of minimal consequences, which down-played media influence (Klapper 1960). The earliest studies of the effects of television in Britain lent further weight to these conclusions. Many anticipated that television would become a powerful new weapon in the hands of political parties but the first systematic survey analysis in Britain emphasized that the overall impact of mediated communications was essentially one of reinforcement not change (Trenaman and McQuail 1961; Blumler and McQuail 1968). After the Erie County studies over twenty years elapsed before another study analysing individual-level change within the American campaign was produced (Mendelsohn and O'Keefe 1976; Patterson and McClure 1976).

Social and Party Alignments: It's Class, Stupid

If campaign communication was largely unimportant for the outcome, what was decisive? Social psychological theories developed by Campbell *et al.* in *The American Voter* (1960) came to provide the conventional understanding of electoral behaviour. This framework became widely influential in Britain following publication of *Political Change in Britain* (1969, 2nd ed. 1974) by David Butler and Donald Stokes, which shared many of the same concepts and theoretical assumptions developed by the Michigan school.

Drawing on the British Election Study from 1963 to 1970, Butler and Stokes argued that politics remained peripheral to most people's lives: the British electorate rarely participated politically and had minimal involvement in civic life. The typical British voter was seen as fairly uninformed about politics, falling far short of the expectations of citizenship in liberal theories of representative democracy. Butler and Stokes concluded that few people had consistent and stable opinion about well-known issues which divided the parties. Yet despite widespread ignorance about politics and minimal interest, nevertheless about three-quarters of the British electorate cast their vote. When faced with the choice of parties at the ballot box, Butler and Stokes concluded that British voters sought cognitive short-cuts, or 'standing decisions', to guide them through elections. As in the United States, during periods of stable partisan alignment, voters in Britain were seen as being rooted for many years, even for their lifetime, to one or other of the major parties.

Communications were critical, but largely operating at the interpersonal level, since political attitudes were believed to be reinforced through discussions with friends, colleagues and family who shared similar party attachments. Socialization theory explained how party loyalties developed when influenced by the family and social milieu of voters, including their neighbourhood, workplace and community. Partisan newspapers were also regarded as important reinforcing mechanisms, since people read the paper which most agreed with their own viewpoint. The role of the press was therefore primarily to mobilize, rather than to convert, partisan voters. For Butler and Stokes, modern party loyalties were founded on the rock of class identities although there was evidence for a weakening relationship as early as the 1960s, partly due to the influence of television (Butler and Stokes 1974: 419).

If voting behaviour is stable, there is little room for the influence of issues debated during the campaign, news coverage of leaders' speeches, or indeed any short-term flux in party support. If voters are anchored for a lifetime, the campaign can be expected to reinforce partisans, to bring them 'home', and to mobilize them to turn out, but not to determine patterns of voting choice. Electoral studies therefore turned to under-standing structural determinants on the vote (see, for example, Heath *et al.* 1985, 1991, 1994). Because of this dominant paradigm, beyond some occasional articles, it was not until two decades after Blumler and McQuail (1968) that a new study re-examined the effects of the news media in British campaigns (Miller 1991).

Yet the traditional Michigan framework is less useful today due to social and partisan dealignment. In common with many advanced industrialized societies, since the early 1970s Britain has experienced a weakening of the traditional social anchors of voting behaviour. *Critical Elections* (Evans and Norris 1999) found that for political reasons the process of dealignment has persisted and deepened in recent years. In the 1997 election, class voting reached its lowest level since the BES series began; the proportion of the middle class voting Labour was far higher than in any previous general election since 1964. The strength of party identification has also weakened over successive elections during the last three decades, a process that continued in 1997, so that the proportion of strong loyalists plummeted from 44 per cent of the electorate in 1964 to only 16 per cent in 1997. The classic left–right divide over the role of the state in the economy, which is usually the basic ideological cleavage in the British electorate, proved to be more weakly associated with Labour voting than in any previous contest. Lacking stable social and partisan anchors, voters may become more open to the influence of campaign factors: evaluations of the government's record, particularly on the economy, preferences about party policies, perceptions of party and leadership images, and the way all these factors are communicated to the public.

It's the Economy, Stupid

Given the evidence of social and partisan dealignment, an alternative school of thought has focused on theories of political economy stressing the importance of 'pocket-book' voting. One popular account of the 1997 election suggests that the outcome was largely decided by the events of 'Black Wednesday' with the currency crisis following Britain's withdrawal from ERM in September 1992. The opinion polls seemed to indicate that as a result of this event public opinion switched decisively towards Labour, and then stabilized at a new level, eventually producing Blair's landslide:

> The fate of the Conservative government was essentially settled in September 1992, shortly after their fourth electoral victory in a row. . . . Only a major political shock could have turned things around after that, and this did not happen. (Whiteley 1997)

The argument suggests that the Conservative government lost its reputation for competent economic management because of the effects of the ERM crisis, almost five years before polling day, and they never recovered subsequently as this proved a 'crystallizing' moment for the other factors troubling voters (Sanders 1997b: 68). In this view the next five years were just a question of waiting patiently for the curtain to fall and the Conservatives to exit stage right. Yet, as Harrop (1997) points out, it is not immediately apparent why the events of a few days in September 1992 should continue to have had major reverberations on party fortunes five years later. The electorate's memory must be unusually sharp for this rather abstract and technical issue to have led to the government's downfall.

This explanation draws on the long tradition of political economy which has attempted to predict party support from a few aggregate-level economic and political variables. During the 1990s this approach has developed increasingly sophisticated modelling techniques to demonstrate that the outcome of elections can be forecast, with some degree of accuracy, well before the launch of the official manifestos. These models have typically sought to explain government popularity by reference to variations in certain core macroeconomic variables, like the rates of inflation and unemployment, combined with a few key political events, such as the outbreak of the Falklands War (see, for example, Lewis-Beck 1988; Norpoth *et al.* 1991; Sanders and Price 1994). Forecasting models differ in terms of the precise specifications and modelling techniques they employ. What they share, however, is the emphasis that campaigns do not matter if the voting outcome can be predicted parsimoniously from a few economic indicators. Economic conditions are believed to lead to predictable outcomes, despite fluctuations in the opinion polls and the intense party and media battle to dominate the political agenda during the official campaign (Gelman and King 1993).

In 1992 this approach seemed to provide a plausible account of the outcome: in November 1990 the 'Essex' model forecast that in the next general election the Conservatives could expect to be returned with 42.5 per cent of the popular vote, based on certain levels of inflation and interest rates (Sanders 1991, 1993). This forecast proved remarkably prescient when the Major government was returned in May 1992 with 42.7 per cent of the popular vote. But in 1997 the Essex forecast failed to hit the mark (Sanders 1996, 1997a). Standard pocket-book accounts have difficulties in explaining why the Conservatives won in 1992 in the middle of a recession while in 1997 they lost in the middle of a boom. In the run up to the 1997 election the economic record of the Major government looked remarkably healthy. During the twelve months prior to 1 May, average earnings were rising at 4 per cent, comfortably outstripping inflation at 2.9 per cent. Economic growth (GDP) was around 2.2 per cent, down from the peak of 1994 but still positive, while the rate of unemployment saw a steady decline to around 7.2 per cent Moreover, reflecting these indicators, consumer confidence did show a modest recovery during 1995–97 (Gavin and Sanders 1997). Yet in 1997, unlike in 1983, 1987 and 1992, the pocket-book economy apparently failed to translate into a recovery for the government at the polls. The magic 'feel-good factor', so much discussed in the popular press, seemed to have lost its powers.

Theories of Cognitive, Agenda-setting and Persuasion Effects

If long-term anchors like class and partisan identification have eroded, and yet if it wasn't 'the economy, stupid', then this leaves us scratching our heads for other factors which could account for Labour's victory. For many observers the role of strategic communications represents the most plausible alternative candidate, suggesting that Labour won because of their superiority in image-building, news-management and political marketing (Butler and Kavanagh 1997: 224–43). In this account Mandelsonian magic rebranded Old Labour under the leadership of Tony Blair into a new centrist image, located between the Conservatives on the right and the Liberal Democrats on the left. In contrast during the campaign the Conservatives usually seemed deeply divided, dispirited and mired in sleaze. An important component of this change has been attributed to the switch in partisanship among the press, with more major newspapers backing Labour than in any previous post-war general election (McKie 1998). But is there systematic evidence to show that political communications played a key role in Labour's landslide, as is so often assumed, and that campaign coverage in the news media influenced voters?

To examine this issue let us outline the schematic model about the process of political communications which guides the thinking behind this book. Ever since Harold Lasswell (1949), the literature has commonly understood the process of communications as divided into a series of steps: who (the source) says what (the content) through which channel (the media) to whom (the audience) with what effect (the impact). The central focus of this book, shown in Figure 1.1, concerns the *process* and *effects* of political communications within election campaigns.

In this model the news can be expected to influence public opinion directly through three main avenues: enabling people to keep up with what is happening in the world and mobilizing them to vote (*civic engagement*), defining the priority of major political issues (*agenda-setting*), and shaping people's political preferences (*persuasion*). In turn, these attitudes can be expected to influence reasoned voting choices. These categories are understood to represent a sequence of effects in a dynamic process: from growing information and awareness of a problem (like the issue of Britain's role within the ERM, long delays in hospital waiting lists, or constitutional reform), to rising public concern about these issues, and finally to persuading voters to shift party preferences. Of these factors, most attention in the British literature has been devoted to the media's (particularly newspapers') powers to alter party support in the short term, without taking into account the intermediate steps which may, or may not, lead to changes or reinforcement in voting choices. Let us examine each of the steps in this sequence.

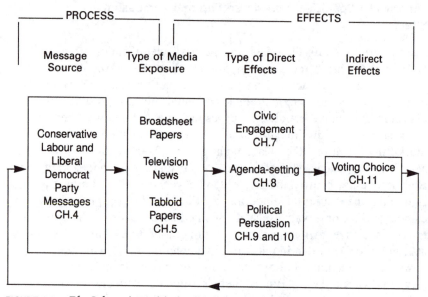

FIGURE 1.1:   *The Schematic Model of Political Communications*

The Process of Campaign Communications

Parties as Communicators

First, a growing literature has emphasized that in many countries parties have become increasingly sophisticated in the use of strategic communications in the attempt to retain control of the agenda or to stay 'on message'. Changes in party campaigning have been richly documented in Nuffield studies covering every British general election since 1945. More recent work has examined how electioneering has been transformed since the 1980s by 'political marketing' and the rise of campaign professionals (Scammell 1995; Kavanagh 1995; Crewe and Harrop 1989; Crewe and Gosschalk 1995). Studies have described the day-to-day party campaigns and the outcome of the 1997 election (Butler and Kavanagh 1997; King 1997; Norris and Gavin 1997; Jones 1997; Geddes and Tonge 1997; Crewe, Gosschalk and Bartle 1998; Evans and Norris 1999). Building upon this foundation, this book highlights and summarizes significant institutional changes in the context of political communications in Britain, notably the rise of a more autonomous press, the growing fragmentation of the electronic media, and how parties have responded to this increasingly complex environment. The development of 24-hour news and the expansion of news outlets makes it far harder than in the post-war era for parties to stay on message in the hurly-burly of the official campaign and to avoid being deflected by unexpected stories, disruptive events, or sudden gaffes. Parties have responded by attempting to maintain control through strategic planning, rapid response and targeted messaging.

After the election the conventional explanation attributed Labour's victory to their effective use of these techniques to stay on message, in contrast to the flubs and flurries experienced by the Conservatives. *The Independent* provided a typical post-election account:

> The party's (Labour) campaign strategy owed much to the success of Bill Clinton's successful campaigns in the United States with its remodelling of his party into New Democrats. . . . The hierarchical structure of the Labour election machine was jettisoned and replaced with a dozen task forces on key seats, party, media, trade unions, attack and rebuttal, presentation, regions, leader's office, message delivery, logistics, and so on. . . . As a result Labour has been following a detailed week-on-week electioneering strategy for almost a year. . . . It also learned from Clinton's people the techniques of how to stay on that strategy and deflect Tory attempts to derail it. Throughout the campaign a central control room at the party's Millbank headquarters provided a rapid rebuttal unit which responded instantly to any new Conservative claims. Its liaison with the media was slick, feeding out approved messages and effectively emasculating attempts to undercut the official version of events. Its use of pagers, the Internet and faxes helped keep its candidates consistently 'on message'. Its advertising was focused and effective. . . . Amid all this the Conservatives were unable to gain any momentum. (Paul Vallely *et al. The Independent*, 3 May 1998)

But much of the popularity of this explanation rests on *post hoc* rationalizations in the aftermath of Blair's victory, reflecting the size of the Labour landslide. If we look more critically at the evidence, did Labour actually 'win' the battle over the campaign agenda? To examine this proposition we need systematic evidence about the strategies of the major parties in the 1997 campaign. One criterion is to see how far the major parties stuck consistently to the themes which they prioritized in daily press releases, party manifestos, and election broadcasts during the 1997 campaign. Parties remaining 'on message' would be consistent throughout the campaign, whereas if they were blown off course they would be more likely to stress different issues on different occasions. Based on content analysis of party messages we examine whether the Labour Party had the most successful campaign in 1997, as commonly assumed, contributing towards its eventual victory.

The News Media

The modern campaign is characterized by a complex and increasingly fragmented news environment. Voters may draw upon information from personal conversations with friends, family and neighbours (Huckfelt and Sprague 1995); direct contact with constituency party canvassers and parliamentary candidates; election coverage in the local and regional press; news and current affairs on regional and national radio; paid party propaganda like posters and newspaper advertisements; party election broadcasts on television and radio; as well as coverage of the campaign in national newspapers; and news and current affairs on terrestrial and satellite television. The local party campaign involving canvassing, leaflets and the local activists, often discounted, is now seen as far more important for voter mobilization (Denver and Hands 1997a). The 'new media' of the internet is rapidly adding another layer of complexity in campaigning (Norris and Jones 1998; Ward and Gibson 1998; Gibson and Ward 1998).

This book focuses in particular upon monitoring the contents and effects of the main evening television news programmes on BBC1 and ITN, and broadsheet and tabloid national newspapers. These media are widely available and are commonly regarded as the most influential in British election campaigns. Our focus therefore provides a strong test of the media effects thesis: if we fail to find any influence from attention to these sources then arguably we would expect to find even weaker effects from many others. These media were also selected because they provide significant contrasts in terms of the coverage of campaign news, and therefore variance in its potential effects. Newspapers are relatively partisan, but television news broadcasts aim to provide more impartial and balanced information. Moreover the differences between broadsheet (quality) and tabloid papers in Britain, as well as between Labour and Conservative-leaning papers, and to a lesser extent between commercial and public service broadcasting, provide important contrasts.

Based on this evidence we examine whether strategic communications actually helped Labour get its preferred messages across via the mass media. Did Labour's communications operation at Millbank Tower influence the news agenda more than the other parties, as many assume? And did television and print journalists follow any party, or were they more autonomous in their priorities? The content analyses allow us to compare the issues stressed by the parties in their press releases with those picked up by television news and the press, to understand who set the media agenda.

The Effects of Political Communications

Part III goes on to consider the impact of political communications on the public. There are multiple ways in which political communications may influence the electoral process and today the literature has moved beyond a narrow focus on voting behaviour (Bryant and Zillman 1994). We argue that we need to distinguish between the impact of political communications on the outcome for government and on individual participants. The 1997 campaign was probably not decisive for the return of the Labour government, but this did not mean that the election broadcasts, or the coverage of opinion polls, or the rallies, meetings and speeches did not affect party supporters.

We also need to draw an important distinction between cumulative and campaign-specific effects from the news. Cumulative media effects are due to repeated exposure to television and the press on the assumption that news habits have a diffuse influence on our values and opinions in a long-term socialization process, analogous to the role of the family, school or neighbourhood. Cumulative effects are monitored by comparing *absolute* differences between groups of media users; for example, whether broadsheet readers are better informed than those who buy tabloids. Since evidence in this study is confined to the period of the long campaign (starting twelve months before polling day), we cannot firmly establish that any persistent differences between groups are due to the news *per se*, rather than the prior predispositions of viewers and readers. Nevertheless we shall argue that, in an interactive process, this seems like a reasonable assumption. Hence, for example, people who are more right-leaning may prefer to buy the *Daily Telegraph*, but over time we would also expect that the paper's culture would influence its regular readers. In the same way the more knowledgeable may turn to the BBC World Service to find out about international affairs, but we would also expect that longtime listeners would learn more about developments from Azerbaijan to Zimbabwe. In this context it is the steady drip-drip-drip of media messages over a prolonged period – for example, the constant repetition of the phrase 'New Labour', the steady series of opinion polls showing the Conservatives in the doldrums, or continuous headlines about government scandal – which is understood gradually to shape our opinions, attitudes and values.

We monitor *short-term media effects* with relative measures which focus on the degree of change among users of different news media within the long (twelve-month) and short (six-week) campaign. For example, as polling day approaches we might expect feelings of political efficacy to increase in general, almost irrespective of the campaign, as citizens come to believe that they can determine the outcome. What we test is whether this sense of efficacy increases more during the campaign among different categories of news users; for example, for regular viewers of television news more than for non-viewers. The focus on relative change, using the time line of the campaign, provides a more satisfactory test of media effects. Relative measures allow us to control for other factors which commonly distinguish both the characteristics of media use and political attitudes, such as higher levels of education among regular readers of broadsheet papers.

As we go on to discuss, we also need to distinguish different types of media effects: on cognitive learning and political mobilization, on agenda-setting, on persuasion, and on voting behaviour. During the course of a campaign citizens may potentially learn more about public affairs, or may alter their issue concerns, without this necessarily translating through into changes in voting behaviour. Reinforcement and mobilization effects are just as important for elections, by generating participation in the democratic process, as the alteration of party preferences.

Lastly, we also need to distinguish *conditional* effects (which specify if *x* then *y*) from *actual* effects which occurred within a given news environment. For example, in practice party political broadcasts are strictly ruled by the conventions of stop-watch balance but it is important to know if this were no longer the case – for example, if Britain adopted political advertising on a commercial basis – whether this would make a difference to party support. Conditional effects often do not appear in the campaign, because of the conventions of news coverage and party campaigning, where there are multiple messages which may cancel each other out. But this does not mean that conditional effects detected through experimental manipulation are any less 'real' than the actual effects of the campaign detected through panel surveys (Hovland 1959). With these distinctions in mind, what sort of effects might we expect from attention to campaign news?

Civic Engagement

Democratic theory suggests that one of the most important impacts of campaign communications is upon civic engagement, including cognitive and mobilization effects. The first and primary function of the news media in a democracy, widely accepted as a guiding principle by British broadcasters, is to transmit information so that citizens can make reasoned choices about their electoral alternatives. Downsian theory stresses that the capacity to make reasoned choices does not require full, comprehensive and encyclopaedic information about every detail of each party's manifesto, which would be unrealistic. Elections are not a civics test with twenty pass/fail questions. Rather, citizens need sufficient information about the government's record on the important issues, about the major policy proposals of alternative parties, and about the competence and trustworthiness of leaders and candidates, to predict the probable consequences of casting a ballot (for a discussion see Downs 1957: 207–259; Lupia and McCubbins 1998). Information costs are reduced by relying upon a few trusted sources and by seeking information only about issues which concern the voter.

Ever since Lazarsfeld *et al.* (1944), one stream of research has considered what knowledge voters acquire from the news media. Recent work has often focused on the role of cognitive short-cuts such as ideology or 'schema' which reduce the time and effort required to monitor the candidates and allow a reasoned choice with imperfect information (Zaller 1993). Much of the literature has stressed the breadth and depth of citizens' ignorance about public affairs and minimal retention of factual knowledge from watching news broadcasts (Delli Carpini and Keeter 1996). But others have emphasized the limited but still significant acquisition of information about candidates and issues derived from exposure to the news in an American campaign (Graber 1984; Neuman *et al.* 1992; Just *et al.* 1996). Popkin (1994) has argued that gains in knowledge, even if modest, may be sufficient to allow voters to cast a meaningful ballot.

The cognitive impact of the media depends upon many factors, including the substance of the message, the form of communication, and the receptivity of voters.

Although generating an increasingly sophisticated body of research, it is not clear how far we can generalize from cognitive effects within the institutional context of American presidential campaigns to British campaigns. In the US political system several institutional features create exceptionally high hurdles in the levels of information required for citizens to make reasoned choices. This includes, *inter alia*, the frequency and number of elections, the largely unknown qualities of non-incumbent candidates at the start of the race, the lack of party cues in primary elections, the weakening of collective party discipline, the fragmented commercial news media lacking a public service culture, the reliance upon 30-second ads as the primary means of candidate communications, the complex choices facing voters in multi-level elections, as well as the common use of state-level referendums. In states like California the briefing book for the latter alone is commonly a few inches thick. Given this context we might expect American voters to start the long campaign knowing far less, but also potentially to learn far more, than their European counterparts.

In Britain, general elections provide an information-saturated context where it is difficult to avoid the campaign. The news media, particularly television, provides wall-to-wall coverage of issues and events during the official campaign, from the launch of the party platforms through to the results on polling day. This is often the most intensive period of exposure to politics that most citizens will ever experience. On the other hand, although coverage is comprehensive, by the time of the long and short campaign, much of it involves the repetition of familiar and well-rehearsed party positions, with few genuine surprises, rather than providing genuinely new or unexpected information. In this regard election campaigns can be seen as largely ritualistic devices, where all the actors go through the familiar steps.

To examine what citizens learn in British general elections we compare the effects of exposure to different types of media which prioritize different types of political news. For example, did tabloid readers learn less than those who bought broadsheet newspapers? If politicians and journalists succeed in their civic education function, we would expect to find cognitive learning effects during the course of the long and short campaign, as citizens acquire more information about party policies, candidates, and civics in general. If parties and the media fail in this role, then voters may end up no wiser at the end than at the start of the campaign.

Moreover, in a democracy the campaign should also function to mobilize citizens to turn out on polling day and to boost interest in public affairs. By this criterion parties and the news media succeed if they stimulate debate and grassroots discussion, if they encourage party members to participate at local level, and if they boost civic engagement. On the one hand, video-malaise theories emphasize that the modern news media often fail in this role, because of an over-emphasis on negative news and 'horse race' strategy, producing turned-off and cynical voters disconnected from civic affairs (Robinson 1976; Fallows 1996). Hence Patterson (1993) suggests that American journalistic values produce an excessive focus on the poll-led horse race and insider strategy, rather than the policy issues. Putnam (1995) argues that attention to American television discourages civic engagement and social capital, while Gerbner (1980) postulated a 'mean-world' effect from television news. Experimental studies have demonstrated the power of negative advertising to discourage electoral turnout in the United States (Ansolabehere and Iyengar 1995). Civic engagement is a matter of considerable concern given the fall in voting participation in the 1997 British election, producing the lowest turnout since 1935.

Yet, on the other hand, traditional social-psychological theories emphasize that partisan newspapers function to mobilize voters, reinforcing their commitment to particular parties as polling day draws near (Butler and Stokes 1974: 114–19). Recent studies have also challenged the video-malaise thesis (see the discussion by Newton 1999). The available evidence suggests that in many advanced industrialized societies the amount of time devoted to watching TV is often associated with civic apathy, but in contrast time devoted to watching news and current affairs is significantly associated with civic engagement (Norris 1996, 1999b; Newton 1997). In this regard it matters *what* you watch as much as how much TV you watch. Given this debate, we re-examine the evidence for the positive or negative influence of the news media on civic engagement within the context of the last British general election.

Agenda-setting

The function of the campaign for agenda-setting has also been a long-standing concern in the literature on political communications. Theories of agenda-setting suggest that the news drives the public's issue priorities, thereby telling people not 'what to think' but 'what to think about'. This idea can be traced originally to Walter Lippmann's *Public Opinion* (1922), before first being tested systematically in the work of McCombs and Shaw (1972). During the last two decades a series of studies in the United States have found that the political agenda is set by a process of competition between politicians, journalists, and the public (for a review see Dearing and Rogers 1996; Protess and McCombs 1991; McCombs 1997). The theory of agenda-setting implies that stories which get most attention in the news become the problems which the public regards as the nation's most important. The theory focuses only on the amount of coverage, not its tone or contents. Should we be concerned about the effects of climate change and global warming? The threat terrorism poses to the Northern Ireland peace process? The impact of the European Union's Exchange Rate Mechanism on Britain's financial markets? The Lewinsky affair in the

United States? Internal civil war and strife in Kosovo? The news headlines are believed to shape public concerns about the most important problems facing the country. This process may have significant political implications if public concerns ultimately feed into government priorities, and thereby help drive the policy process. Theories of issue ownership also stress that the campaign is largely a battle about which policies are prioritized, whether those like defence where right-wing parties usually have a distinct advantage, or issues like welfare where left-wing parties have ownership (Budge and Farlie 1983).

Despite the extensive literature elsewhere, previous studies found little support for the media's agenda-setting role in the context of British general elections. In the 1987 campaign, for example, Miller (1990: 232) concluded that 'Television failed to set the public agenda and the public failed to set the television agenda. Each influenced the other to a very modest extent but they remained poles apart.' (See also Miller 1991; Norris 1997a.) To see whether the adoption of strategic communications helped Labour set the news agenda in the 1997 campaign, we compare the issues which each major party tried to highlight during the campaign, those headlined by the news media, and those of concern to the electorate.

Persuasion

Lastly, the effects of the media in shaping electoral preferences, including images of the parties and party leaders, has long been regarded as important, ever since early studies of propaganda. Party managers, advertising consultants and market researchers think that strategic communications matters for persuading voters, and that this was a vital component in Blair's 1997 victory. The increased importance parties place on campaigning is demonstrated by the escalation in expenditure: the three major parties in Britain spent an estimated total of £56.4 million on the 1997 general election, compared with only £7.7 million in 1983. In the last campaign £21.5 million was spent on advertising alone, including newspapers, posters and the production of election broadcasts (Neill Report 1998). While there are serious doubts about whether some of the advertising spending was effective, nevertheless in an escalating 'arms race' more and more party resources are devoted to news management, election publicity and voter targeting.

Survey evidence provides some grounds to support the assumption that parties can use campaigns to reach undecided voters. The British Election Study has regularly asked voters: 'When did you decide who to vote for?' In 1997 27 per cent of the electorate reported making up their minds 'during the election campaign' (see Chapter 11). Moreover, about one-quarter (23 per cent) of the electorate fell into the category of 'waverers', defined as those who considered voting for another party during the campaign. This suggests that in the 1997 campaign many people were still potentially open to persuasion about how to vote, even close to polling day, rather than fixed with party anchors. The proportion of late deciders and waverers was particularly high among Liberal Democratic voters. As discussed further in the conclusion, other evidence on the flow of the vote from 1992 to 1997, as well as net indicators like the 'Butler' swing and the Pedersen Index, indicate considerable electoral volatility in 1997, more so than in most previous general elections.

Yet previous studies have found limited evidence for the power of parties and the news media to change voting behaviour within British campaigns, but most scholars have been fairly sceptical about some of the larger claims made by political consultants. Miller (1991) conducted the most thorough previous study of the news media during the 1987 general election, based on a panel survey of voters and content analysis. The research found that the press had a significant but limited impact upon party images, leadership preferences and voting choice. But television viewing, with its more balanced and non-partisan messages, had relatively little influence upon viewers. Curtice and Semetko (1994) analysed the 1987–1992 BES panel and found that over the longer term newspapers had a modest influence upon their readers' voting choice and economic evaluations, although there were few other short-term effects (see also Newton 1991; Webber 1993; Gavin and Sanders 1996; Gavin 1998). Their studies are suggestive but one problem is that most previous British research has been based upon cross-sectional surveys, where it remains impossible to disentangle the direction of causal effects: people may vote for a party influenced by the political content of newspapers, but they may also buy a newspaper sympathetic to their party choice, or both. To overcome these limitations we re-examine persuasion effects using a triangulated research design combining content analysis, panel surveys and experiments.

Feedback Loop: From Voting Choice to Party Messages

We would also expect a feedback loop in this process, where public opinion expressed through the outcome of the election may have a significant impact 'upwards' on party leaders. The views of the electorate, expressed directly through opinion polls, focus groups, and canvassing operations, and indirectly through the filter of the news media, may shape party policies and communication strategies. Should Labour prioritize tax credits for families or child care places? Should the Conservatives adopt a policy of outright opposition to ERM, or a more cautious 'wait and see' approach? Party manifestos are influenced by the popular mood, as well as by the attitudes and opinions of party members, elected MPs and leaders.

At an informal level there is nothing new in this process: this occurs whenever MPs go home to the constituency to listen to the views of party activists and supporters on particularly controversial or divisive matters. Door-stepping during the campaign is part of the long tradition of the election hustings. But in recent years the feedback loop has become far more intensive, systematic, professional, and centralized (Scammell 1995; Kavanagh 1995; Jones 1995). The Labour Party's attempt to organize town hall meetings around the country, in their 'Labour Listens' campaign (subsequently emulated by the Conservatives under Hague) can be regarded as a cynical exercise in the manipulation of public opinion or alternatively it can be seen as a genuine attempt to reach out and connect with the concerns of people in Britain, or a bit of both. The Blair government's use of specially commissioned opinion polls and focus groups represents a natural extension of this process. The feedback loop operates primarily after election day, especially among politicians thrown onto the opposition benches who are searching for the best way to regain public popularity. This process is a critical function of elections but because we focus upon only the period of the long campaign this is treated as essentially exogenous to our model.

The Plan of the Book

To summarise the discussion so far, theories of the effects of political communications have developed from the pre-war accounts deeply fearful of the impact of 'propaganda' on the gullible mass public, through the post-war orthodoxy of the Erie County and Michigan studies stressing partisan reinforcement, to more recent work on cognitive, agenda-setting and persuasion effects. British elections are often explained on the basis of long-standing cues like social identities and medium-term evaluations of the state of the economy. Yet the standard social and economic variables have had decreasing success in predicting voting behaviour, owing to the process of class and party dealignment during the last thirty years (Evans and Norris 1999). Building upon the schematic model already discussed, political communications is conceptualized in this book as a sequential process from message through successive steps of information and mobilization, agenda-setting, and persuasion, to the act of casting a ballot paper.

Part I of the book sets the general context for the study. **Chapter 2** outlines the changing pattern of political communications in British election campaigns. We argue that the evolution of the post-modern campaign has produced the rise of a more autonomous press and a more fragmented electronic news environment, and that parties have been forced to respond to these new challenges. **Chapter 3** considers some of the methodological challenges surrounding studies of media effects and outlines the multi-method research design used in this book, including the content analysis of party and media messages, the 1997 British Election Study (BES) cross-sectional and campaign panel surveys, and an experimental study of television news. These methodological considerations are important for weighing the evidence for our arguments but readers who prefer to skip over the technical details should move directly to the next section.

Part II examines the inputs into the process of campaign communications. **Chapter 4** analyses the contents of party manifestos, press briefings and party election broadcasts during the 1997 election to address three core questions: what were the campaign strategies of the major parties in 1997; what were their priority issues; and how far did they stay 'on message' with a consistent agenda throughout the official campaign? **Chapter 5** examines the coverage in the news media. Based on content analysis of national newspapers and television news in 1997, we examine the amount of attention devoted to the election campaign; the breakdown of this coverage between different issues; and which party was most successful in setting the news agenda in the campaign. **Chapter 6** considers the public's reaction to the coverage, who proved most attentive towards campaign news, and how far people were turned on or turned off by the election.

Part III examines the effects of the news media on voters. The issue of **civic engagement** has long been a matter of concern. In democratic theory the most basic function of the campaign is to inform voters about the choices before them and to mobilize citizen participation. As we have seen, there is considerable controversy in the literature about how far the news media succeed in this function. **Chapter 7** analyses what the public learnt from the campaign in the British election, whether the news media influenced political cynicism among the public, and whether the news media discouraged electoral participation.

Chapter 8 compares the role of parties, the media and the public in agenda-setting. We focus in particular on whether the issue agenda of parties, the media and the public moved together, or apart, during the campaign. The issue of Europe, which suddenly attracted news headlines in mid-April, is examined as a case-study in media agenda-setting. Agenda dynamics are analysed using the panel survey and the experimental study.

Chapter 9 goes on to examine the influence of television news. We hypothesize that there are three primary ways in which the contents of television news could influence party support: through the amount of time devoted to each party (*stop-watch* balance), through positive or negative news about each party (*directional* balance), and through prioritizing certain issues over others (*agenda* balance). Chapter 9 analyses the results of the experiments which manipulated these factors in a montage of news and monitored the effects on party preferences.

Chapter 10 focuses on the impact of the press on party support. The post-war decade saw a rough division of newspaper support between the major parties but the balance swung towards the Conservatives in the mid-1970s. In 1992 the Conservatives campaigned assured of a largely sympathetic press. By 1997 this had changed, with an historic shift in editorial allegiances, particularly the defection to Labour of *The Sun*. The central issue this chapter examines is whether the change in newspaper partisanship led, or followed, their readers. Did *Sun* readers become more

Labour after the paper declared their backing for Blair on the first day of the campaign? This provides a 'natural experiment' to test for the effects of newspapers' partisanship.

The conclusion **(Chapter 11)** draws together the central themes, provides a summary of the core findings throughout the book, and considers the implications for our understanding of the role of parties, the news media and the public in a mediated democracy.

2 The Campaign Context

This chapter outlines changes in the overall context within which parties and the media operate within British political campaigns, and how these trends shaped the communications environment during the 1997 British general election. We first identify how the process of political campaigning has evolved over the years, including major developments in the national press and electronic news media. We then consider how parties used strategic communications within an increasingly complex news environment during the 1997 campaign. Voting studies often focus exclusively on individual citizens, using survey data to monitor the relationship between social characteristics, political attitudes, and party choice. But the process of political communications functions within a broader structural framework. We therefore need to understand the changing roles of parties and the news media before we can go on to analyse the public's response to campaign communications.

The Evolution of Political Campaigning

Modernization theory suggests that during the post-war era political campaigning has been transformed by the decline of direct linkages between citizens and parties and the rise of mediated relationships. One of the most persuasive accounts has been provided by Swanson and Mancini (1996) who argue that similar, although not identical, developments are recognizable across advanced industrialized societies.

In the earliest era, the *pre-modern* campaign was characterized by the predominance of the partisan press; a loose organizational network of grassroots party volunteers in local constituencies; and a short, *ad hoc* national campaign run by the party leader with a few close advisers. In Britain this period of campaigning gradually evolved in the mid-nineteenth century following the development of mass party organizations registering and mobilizing the newly enfranchised electorate. In the local constituencies most contact was on a face-to-face basis between candidates and voters, with campaign rallies, canvassing and party meetings, as well as mediated through local newspapers. Despite the introduction of wireless broadcasting in 1922, this pattern continued in recognizable form until at least the late 1950s (Norris 1997a).

In most advanced industrialized democracies the critical shift towards the *modern* campaign developed with the rise of television during the 1950s. The British watershed occurred in 1959, with the first televised coverage during a general election campaign (rather than simply reporting the results after the event). The evolution of the modern campaign gradually shifted the location of political communications, from the print media towards the electronic, from the constituency towards the central party leadership, and from amateurs towards professionals. Within this news environment parties developed a coordinated national campaign with communications designed by specialists skilled in advertising, marketing, and polling. The 'long campaign' in the year or so before polling day became as important strategically as the short 'official' campaign. In Britain these changes did not occur overnight, nor did they displace grassroots constituency activity, as the timeless ritual of canvassing and leafleting continued (Denver and Hands 1997a; Denver *et al.* 1998). Dedicated party volunteers and candidates continue to engage in the day-to-day activity of organizing, canvassing, leafleting, telephone polling and mobilizing support. Nevertheless even local activity is now increasingly tightly coordinated by the central campaign headquarters. The mediated campaign reduced the importance of personal contacts as politicians became more reliant on television and the press to convey their message, particularly partisan mass-circulation tabloids sympathetic to their cause.

Lastly, in the late twentieth century advanced industrialized societies have been experiencing the rise of the *post-modern* campaign. The most obvious characteristics include the emergence of a more independent dealigned press following its own 'media logic'; the growing fragmentation and diversification of electronic media outlets, programmes and audiences; and, in reaction to these developments, the attempt by parties to reassert control through strategic communications and media management during the permanent campaign. Let us examine the most important recent developments which became particularly evident in the 1997 British election, focusing in particular on the rise of a more autonomous and sensationalist press and the fragmentation of the electronic media, and how political parties have been forced to respond to these challenges by more professionalized and sophisticated communication strategies.

The Rise of an Autonomous and Dealigned National Press

In recent decades the press has experienced an era of long-term secular decline: circulation of national newspapers peaked in the late 1950s and sales have subsequently dropped by one-third (see Figure 2.1). The fall was sharpest among tabloids, pushing these further down-market in the search for readers (Seymour-Ure 1996). Between 1981 and 1995 the proportion of the public reading a daily paper dropped substantially (from

76 to 62 per cent of men and from 68 to 54 per cent of women) (*Social Trends* 1997). The most important consequences of this process for campaign communications is the way that fierce competition for readers has transformed the press, producing growing dealignment in the linkages between parties and newspapers, and the growth of a more autonomous print media following the commercial logic of sales.

In the post-war decade British parties had long-standing and stable links with the press. In 1945 there was a rough partisan balance with about 6.7 million readers of pro-Conservative papers and 4.4 million readers of pro-Labour papers. This balance shifted decisively in the early 1970s, with the transformation of the left-leaning *Daily Herald* into the pro-Conservative *Sun*, and the more aggressively right-wing tone of *The Times*, both under Rupert Murdoch's ownership. By 1992 the cards had become overwhelmingly stacked against the left, since the circulation of the Conservative-leaning press had risen to about 8.7 million compared with only 3.3 million for Labour-leaning papers (see Figure 2.1). Throughout the 1980s Mrs Thatcher could campaign assured of a largely sympathetic press, which provided a loyal platform to get her message across (Ingham 1994). One of the most striking developments of recent years, which became particularly evident in the run-up to the 1997 election, has been the crumbling of these traditional press–party loyalties.

The evidence comes partly from editorial policy (Seymour-Ure 1997). The Conservative press had started to turn against Mrs Thatcher in 1989–90, when the economy was in recession and her leadership became deeply unpopular, and this constant barrage of criticism probably contributed towards her eventual demise. During the 1992 election, while

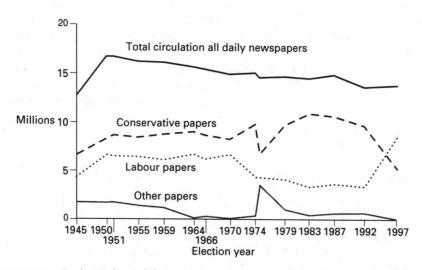

FIGURE 2.1 *Partisan Balance of the Press, 1945–97. Note: Party affiliation defined by editorial endorsements.*

The Sun and the *Daily Express* continued to beat the Tory drum, comment from some of the other pro-Conservative press like the *Mail* and *The Sunday Times* was more muted, and four out of eleven daily papers failed to endorse a single party (Harrop and Scammell 1992). The new government enjoyed a brief respite on returning to office but press criticism of John Major's leadership deepened following the ERM debacle on 16 September 1992, with only the *Daily Express* staying loyal. Journalists continued to highlight the government's difficulties over Europe, and internal splits over the debate on the Maastricht Treaty. By the winter of 1993, a succession of scandals involving Conservative politicians created headline news while editorials regularly denounced the government, and particularly the Prime Minister. By the time of the July 1995 leadership challenge only the *Daily Express* backed John Major solidly, while *The Sun*, the *Mail*, *The Times* and the *Telegraph* all argued that it was time for him to be replaced (Seymour-Ure 1997), an embarrassment for their leader writers given the outcome.

The question, in the long run-up to the election, was whether the Tory press would return home, once the future of the Conservative government was under real threat. In the event, the 1997 election represents a historic watershed. In a major break with tradition, six out of ten national dailies, and five out of nine Sundays, endorsed the Labour Party in their final editorials (see Table 2.1). This was twice the highest number previously, and it reversed the long-standing pro-Conservative leanings in the national press. With impeccable timing, *The Sun* led the way on the first day of the campaign, (THE SUN BACKS BLAIR), with a front page

TABLE 2.1: *National Daily Press: Ownership, Circulation and Partisanship*

Paper	Owner	Editor	Circ. April 1997 (000s)	Preferred winner
Daily Mail	Associated Newspapers/ Lord Rothermere	P. Dacre	2,151	Conservative
Mirror	Mirror Group	P. Morgan	3,084	Labour
Daily Star	MAI/United/ Lord Hollick	P. Walker	648	Labour
Daily Telegraph	C. Black/ Hollinger	C. Moore	1,134	Conservative
Express	MAI/ United/Lord Hollick	R. Addis	1,220	Conservative
Financial Times	Pearson/ Lord Blakenham	R. Lambert	307	Labour
Guardian	Scott Trust	A. Rusbriger	401	Labour
Independent	Mirror Group	A. Marr	251	Labour
Sun	News Int./R. Murdoch	S. Higgins	3,842	Labour
Times	News Int./R. Murdoch	P. Stothard	719	Conservative

Source: Colin Seymour-Ure (1997).

claiming Blair is a 'breath of fresh air' while the Conservatives were 'tired, divided and rudderless', and its defection stole the headlines and damaged Tory morale. Throughout the campaign *The Sun*, with ten million readers a day, provided largely unswerving support for Blair, although opposing Labour policy on Europe and the unions, and many commentators predicted that the switch, based on Murdoch's commercial considerations rather than political affinities, would not last long. Labour's traditional tabloid, *The Mirror*, with six million readers, continued its brand of centre-left journalism ('the paper for Labour's TRUE supporters'). On the last Sunday of the campaign, influenced by Murdoch, *The News of the World* decided to follow the lead of its sister paper, *The Sun*, and backed Labour.

Among the broadsheets *The Guardian* called for tactical voting for the Liberal Democrats in seats where it made sense, but broadly endorsed Labour. *The Independent* was more restrained in its backing, casting its editorial vote for Labour 'with a degree of optimism that is not entirely justified by the evidence'. The paper was clearly more anti-Tory than pro-anything. *The Times* advised its readers to back Eurosceptic candidates from whatever party, although, in practice, nearly all were Conservatives. Only leads in the *Daily Telegraph*, and the *Daily Mail* ('LABOUR BULLY BOYS ARE BACK' 'LABOUR'S BROKEN PROMISES') remained strongly in the Tory camp. Even the *Daily Express* was more neutral than in the past: a double-page spread was divided between Lord Hollick, its chief executive, arguing for Labour and its chairman, Lord Stevens, arguing for the Conservatives. The front page of the election-eve *Mail* carried a colourful Union Jack border and the apocalyptic warning that a Labour victory could 'undo 1,000 years of our nation's history'.

Yet any comparison of editorial policy probably underestimates the balance of partisanship in news coverage during the overall campaign. For example, the *Mail* ostensibly endorsed the Conservatives during the campaign, but in practice it probably deeply damaged the government by headlining sexual scandals in the party, and reinforcing images of disunity with leading articles highlighting the number of Tory Eurosceptics. With friends like this, the Conservatives did not need opponents. To understand this pattern we need to go beyond the leaders, which are rarely read, and even less heeded, to examine the broader coverage of stories. The most plausible evidence for *dealignment* is that certain papers like *The Sun*, traditionally pro-Conservative, switched camps, but also that front-page stories were often so similar across all the press, driven by news values irrespective of the paper's ostensible partisanship.

Table 2.2 covering six national papers shows the overall tone of campaign stories when classified as favourable or unfavourable from the perspective of each party in the 1997 campaign. The balance is calculated by deducting the proportion of negative from the positive news stories for each party and paper. The results show that on balance Labour received positive press coverage from every paper except for the very critical *Daily Mail* and (very modestly) *The Guardian*. Labour also scored the highest

TABLE 2.2: *Favourability of the Press, 1997 Campaign*

	Conservative Party				Labour Party				Liberal Democrat Party			
	Neg	Mix	Pos	**Bal**	Neg	Mix	Pos	**Bal**	Neg	Mix	Pos	**Bal**
Mail	15	73	13	–2	28	66	6	–22	5	96		–5
Times	16	81	3	–13	7	85	8	+1	1	95	4	+3
Sun	19	81		–19	2	81	17	+15	2	98		–2
Independent	26	73	1	–25	8	78	14	+6	4	93	3	–1
Guardian	34	61	6	–28	13	77	10	–3	5	89	6	+1
Mirror	40	61		–40	2	73	24	+22		96	4	+4
Total	**24**	**73**	**3**	–21	**9**	**79**	**12**	+3	**2**	**98**	**0**	–2
Mean Favourability	3.70				4.06				4.01			
No. of Stories	N.464				N.488				N.511			

Note: Content analysis of political stories in six papers. The Favourability Score is calculated based on the tone of the story as a whole from the perspective of the party's campaign using a 7-point scale from 1 (Negative) to 7 (Positive). The scores were recoded into Negative (1–3) Mixed (4) Positive (5–7). The Balance is calculated as the negative minus the positive proportion.

Source: Semetko and Scammell 1997 British General Election Campaign Content Analysis.

mean favourability rating of any party. In contrast, on balance the Conservatives received more negative than positive news from every paper, notably the traditional left-leaning *Mirror* and *The Guardian*, but also from *The Independent*, *The Sun* and *The Times*, in that respective order. Their only real ally remained the *Daily Mail*, and that paper proved distinctly lukewarm, at best. Overall the Conservatives scored the most negative average rating of any party. Lastly the Liberal Democrats received overwhelmingly mixed or neutral coverage (in 98 per cent of stories) and an overall score neatly balanced between the two major parties.

The process of dealignment becomes apparent if we compare the pattern in 1997 with coverage in the same six papers in the 1992 campaign. As Table 2.3 shows, the press proved more polarized by party in 1992. In that campaign the *Daily Mail* was unswervingly positive towards the Conservatives and the most critical paper towards Labour, with a similar pattern of right-wing bias clearly evident in *The Sun*. At the other extreme *The Mirror* showed rock-solid Labour colours, and *The Guardian* followed with more subdued pro-left support. In contrast, among the broadsheets *The Independent* stood by its name and provided almost exclusively mixed or 'straight' reporting, while *The Times* also proved relatively even-handed in its criticisms. As widely discussed by commentators, the defection of *The Sun* in 1997 therefore reversed party camps most dramatically, in its editorial policy as well as the contents of its news columns. But what has not been revealed in previous studies is that from 1992 to 1997 there was an important shift towards less partisan reporting in the balance of positive-negative coverage across many papers, not just Conservative ones. The amount of mixed or straight reporting increased substantially, indicating dealignment on both sides of the party divide.

The Major government was damaged, not just by weakening partisan linkages, but also by the news values inherent in the growing tabloidization of the press. Since the early 1970s fierce competition for readers has encouraged far more sensational coverage in the popular press, fuelling an endless diet of stories about 'scandals' (mostly sexual but also financial), infotainment, and the Royals, preferably all three. This process started when Rupert Murdoch bought the *News of the World* in 1968, and *The Sun* a year later. It accelerated in the cut-throat competition produced by the launch of the *Daily Star* in 1978, which sought to out-do *The Sun* in its relentless search for sex, investigative 'exclusives' about celebrities, violent crime, and graphic coverage of the bizarre. Those who thought British newspapers had reached their nadir at this point had underestimated the soft-porn *Sunday Sport*, launched in 1986 (McNair 1994). The tackiness of the popular press, such as their exhaustive gossip about the goings-on of the younger Royals, gradually infected and corroded the news culture of the broadsheets as well. By the mid-1990s, the journalism of scandal trumped party loyalties, hands down. This fuelled the series of sleaze stories about senior Conservative politicians throughout John Major's years in government, and there was no let-up during the campaign. As documented in detail in Chapter 8, the first two weeks of the election were dominated by a succession of stories about corruption in public life and sexual 'scandals', providing a steady diet of negative news for the government which swamped their message about the economy. The way that this process has continued under Blair, with a

TABLE 2.3: *Favourability of the Press, 1992 Campaign*

	Conservative Party				Labour Party				Liberal Democrat Party			
	Neg	Mix	Pos	**Bal**	Neg	Mix	Pos	**Bal**	Neg	Mix	Pos	**Bal**
Mail		63	38	**+38**	79	21		**–79**	30	70		**–30**
Times	12	69	18	**+6**	10	77	14	**+4**	2	79	19	**+17**
Sun	4	35	61	**+57**	74	20	7	**–67**	27	59	14	**–13**
Independent	6	94		**–6**		98	2	**+2**		97	3	**+3**
Guardian	43	49	8	**–35**	14	51	35	**+21**	11	69	20	**+9**
Mirror	85	14	2	**–83**		19	81	**+81**	10	76	14	**+4**
Total	**40**	**43**	**18**	**–22**	**27**	**42**	**31**	**+4**	**9**	**74**	**16**	**+7**
Mean Favourability	3.48				4.15				4.09			
No. of Stories	N.776				N.752				N.373			

Note: Content analysis of political stories in six papers. The Favourability Score is calculated based on the tone of the story as a whole from the perspective of the party's campaign using a 7-point scale from 1 (Negative) to 7 (Positive). The scores were recoded into Negative (1–3) Mixed (4) Positive (5–7). The Balance is calculated as the negative minus the positive proportion.

Source: Semetko and Scammell 1997 British General Election Campaign Content Analysis.

steady stream of stories about sleaze in the new Labour government, suggests that this represents a permanent shift in the news culture in Britain, not just a passing phase caused by eighteen years of one-party predominance.

Trends in Britain seem, therefore, to have followed those in many other European countries which used to have a strongly partisan press, like The Netherlands, but where political coverage is now driven more strongly by an autonomous 'media logic' in the fierce competition for readers rather than by traditional allegiances or the politics of their proprietors. 'Modern media are more powerful, more independent, and more determined to pursue their own interests through a professional culture of their own making' (Swanson and Mancini 1996: 15). This dealignment has increased the complexity and uncertainty of media management for parties, who can no longer rely on getting their message out through a few well-known and sympathetic sources.

The Fragmentation of the Electronic Media

Parties face, not just a more autonomous press, but also an increasingly fragmented and complex electronic news environment. In Britain the legal framework for the BBC/ITV duopoly has always been suffused by a strong public service ethos which required broadcasters to maintain 'party balance' and impartiality in news coverage, to 'inform, educate and entertain' according to high standards, and to provide an agreed allocation of unpaid airtime to party political broadcasts (Blumler and Gurevitch 1995). Within this familiar context, in the early 1960s and 1970s news coverage on television channels served to centralize the campaign and heightened the visibility of party leaders: what appeared on BBC1's flagship *Nine O'Clock News* and ITN's *News at Ten*, and in related news and current affairs studios, was the principal means by which politicians reached the vast majority of voters. This pattern persists but it is being gradually, perhaps evenly sharply, eroded today.

British broadcasters continue to reflect a high standard of public service. The BBC Producer Guidelines stress the strict need for political impartiality, written into the BBC Charter, but are fairly vague about how this is to be achieved in practice: 'There is an absolute obligation for the BBC's journalism to remain impartial as the people of the United Kingdom exercise their right to vote. . . . Editors should ensure that, through the course of the campaign, their coverage has proved wide-ranging and fair.'[1] Requirements of 'due impartiality' are also written into the Independent Television Commission's Programme Code.[2] Like much British electoral law, the regulations governing broadcasting embodied in Section 93 of the Representation of the People Act only controls coverage of parliamentary candidates standing in particular constituencies.[3] Television coverage of parties is determined less by law than by conventions which have evolved since the creation of the BBC in 1922 (Blackburn 1995: 258–61).

During British election campaigns broadcasting is dominated by the concept of 'stop-watch' balance, meaning proportional (not equal) coverage of political parties. The allocation of free party political broadcasts is determined by the Committee on Political Broadcasting, created in 1947, a body whose proceedings are never published and which has not actually met in person since 1983, but which is composed of senior representatives from the broadcasters and the parties. Through negotiations this body agrees the time allocation for regular party political broadcasts (PPBs) outside of elections, and also for party election broadcasts (PEBs) during the official campaign (for details see Scammell and Semetko 1995). As shown in Table 2.4, during the 1997 general election, in line with many previous contests, the ratio was 5:5:4, meaning that the Conservatives and Labour were each given five ten-minute PEBs, while the Liberal Democrats were allowed four, and minor parties which mustered a minimum of fifty candidates, like the UK Independence Party and the Greens, received at least one five-minute broadcast each, with additional arrangements for Scotland, Wales and Northern Ireland (for details see Harrison 1997: 149–54).[4]

Most importantly, the agreed ratio of time allocated to each party also operates in election newsrooms. During the official campaign, coverage of parties in election news on all public and commercial television channels reflects the agreed proportion of time allocated to parties for election broadcasts. The stop-watch principle does not apply to each daily broadcast, but rather to party coverage for each news or current affairs programme during the course of the campaign. Participant observation studies of newsrooms during campaigns have found that the 'stop-watch'

TABLE 2.4: *Ratio of Election Broadcasts and Proportion of Election News, Major Parties 1964–1997*

	Party Election Broadcast			Proportion of BBC TV Election News			Proportion of ITV Election News		
	Con	Lab	LDem	Con	Lab	LDem	Con	Lab	LDem
1964	5	5	3	42	41	17	41	39	20
1966	5	5	3	39	42	16	43	40	16
1970	5	5	3	46	42	10	45	43	11
1974F	5	5	3	39	40	18	37	36	22
1974O	5	5	4	35	35	26	37	37	21
1979	5	5	3	35	35	22	37	37	21
1983	5	5	4	34	36	26	34	37	27
1987	5	5	5	35	31	25	38	31	26
1992	5	5	4	32	32	31	31	34	32
1997	5	5	4	35	31	24	35	30	28

Sources: Information about PEBs from Margaret Scammell and Holli Semetko 1995 'Political Advertising on Television' Table 3.1. In Lynda Lee Kaid and Christina Holtz-Bacha (eds.) *Political Advertising in Western Democracies* (Thousand Oaks, Sage). The proportion of election news per party from successive volumes of *The British General Election of . . .* by David Butler *et al.*

principle is conscientiously implemented and continually monitored by news organizations and by parties (Blumler and Gurevitch 1995; Scammell and Semetko 1995). In 1992 ITN put slightly greater emphasis on news values driven by editorial judgements rather than the stop-watch rule, but in practice the overall time ITN allocated to parties differed little from the 5:5:4 formula which would otherwise have applied (Tait 1995: 60). 'Stop-watch' balance is one of the prime ways that British broadcasters try to be impartial. The 1997 campaign followed this pattern: the proportion of coverage given to each of the parties in television news closely reflected the allocation of time for PEBs (see Table 2.4). Nevertheless other criteria of impartiality are also applied by producers; for example, even-handedness in the relative position of parties in the running order and equivalence of tone in reporting campaign events. Leader is matched against leader, issue against issue, and press conference against press conference. In this sense other notions of neutrality are also pervasive in election newsrooms.

The core question raised by these conventions is whether 'due impartiality' is achieved in practice. The situation is carefully monitored by broadcasters and campaign managers alike, with vociferous complaints if the party balance is seen as unfair. The ITC regularly surveys the public's perceptions of bias in the media (see, for example, Gunter *et al.* 1994). When asked after the 1997 campaign how far the major channels provided news programmes which were 'balanced', viewers tended to give high marks to Channel 4, and about half thought that BBC2 and ITV achieved this 'just about always' or 'most of the time', compared with one-third who thought this of BBC1's news (Norris 1998a). If we examine the favourability of television news during the 1997 campaign based on the content analysis, shown in Table 2.5, then we find that overall the vast majority of stories were internally 'mixed' or balanced in tone, including positive and negative statements. This pattern on television was far more common than in the press. Nevertheless the analysis also reveals some interesting differences in party coverage. On BBC1, ITN and Sky News the Conservatives received more unfavourable than favourable stories, giving a negative balance overall. This pattern was particularly evident on BBC1's *Nine O'Clock News*. In contrast, coverage of the Labour Party was on balance modestly positive while the Liberal Democrats received the most favourable treatment, attracting almost no negative coverage at all. In terms of directional bias, therefore, television was more neutral than the press but this does not mean that the overall picture was absolutely balanced. We will come back to this pattern when considering its implications in the conclusion.

Yet foundations for the traditional framework governing election broadcasting during the last four decades are starting to creak and settle into a new pattern. In January 1998 the broadcasting authorities published a joint consultation paper suggesting, given the rise in current affairs programming, that routine party broadcasts outside of election time

TABLE 2.5: *Favourability of Television News Coverage, 1997 Campaign*

	Conservative Party				Labour Party				Liberal Democrat Party			
	Neg	Mix	Pos	**Bal**	Neg	Mix	Pos	**Bal**	Neg	Mix	Pos	**Bal**
BBC *Nine O'Clock News*	16	79	4	–12	8	82	10	+2	1	91	8	+7
ITN *News at 10*	11	82	7	–3	5	85	10	+5	1	90	9	+8
Sky News	9	86	5	–4	6	88	7	+1	1	93	5	+4
Total	**12**	**83**	**5**	**–7**	**6**	**85**	**9**	**+3**	**1**	**92**	**7**	**+6**
Mean Favourability	3.92				4.04				4.08			
No. of Stories	1267				1276				1269			

Note: Content analysis of political stories in television news. The Favourability Score is calculated based on the tone of the story as a whole from the perspective of the party's campaign using a 7-point scale from 1 (Negative) to 7 (Positive). The scores were recoded into Negative (1–3) Mixed (4) Positive (5–7). The Balance is calculated as the negative minus the positive proportion.

Source: Semetko and Scammell 1997 British General Election Campaign Content Analysis.

should be abolished. The Neill Report (1998: 13.21) rejected this argument and favoured few reforms to the existing system but the report notes that changes are probably coming in the near future: ' "Broadcasting" is gradually giving way to "narrowcasting", with an increasing fragmentation of television and radio audiences. The advent of satellite and cable television and digital broadcasting means that the current arrangements governing political broadcasting may soon no longer be relevant. The increasing use of the internet, and the widespread availability of desktop publishing, raise similar kinds of issues.'

One striking development in the post-modern campaign has been the increasing fragmentation of the electronic media, news programmes, and audiences. The erosion of the BBC/ITV duopoly of viewers has proceeded slowly in Britain, compared with the fall in the network share of the audience in Europe and North America. The *Six O'Clock* and *Nine O'Clock News* on BBC1, BBC2's 10.30pm *Newsnight*, ITN's early evening programme and ITN's *News at Ten*, and Channel 4's *Seven O'clock News* continued to have the broadest appeal for the mainstream audience (see Figure 2.2), along with regional news programmes and more specialist current affairs like *Panorama* and *A Week in Politics*. The sheer amount of news coverage produced by British television is substantial: in 1996/7 BBC television broadcast 1,687 hours of news programmes on both channels and 1,947 hours of current affairs, representing one-quarter of its total output (BBC Annual Report 1996/7).

The four main terrestrial channels continued to devote considerable resources to their public service functions in the campaign. During April 1997, election news absorbed more than half of the main BBC and ITV evening news programmes, only dipping at Easter and during the weekends, while over three-quarters of all coverage on Channel 4's *Seven O'Clock News* was devoted to election news (Harrison 1997). News junkies surfing from one channel to another during April could catch around ten hours of election news on average each weekday, from the *Breakfast News* in the morning to *Newsnight* in the late evening. Newspapers gave slightly less space to the campaign in 1997 than in previous contests, but nevertheless almost half of all editorials during April were devoted to the election (Scammell and Harrop 1997). There were special political supplements in many papers and during the campaign the election occupied more than a quarter of domestic news in the broadsheet press and one in seven stories in the tabloids. Chapter 6 goes on to analyse the audience for the news media, who watched, read and listened to this outpouring of stories, and their reaction to the coverage.

Nevertheless, the BBC and ITN flagships news programmes face rapidly increasing competition from the evolution of digital, cable and satellite television 'narrowcasting', and also from new forms of interactive communications like the internet. The first satellite services became available in

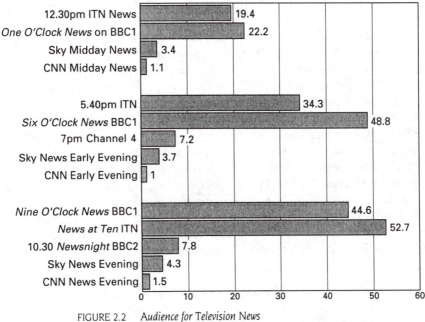

FIGURE 2.2   Audience for Television News
(% 'Usually watch at least one edition per week')
Source: ITC Television The Public View 1996.

Britain from Sky TV in February 1989, followed by BSB the following year. By 1992, about 3 per cent of homes had access to cable TV, while 10 per cent had a satellite dish. In contrast by 1997 almost a fifth of all households could tune in to over fifty channels on satellite and cable. In these homes, more than a third of all viewing was on these channels. During the campaign, between 10 and 15 per cent of the audience usually watched cable and satellite programmes every evening. Occasionally when there was wall-to-wall election on the terrestrial channels, as on Thursday 24 April 1997, a week before the election, the proportion of cable and satellite viewers jumped to almost a quarter of the audience. Moreover, Sky News, CNN, News 24, Channel 5, and BBC Radio's Five Live have altered the pace of news, to brief headlines on the hour every hour.

The internet also promises to transform news habits. In 1997 the availability of the BBC's *Election '97, ITN Online*, the online headlines from the Press Association and Reuters, party home pages, as well as electronic versions of *The Times* and the *Telegraph*, dramatically accelerated the news cycle. BBC's Online (http://news.bbc.co.uk/) with easy access to RealAudio broadcasts of its major political programmes and live parliamentary coverage, promises the shape of things to come. With 24-hour coverage, the acceleration of the news cycle has dramatically increased the need for parties to respond to, or get knocked off their feet by, a suddenly shifting agenda. By November 1997 almost one in ten citizens in Britain had access to the internet, or about five million people, close to the average for the EU (EuroBarometer 1997; Ward and Gibson 1998). In the United States the figures are higher: a Pew survey in May 1998 found that one-third of Americans (36 per cent) said they *ever* went online over the internet or World Wide Web, up from 21 per cent in April 1996. As well as access, regular use has also surged dramatically in just a few years. Pew estimated that in 1998 one-fifth of Americans went online at least once a week to get news, more than the size of the audience for news magazines, talk radio and many other traditional news outlets. Data from BBC Research and Development shows in mid-summer 1998 at least 1.3 million users access BBC Online each month. In the long run the internet promises to provide new resources for the politically mobilized and attentive (Norris 1998b). The internet has not yet displaced traditional reliance upon television and newspapers in Britain; nevertheless, by the next election it seems likely to change the news environment. The key issue here remains the consequences of these developments in the press and television for the process of campaign communications.

Party Communications during the Permanent Campaign

As press–party loyalties have declined, and the outlets for electronic news have diversified, politicians have been forced to respond to a more complex communications environment. The key indicators of the post-modern campaign include professionalization of campaign personnel, more sophisticated targeting of key voters and seats, increased expenditure on publicity, and the growing use of campaign techniques in government.

Parties have been transformed by the gradual evolution of the permanent campaign where the techniques of spin doctors, opinion polls, and professional media management are increasingly applied to routine everyday politics. The professionalization of party communications has increased in recent years although it has not yet reached the level evident in the United States. In Britain a few trusted experts in polling and political marketing are influential during the campaign in each party, such as Maurice Saatchi, Tim Bell and Gordon Reece at Conservative Central Office, but this role continues to be as part-time outside advisers, not integral to the process of government, nor even to campaigning which is still run by politicians. Unlike in the United States, no political marketing industry has developed, in large part because the only major clients are the Labour and Conservative party leaderships: the minor parties have limited resources, while parliamentary candidates run retail campaigns based on shoe-leather, grassroots helpers, and tight budgets. But the effect of television during recent years has been to shift the primary focus of the campaign from unpaid volunteers and local candidates towards the central party leadership flanked by paid, although not necessarily full-time, professionals (Scammell 1995; Kavanagh 1995; Denver and Hands 1997a). The daily cut and thrust of the 1997 campaign has already been described in detail in earlier accounts (Norris and Gavin 1997; Butler and Kavanagh 1997; King 1997) so here we will focus on highlighting the major developments in strategic communications and their consequences.

The Labour Campaign in 1997

The essential motto for Labour during the long and short campaign was 'play safe', a strategy memorably described by Lord Jenkins as similar to an elderly butler carrying a very precious Ming vase from one end of the room to the other. Three things about the campaign determined this strategy. First, Labour had been comfortably ahead in the polls almost ever since the previous election. Second, despite this, memories of 1992, which slipped from their grasp, and memories of eighteen years confined to the back-benches, meant that despite the polls few politicians or commentators believed that the outcome would be as cut and dried as all that. Lastly, after the fiasco of the opinion polls in 1992 there were serious doubts about their predictive ability.

As discussed earlier, the long-term collapse of Conservative support in the opinion polls and local and by-elections seems to have started on 'Black Wednesday' (16 September 1992) with the withdrawal of Britain from the European Monetary Union. On a single day, base interest rates at the bank bounced from 10 to 12 per cent, then 15 per cent a few hours later, then back to 12 per cent by the end of the day. The ERM debacle was widely believed to have destroyed notions of Conservative economic competence and simultaneously sowed the seeds for bitter internal divisions within the government over Britain's future within the European Union, although why this single event should have such profound political consequences remains a puzzle. After this, poll after poll reported the government in the doldrums (see Figure 2.3). Labour support hovered comfortably between 40 and 50 per cent. The election of Tony Blair as Labour leader after the sudden death of John Smith, in May 1994, and the transformation of 'New Labour' consolidated and boosted their lead in the opinion polls. Throughout 1995 the Conservatives languished at the lowest point for any government since regular polling began in 1945.

Labour's election machine in 1997 was widely regarded as effective, controlled in remaining on message, and sophisticated in targeting. The high-tech developments in media management at Millbank Tower were widely discussed in the press. Supposedly modelled on the war room in the Clinton campaign, the Millbank organization had a tight inner core, including Peter Mandelson, Gordon Brown, the press secretary Alastair Campbell, the pollster Philip Gould, Blair's personal assistant Anji Hunter, Lord Irvine of Lairg and Jonathan Powell. The interior circle was surrounded by about 200 staffers connecting via fax, modem and pagers to key shadow spokespersons and candidates in marginal constituencies, to keep the party 'on message'. Briefings were sent out nightly, sometimes twice a day. The Labour Party designed their communications strategy down to the smallest detail, with a rebuttal unit (and the Excalibur

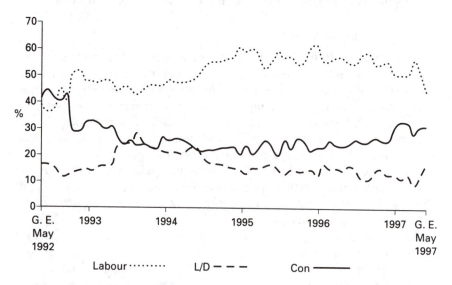

FIGURE 2.3 *Party Popularity 1992–97*
Source: Gallup Opinion Polls.

programme) under the direction of Adrian McMenamin, ready for a rapid response to anticipated attacks.

After 1992 Labour realized that elections are not usually won or lost in the official campaign, and they subsequently designed their strategy for the long-haul. Labour renewed their interest in constituency campaigns, although local contests became increasingly professionalized by strategic targeting of key voters under the guidance of Millbank Tower. Two years before polling day, a Labour task force was created which aimed to switch 5,000 voters in each of 90 target marginals. Those identified as potential Labour converts in these seats were contacted by teams of volunteers on the doorstep, and by a canvassing operation run from twenty telephone banks around the country, coordinated from Millbank during the campaign. In January 1997 'get out the vote' letters were sent to each type of target voter, and young people received a video of Tony Blair (Kavanagh 1997). Candidates in marginals were each asked to contact at least 1,000 switchers. Information from the canvassing operation, especially issues of concern raised by voters, was also fed back to Philip Gould, to help shape Labour's presentations (Gould 1998b).

Opinion polling was carried out regularly from late 1993, and Philip Gould and Deborah Mattinson conducted a programme of focus group research to monitor reaction to Labour's policies. Strategy meetings were conducted almost daily from late 1994, tackling Labour's weaknesses on taxation, trade unions, and crime well before the official campaign came close. The manifesto, *New Labour: Because Britain Deserves Better*, was designed to focus on five specific pledges: cutting class sizes for under seven-year-olds; fast-track punishments for persistent young offenders; reducing NHS waiting lists; moving 250,000 young unemployed into work; and cutting VAT on heating. By launching the draft manifesto *New Labour, New Life for Britain* as a dry run a year earlier, Labour had ample opportunity to iron out any pledges which proved unduly controversial. The main theme of Labour's advertising was 'Britain Deserves Better', fairly bland and safe, if unmemorable. To press home the message, Tony Blair visited 60 constituencies, travelling about 10,000 miles by road, rail and air, and providing controlled photo-opportunities rather than press conferences for the media. The membership drive launched by Blair was also part of this long-term strategy, increasing grassroots membership by almost two-thirds, up from 261,000 in 1991 to a peak of 405,000 in January 1998. This achievement was in stark contrast to Conservative Party membership which fell, from an estimated 1,000,000 in 1987 down to 400,000 at the time of the election, before falling further to around 300,000 eighteen months later (Evans and Norris 1999). Lastly Labour's assiduous courting of the City, including launching the special business manifesto, was all part of this careful planning to anticipate and batten down any lines of potential weakness.

Labour suffered a wobbly day or two in early April, over privatization of the air traffic control service, with contradictory messages coming from

Blair and Prescott. There were also some modest semi-trembles in the second week over the unions; for example, when Blair made an embarrassing 'parish council' slip over Scottish devolution. In the sixth week a poll by ICM for *The Guardian*, suggesting the Labour lead was closing, also induced concern in the Labour camp (Crewe 1997). But these were regarded as minor hiccups in an otherwise play-safe strategy which rolled inexorably towards victory.

The Conservative Campaign

In contrast, in the 1997 campaign Conservative Central Office more often appeared to be knocked off message by events out of their control, with the topics planned for press conferences torn up at the last minute. The campaign was led by the party chairman, Brian Mawhinney, the deputy leader Michael Heseltine, Danny Finkelstein, head of Tory Party research, and advised by Lord Saatchi, although up to twenty people attended strategy meetings, each with different priorities. During the long campaign the Conservatives seemed unable to decide whether the most effective strategy was to attack Old Labour (the party of trade unions and taxes) or New Labour (the party of 'smarmy', 'phoney' and untrustworthy Blair). Tory briefings, and posters, veered back and forth uncertainly. Their most effective slogans were probably 'Britain is Booming – Don't let Labour Blow it', or 'New Labour, New Danger', but their advertising was generally regarded as unconvincing (indeed their 'Tony and Bill' poster was widely believed to be a Labour advertisement).

In the midst of the campaign the Conservatives became deeply mired in divisions, arguing with each other rather than addressing the public, as the splits over Europe burst open again. On 14 April the *Mail* published a list of 183 Conservative candidates who had come out against the Euro in their constituency leaflets, in contradiction to the official 'wait and see' line. In response John Major tore up the PEB planned for 17 April, and instead broadcast an impromptu appeal on Europe. But the internal row only intensified the following day with publication of a Conservative advertisement showing Blair as a puppet on Kohl's lap, which brought public criticism from Edward Heath and Ken Clarke (as well as offence from Germany), thereby only highlighting Conservative splits. Other diversions included speculation about the Tory leadership election to replace Major, and comments like Edwina Currie's prediction of Conservative defeat in the twilight days of the campaign. In short, the Conservative message of Britain's economic health was drowned out as much by internal conflicts, fuelled but not caused by the media, as by anything the opposition did or said. The *Mail* may have tossed the lighted match, but the row between Eurosceptics and Europhiles was a conflagration waiting to happen, based on years of a party tearing itself apart.

After the event, when the sums were added up, both major sides had gone into debt because of record expenditures. The increasing importance attached to strategic communications is demonstrated by post-war levels of central party expenditure which have risen dramatically in recent decades (see Tables 2.6 and 2.7). The figures are not strictly comparable across parties but the most reliable estimates were compiled for the Neill Report (1998). According to these figures, in the twelve months prior to 1 May 1997 the three major parties spent around £56.4 million at national level, up from £23.2 million in 1992, £15.3 million in 1987, and £7.7 million in 1983. In real terms, controlling for inflation (at 1997 prices), total expenditure by all three major parties has risen from £14.1 million in 1983 to £56.4 million in 1997, a four-fold increase.

In 1997 total campaign expenditure by both major parties was fairly evenly balanced, but the Liberal Democrats lagged far behind. The Conservatives spent £28.3 million in the twelve months before polling day. Since the party was already £19 million in debt in 1996 this created serious financial problems and subsequent staff cuts at Central Office and in the regions. Labour spent £26.0 million at national level but the Liberal Democrats were the poor relations, spending only £2.1 million. The type of expenditure also varied between parties (see Table 2.8). The highest item for every party at national level, absorbing almost half their funds, remained 'traditional' campaigning including the costs of rallies, events, leadership tours, election personnel and opinion polling. But Labour invested far more heavily than the Conservatives on this approach to getting out the grassroots vote. The next highest item was for outdoors advertising and the 'poster wars'. The Conservatives spent £11.1 million on bill-boards, compared with only £4.8 spent by Labour. Whether the Conservative investment paid off seems doubtful, in view of the critical

TABLE 2.6: *General Election Expenditure, 1983–97 (£m)*

	1983	1987	1992	1997	Total
Labour	2.2	4.4	10.2	26.0	42.8
Conservative	3.6	9.0	11.2	28.3	52.1
Liberal Democrat	1.9	1.9	1.8	2.1	7.7
Total	7.7	15.3	23.2	56.4	102.6

Note: Expenditure calculated at 1997 prices.

Source: 5th Report of the Committee on Standards in Public Life chaired by Lord Neill. 1998. Table 3.10. Cm 4057 London: The Stationery Office.

TABLE 2.7: *General Election Expenditure at Constant Prices, 1983–97 (£m)*

	1983	1987	1992	1997	Total
Labour	4.0	6.6	11.2	26.0	+22.0
Conservative	6.6	13.8	12.7	28.3	+21.7
Liberal Democrat	3.5	2.9	2.0	2.1	-1.4
Total	14.1	23.3	25.9	56.4	42.3

Note: Expenditure calculated at 1997 prices.

Source: 5th Report of the Committee on Standards in Public Life chaired by Lord Neill. 1998. Table 3.11. Cm 4057 London: The Stationery Office.

TABLE 2.8: *Type of Campaign Expenditure,* 1997

	Conservative	Labour	Liberal Democrat	Total	per cent of Total
Rallies, events, campaign tours, polling, personnel, touring, etc.	10.2	15.5	1.3	27.0	48.2 per cent
Outdoor advertising	11.1	4.8	0.1	16.0	28.4 per cent
Direct mail	2.2	1.8	0.2	4.2	7.5 per cent
Newspaper advertising	3.2	0.9		4.1	7.3 per cent
Publications	1.0	1.5	0.2	2.7	4.8 per cent
Party political broadcasting	0.5	0.6	0.2	1.3	2.3 per cent
Telemarketing	0.0	0.5	0.3	0.8	1.4 per cent
Other advertising	0.1	0.1		0.2	0.3 per cent
Total	28.3	25.7	2.3	56.3	100 per cent

Source: 5th Report of the Committee on Standards in Public Life chaired by Lord Neill. 1998. Tables 3.5, 3.7, 3.9. Cm 4057. London: The Stationery Office.

reception given to many of their posters. After the election Lord Parkinson, Chairman of the Conservative Party, expressed some regret at this priority: 'The emphasis was on poster boards and a lot of money was spent on this. I am not sure that one could say, in the light of the result, that one got a lot of value out of it.' (Neill Report 1998: Vol. 2:121). Parties also spent £4.2 million on direct mail, allowing more sophisticated voter targeting with specific messages, £4.1 million on newspaper advertising, £2.7 million on publications like leaflets and the manifesto, and only £1.3 million on the production of party political broadcasts. Although television is widely regarded as one of the most important resources in modern election campaigns, direct party expenditure on PPBs is relatively low. It should be noted that there are also substantial hidden subsidies in the present system, notably the provision of free airtime for party broadcasts. If parties had to pay for this on a commercial basis the Neill report estimates that the airtime would have cost £20 million each to Labour and the Conservatives, and £16 million to the Liberal Democrats.

Conclusions

The shift towards the permanent campaign in Britain has still not gone as far as in the United States, in part because of the pattern of longer electoral cycles at Westminster. Nevertheless the way that the techniques for campaigning are becoming merged with the techniques of governing was symbolized by the way that Tony Blair, once elected Prime Minister, announced monthly 'meet the public' sessions, to attract popular support and publicity outside of his appearances in the Commons, following the example of President Clinton's 'town-hall' meetings. Moreover, many of those who played a key role in controlling Labour campaign communications were transferred to Number 10, with the aim of adopting the same techniques in government. Given a more complex communications environment, modern parties have been forced to adapt, with greater or lesser success, to the new communications environment if they are to survive unscathed.

The 1997 election suggests that the evolution to a post-modern campaign currently remains in transition in Britain and certain components are more clearly developed than others. In particular, the full impact of the digital television revolution and the internet remains uncertain, and if Britain experiences an explosion of channels the next election is probably going to be fought in a very different broadcasting environment. Nevertheless, these trends are producing a distinctively new context for the process of political campaigning in Britain, as elsewhere, characterized by dealignment of the press, an increasingly fragmented electronic media, and, in response, more strategic attempts by parties to maintain control and remain on message. The term 'post-modern' captures a communication process which has become increasingly diverse, fragmented, and complex. Similar developments have been identified in many advanced industrialized societies, although the timing and impact of these changes is mediated by each nation's culture, political system, and media structure (Butler and Ranney 1992). The consequences of this transition remain a matter of dispute. Some critics, reflecting on similar patterns in the United States, fear these developments will serve to disconnect leaders and citizens, over-simplify and trivialize political discourse, and produce a more cynical and disengaged public which tunes out from politics altogether (Franklin 1994). Others, however, remain more sanguine (Kavanagh 1995), while some speculate that the fragmentation of media outlets may provide a positive opportunity for more varied, and less mainstream, cultural voices to be heard.

What have been the consequences of the news coverage? During the 1997 British election many voices expressed disquiet about media coverage and its possible effects upon voters. We can identify two major types of criticism. One school of thought claimed that television failed to provide serious, critical and informed debate about public policy issues. The news media were frequently overtaken by a feeding frenzy focusing on sexual and financial sleaze, and later the high drama of Conservative Party splits over Europe. The obsession with sensationalism and party conflict may have obscured debate about many complex issues facing Britain and hindered critical scrutiny of the new Blair agenda. Yet another school argued that, far from providing too little serious coverage of the election, television – particularly the BBC – provided far too much (Semetko, Scammell and Goddard 1997). In this view the news media was charged with presenting a saturation diet of politics during the long campaign, including BBC1's specially extended *Nine O'Clock News*, as well as the extensive campaign supplements in all the broadsheet newspapers, and this, some suggest, may have contributed towards bored and turned-off voters. Establishing how the party campaign reached voters, and whether the contents of the news coverage had these effects upon readers and viewers, as commonly assumed, is the task of subsequent chapters.

Notes

1. See the BBC Producer Guidelines 1996 Chapter 19, (5.1): *http://www.bbc.co.uk/info/editorial/prodgl.*
2. See ITC Programme Code: *http://www.itc.org.uk/regulating.*
3. Section 93 of the Representation of the People Act is designed to ensure strict impartiality by requiring the prior consent of every candidate in a seat to any broadcast about the constituency during the campaign. But it only regulates coverage of particular parliamentary candidates running in particular constituencies, not the national campaign.
4. It should be noted that the parties determine the editorial contents of the programmes although as the publisher the broadcasters must ensure that the programmes follow the law on libel and contempt, and also follow accepted standards of taste and decency. The precise timing of election broadcasts is also within the hands of the television companies.

3 Understanding Media Effects

Although assumptions about the impact of political communications are commonplace, finding systematic evidence to test these claims raises complex theoretical and methodological challenges. Did viewers learn from the extensive coverage of issues like pensions and taxation on the extended BBC News? Did *The Sun*'s defection to Labour switch their readers? Did negative campaigning turn off the public? Did the focus upon Europe raise the importance of this issue in the minds of voters? Many approaches are available to test these claims, usually combining alternative methodologies so as to understand the process of message production, contents and effects (see, for example, literature reviews by McQuail 1992; Bryant and Zillmann 1994; Lowery and DeFleur 1995; Baran and Davis 1995). Any single methodology – such as panel surveys or content analysis – provides insights into only one dimension. In an attempt to overcome these limitations this study adopts a multi-method research design drawing upon many interrelated sources of data. This includes five main elements:

- the content analysis of news and party messages
- aggregate trends in public opinion polls
- the 1997 British Election Study (BES) cross-sectional survey
- the 1997 British Election Study (BES) campaign panel survey
- the experimental study of television news.

The logic of the integrated research design is summarized in Figure 3.1 with full details provided in the Technical Appendix. The advantage of this design is that content analysis enables us to understand the process of campaign communications and the messages which the public received. The experiments allow us to test assumptions about possible causal mechanisms (if x is true then y is possible) and the panel study allows us to see whether these relationships existed in the actual campaign. Each component has certain strengths and weaknesses but in combination they provide an invaluable set of research tools.

Content Analysis of News and Party Messages

First, we need a systematic and reliable map about the contents of the campaign, including the messages disseminated by parties and those covered in the national news media. How much news was devoted to each of the major parties? What issues were prioritized? What was the balance of 'positive' and 'negative' messages? How did coverage vary between news media and during the course of the campaign? The first component of this research design therefore involved content analysis of the media coverage and party messages during the official general election campaign.

We monitored BBC1's *Nine O'Clock News*, ITN's *News at Ten*, and Sky evening news, along with a representative sample of the national daily press (*The Sun, The Mirror, Daily Mail, The Independent, The Guardian, The Times* and in Scotland two major tabloids and one broadsheet). The content analysis covered all front-page stories mentioning British politicians or political parties, including the stories' placement, type, subject, actor, sources, direction, and visuals. The data allows comparison with the 1987 and 1992 elections, and the coding scheme was designed to allow daily comparison with public opinion trends monitored in the 1997 BES campaign panel survey and in commercial polls. The variables for the content analysis are based on those developed by Semetko *et al.* (1991), which have also been used to study media coverage of recent elections in Germany (Semetko and Schoenbach, 1994), Spain (Diez-Nicolas and Semetko 1995), and the United States.

Parties attempt to contact voters using a variety of sources, from local leaflets and personal canvassing to advertising on bill-boards and in national newspapers. Leadership speeches, rallies and photo-ops are all important ways in which parties try to capture attention. Yet it is difficult to get a systematic overview of the national campaign from such sources which vary from one place to another. To provide an accurate picture of the party messages at national level we analysed the contents of the party manifestos, the daily press releases and party election broadcasts. Manifestos provide the fullest official statement of each party's policy proposals and have been widely used to analyse their position across the left–right ideological spectrum (Budge and Farlie 1983; Klingemann, Hofferbert and Budge 1994; Budge 1999). The manifesto is rarely read by the public but it provides the official programme which is designed to set out each party's stall. Manifestos are launched with great fanfare at the start of the official campaign and the contents are carefully scrutinized by commentators and other parties. The press releases provide an alternative source which more closely reflects the daily campaign. In these documents parties try to launch their main theme de jour, whether health, education or taxation, which may then be coordinated with other events and photo-ops.

Lastly, without the ability to pay for television advertising, the party broadcasts represent the only opportunity for parties to present unmediated messages to the television public. In Britain the PEBs are regulated with an agreed allocation of time. During the 1997 general election, in line with many previous contests, the ratio was 5:5:4, meaning that the Conservatives and Labour were each given five ten-minute PEBs,

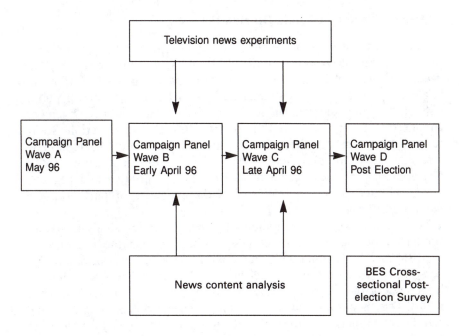

FIGURE 3.1   *The 1997 British Election Study*

while the Liberal Democrats were allowed four. Minor parties which mustered a minimum of fifty candidates, like the UK Independence Party and the Greens, received at least one five-minute broadcast each, with additional arrangements for Scotland, Wales and Northern Ireland (for details see Harrison 1997:149–54). We analysed what messages the parties sought to convey through these broadcasts, whether issues like health, the economy or pensions. To understand the thinking behind party strategies, we also conducted interviews with party managers and campaign strategists. Based on these data we compare the contents of the party and the news agenda, to see how far these converged or diverged during the course of the campaign, and which party was most successful in getting 'its' issue agenda covered in the news media.

Nevertheless, content analysis is silent, in itself, about the effects of coverage. In Britain one body of research in the 1970s, by the Glasgow Media Group, content-analysed the news and focused on the extent to which supposedly 'objective' broadcasts exhibit different sorts of political bias as a result of the 'news values' espoused by programme editors (Glasgow Media Group 1976, 1980; for a critique see Harrison 1989). Although these studies have revealed much about the way in which news values influence contents, they have not explicitly analysed whether the identified 'biases' in news coverage have any consequences for public opinion. Indeed, they have not investigated the links between news contents and public opinion at all.

Aggregate Trends in Public Opinion Polls

To establish the effects of the news we need to link what was covered in the media with the response of the electorate. One common strategy has been to analyse changes in the contents of campaign messages and to relate this, more or less systematically, to changes over time in public opinion at aggregate-level. The national opinion polls conducted by major commercial companies as well as the 1997 British Election Study campaign panel survey allow us to monitor the pulse of public opinion on a regular basis throughout the official campaign. In Chapter 9 we utilize this approach, comparing the overall balance of positive and negative news for each party on television with the levels of party support monitored in campaign polls during April 1997.

The methodology is exemplified by the cultivation analysis studies conducted by George Gerbner (1980) who explored the influence of television violence on public perceptions of a 'mean world'. In this perspective what we watch on television, whether violent police dramas, local news or the soaps, is believed gradually to shape our views of social reality. This theory assumes that the media have a diffuse, long-term and cumulative influence on the political culture. It's the steady drumbeat of messages, not individual exposure, which is believed to entrench mainstream orientations for most viewers. Content analysis provides a systematic description of the media landscape. Using this approach, for example, Patterson (1993: 23) documented growing negative coverage of politicians in news magazines from 1960 to 1992 which mirrored trends in declining political trust in American public opinion during these years. Studies in Germany and Sweden have shown increased coverage of scandals and negative news which has parallelled falling confidence in political leaders (Westerstahl and Johansson 1986; Kepplinger 1996; Friedrichsen 1996).

In Britain this research design has been used by Gavin and Sanders (1996) to explore the impact of economic news using content analysis of news on the major UK television channels over a 15-month period. Coverage, across a range of sub-categories, was coded as 'positive' (i.e. favourable to the government), 'negative' (unfavourable), or neutral. Weekly variations in the balance of coverage (positive versus negative) were compared with aggregate movements in voters' political preferences and economic perceptions. The study found significant relationships between the pattern of coverage over time and changes in public opinion, but its conclusions were necessarily tentative.

Nevertheless, there are some important limitations with this approach. Aggregate-level analysis of this sort involves making quite strong (critics would say heroic) assumptions about what is going on at the individual level. In order to draw causal inferences about individual attitudes and behaviour, it must be assumed that the 'typical voter' is exposed each week to the balance of news coverage indicated by the aggregate-level coverage measure and that s/he responds to changes in that balance in a more or less consistent fashion. The limitations of these assumptions are self-evident. Aggregate-level correlations, since they reveal nothing about individuals, can be highly misleading. The parallel trends over time may be independent, or the association may be spurious, as the result of other causal factors, or the direction of causality may be reversed. Nevertheless it is important to analyse baseline trends in the contents of the news coverage during the 1997 campaign, and to compare these with baseline trends in public opinion monitored by surveys. If we can establish an association – for example, between growing negative news coverage of one party and a decline in public support for that party – this can be understood as at least indicative of a significant association, even if we cannot yet regard it as evidence of a causal relationship.

The 1997 British Election Study Cross-sectional Survey

Another stream of research has examined evidence for the effects of the media at individual level using cross-sectional surveys, notably the series of British Election Studies from 1964 to 1997. The behavioural approach has focused on understanding the conditions which are believed to produce certain effects, including variations in the source, content, channel, receivers and destination (McQuail 1997). Most commonly, studies have compared the attitudes and behaviour of regular users of different types of media, such as newspapers and television news in Britain, or viewers of television debates and campaign ads in America.

The first academic surveys of voting behaviour in Britain were carried out in constituencies in the 1950s and 1960s (Milne and MacKenzie 1958; Birch 1959; Bealey *et al.* 1965). Some of these pioneered the analysis of the effects of television (Trenaman and McQuail 1961; Blumler and McQuail 1968). The field was transformed by the series of British Election Study (BES) surveys initiated in 1963 and carried out in every subsequent general election (see the Technical Appendix). The 1997 British Election Study post-election cross-sectional survey was selected by probability sampling methods from Post Office Address Files. Some 3,615 people from throughout Britain (including a booster sample of 882 Scots) were interviewed face-to-face using laptop computers (CAPI). Respondents were also given a self-completion supplement. The principal purpose of the regular cross-sectional study was to measure long-term change in electoral attitudes and behaviour. The BES builds on surveys of the electorate undertaken at each of the last ten general elections, spanning some three decades. These allow us to explore the relationship between use and attention to the media and a wide range of political attitudes.

Nevertheless, there are well-established difficulties in disentangling the reciprocal relationship between media use and political attitudes using only cross-sectional surveys. For example, Putnam (1995) analysed the US

General Social Survey to demonstrate that the heaviest users of television were least socially trusting and least willing to join community groups. Putnam related these findings to broader trends in civic engagement. He argued that as television saturated American homes in the 1950s this produced a post-civic generation. This helped to explain the cohort patterns of political mobilization and why citizens raised in this cultural environment were less likely than their parents to trust others, to join voluntary associations, and to vote. Television is thereby indicted for the dramatic erosion of civic engagement and social capital in America. Yet other research has challenged the pernicious effects of television news. Watching a lot of British television news, for example, is associated with some modest levels of mobilization (Newton 1991, 1997; Norris 1997a). What we cannot establish through these surveys is the direction of causation: whether people who watch TV news are the most politically interested, or whether those who watch TV news become more interested in the election, or both.

Butler and Stokes (1974) first asked respondents about their television-watching habits in 1964 and the questions they posed have been supplemented, in subsequent BES surveys, by questions about voters' perceptions of bias in the news coverage provided by BBC and ITN. The data thus obtained, however, have provided limited insight into the effects of television news on voters' preferences. Mughan (1996), for example, found that voters' perceptions of bias in news coverage were linked to their partisan identifications: party supporters tended to believe that news coverage on both major channels was biased against 'their' party. This relationship, however, in no way helps to 'explain' voters' partisan preferences. It indicates that partisan preferences affect voters' perceptions of television news, not that news influences preferences. Unless we can link the contents of news programmes which respondents have seen to their political attitudes it is not possible to specify and test convincing causal models that seek to assess the effects of television news on voters.

The problem with individual-level studies of cross-sectional data is that, while more persuasive than aggregate analysis, this approach still cannot establish the classic chicken-and-egg direction of causality. Does political interest cause us to turn on Channel 4's *Seven O'Clock News* or *Panorama*, or does watching these programmes make us more politically interested? Does watching television produce less social trust and community involvement? Or do people who don't trust others and are not engaged in their community prefer, as a matter of personal choice, to stay home and watch TV? Do people pick up a paper which reflects their party leanings, or does their partisanship flow from the papers they read? We cannot tell. The 'uses and gratifications' approach argues that we select the programmes to watch which are most in tune with our prior predispositions and tastes (Blumler and Katz 1974). Hence Blair supporters would be more likely to watch another Labour party political broadcast. This process thereby reinforces, but does not change, our political attitudes.

There are other difficulties of interpretation. Patterns of media use are closely related to many other factors, like education and class, which are usually associated with political attitudes. Moreover, our claims often make generalizations about 'television' as though there is a single experience of this medium. Ideally we need to compare the effects of variance in the media messages, so that we can see whether people who consistently use one source (such as crime-focused tabloid newspapers) differ from those who use others (like the politically-focused *The Week in Westminster*). Unfortunately in practice with survey research it is often difficult to disentangle television sources: our measures of media habits are often diffuse and imprecise; there is little variance in the contents of mainstream sources like television news on different channels; and lastly we usually have multiple and overlapping uses of different media (readers of tabloid newspapers, for example, often watch much popular entertainment on television).

The 1997 British Election Study Campaign Panel Survey

Cross-sectional surveys can therefore demonstrate an association between media use and political attitudes, but this, by itself, fails to unravel the direction of causality. Moreover, many available measures of media use in past surveys are problematic since they usually fail to capture the complexity of patterns of attention to different sources. The experience of regularly watching current affairs programmes like *Panorama* or *A Week in Politics*, for example, could be expected to be very different from occasionally catching the local news headlines while tuning in to catch the football results. Just as we commonly distinguish between use of the tabloids and broadsheet papers, so we also need to distinguish the effects of different patterns of television watching. To overcome these limitations we need research designs which analyse the dynamics of public opinion over time. Panel surveys allow us to monitor changes during the campaign in political attitudes, or media habits, or both.

The 1997 campaign panel survey was part of the British Election Study (BES). The baseline face-to-face interviews (Wave A) were conducted by SCPR as part of the 1996 British Social Attitudes survey among a random sample of the adult British population. The first wave, in May–July 1996, represented the start of the 'long campaign' during the twelve months prior to polling day. Respondents were re-contacted by telephone for three subsequent waves of the survey. The official campaign ran for six weeks from the dissolution of Parliament on 17 March to 1 May 1997. Wave B interviews were completed during the first two weeks of April. Wave C interviews occurred during the last two weeks of April. Lastly respondents were re-contacted for the last post-election interview just after polling day on 1 May (Wave D).

The BES campaign panel survey contained questions on voting

intentions, political trust and efficacy, political issues, media use, knowledge of party policies, economic evaluations, political competence, party image and party leadership. These items were repeated in successive waves. Those interviewed on any one day during the campaign were a random sub-set of the respondents to allow a 'rolling thunder' analysis of change on a daily basis.

The BES campaign panel allows us to monitor the short-term effects of media use, as well as long-term effects, by comparing different categories of media users. The advantages of the panel design is that it allows us to document 'real' change among a representative sample of the electorate. Analysis is based on the 1,422 persons who responded to all four waves.

Experimental Studies

The panel helps us to understand how the public reacted to the news during the course of the official campaign. But panel surveys remain limited when looking at the effects of specific types of messages; for example, the short-term effect of a particular party election broadcast, or a leadership speech, or an event occurring during the campaign. Ever since early work at Yale (Hovland *et al.* 1949, 1953), studies have used experiments to monitor the process of short-term individual-level opinion change in response to specific media messages. Early research looked at the impact of war propaganda for the Allies. Experiments have the potential to provide some of the most convincing evidence for significant effects from exposure to the mass media. In recent years this approach has undergone a revival, largely as a result of the work of Shanto Iyengar (Iyengar and Kinder 1987; Iyengar 1991). One influential recent study (Ansolabehere and Iyengar 1995) demonstrated that watching negative or 'attack' television advertising discouraged voter turnout and decreased political efficacy in the United States. Other experiments have found American network news guilty of sensationalizing and over-simplifying complex issues like health care, producing a 'spiral of cynicism' among the public (Cappella and Jamieson 1997).

During the 1990s experimental methods have gradually entered the standard repertoire of political science. Nevertheless, because this approach remains less familiar than survey analysis we will outline our research design in some detail. Sanders and Norris were funded by the ESRC to study the effects of television news on negative news, agenda-setting and party balance in the 1997 general election. To examine the effects of news coverage on voters' perceptions, we carried out a series of experiments in a central London location (Regent Street). We included 1,125 respondents in total, more than most experimental designs. Participants were drawn primarily from Greater London and south-east England. Respondents were not selected explicitly as a random sample of the British electorate, but they did generally reflect the Greater London population in terms of their social background and party preferences. We chose a busy central London location during the day to provide a diverse group of Londoners including managers, office-workers and casual shoppers. The generalizability of the results rests not on the selection of a random sample of participants, as in a survey design, but on the way that subjects were assigned at random to different experimental groups. Any difference in the response of groups should therefore reflect the stimuli they were given rather than their social backgrounds or prior political attitudes.

One potential problem of experiments is that participants may alter their own behaviour given the artificiality of the research setting and their perceptions of the aims of the study. In order to counter this, respondents were told that they would be participating in research to learn how people evaluate and understand television news. Prior to the experiment, we informed respondents (falsely) that we were primarily interested in 'selective perception', that is, whether young people and older people, or men and women, are interested in different stories in the news. We did not mention that the news would be about the election, which might well have discouraged participation by the politically apathetic, and we found that many participants believed we were carrying out television market research. We used a single-shot rather than a repeated design so that respondents would not become unduly conditioned by the research process itself.

Participants completed a short (15-minute) pre-test questionnaire about their media habits, political interests and opinions and personal background. They were then assigned at random to groups of 5–15 to watch a 30-minute video compilation of television news. Respondents subsequently completed a short (15-minute) post-test questionnaire. The experiments were carried out in April 1997 during the middle of the official general election campaign. This timing was deliberate: we wanted to examine the attitudes of participants who had been subjected to the intensive barrage of political coverage that characterizes television news during an election period.

The video compilations of news stories were chosen to represent a 'typical' evening news programme during the campaign. We drew on stories recorded from mid-February until early to mid-April 1997. The programmes sampled were *Nine O'Clock News* (BBC1), *News at Ten* (ITN), *Channel 4 News* and *Newsnight* (BBC2). The videos all had the same format. They consisted of a 'sandwich', with ten minutes of identical, standard footage at the top and bottom of each programme and one of fifteen different experimental video stimuli in the middle 'core'. Respondents were not told which video was being shown to which group or even that different videos were being watched by different groups of respondents. Details about the videos are provided in the Appendix and described in subsequent chapters. Full transcriptions of the content of the videos are available from the authors. In addition to the treatment groups, we also monitored the reactions of control groups shown different news stories. Throughout the analysis we compare pre- to post-test changes in the response among the group shown a particular video stimuli compared with the control. As with other methodologies, experiments commonly suffer from certain shortcomings, particularly the generalizability of the results to the population at large. The triangulation of the research design, combining content analysis of the actual news environment with the panel survey, measuring the public's reaction during the campaign, and the experiments monitoring responses to changes in television news, provided the best mix of approaches.

Conclusions

There is no single ideal methodology to explore the complex and difficult issue of media effects. Alternative approaches have different strengths and weaknesses. Previous empirical studies have utilized a variety of alternative types of research designs, notably:

- macro-level studies comparing content analysis of the news media messages with trends in public opinion
- cross-sectional surveys monitoring the association between individual-level media use and political attitudes
- panel surveys measuring changes in media exposure and political attitudes during the course of the campaign
- experiments measuring the conditional effects of media messages on changes in political attitudes.

We concluded that the most satisfactory approach was a multi-method research design which combined different methods and data. If we establish similar patterns in each of the alternative approaches then this increases confidence that our results are not simply a methodological artifact. The sum of the research project is more than the parts, and the integration allows us to generalize more widely from the findings. If we establish significant differences in the results, then this also has important implications for our research. We can go on to explore the evidence for how far the roles of parties and the news media have been transformed in recent years by the modernization process.

PART II

PROCESS

4　The Party Strategy

The 1997 election was a landmark in British campaigning. The territory marked out was all Labour's, and, especially Tony Blair's. By common consent their campaign was a major leap in the techniques of controlled electioneering (Butler and Kavanagh 1997: 243). It was the most determinedly professional piece of political communication in British electoral history, constructed around a tight corps of party leaders who stayed ruthlessly on message to the point of near-robotic incantation of key themes and slogans. Labour's remarkable triumph has reverberated across the Atlantic and over Europe. It is a measure of its international impact that Labour and Blair now provide the campaigning models for comparison, not just in Britain, but in assessments of Europe's social democrat parties. Technically, Labour's campaign may have been 'a thing of grace and beauty' (Harrop 1997: 315) but what is the hard evidence that it ran the best campaign?

The evidence of the result is clearly not sufficient. There are competing explanations of the outcome, not least that the Conservatives lost it, through years of infighting, sleaze and, especially, an economic reputation severely damaged by ejection from the European Exchange Rate Mechanism on 'Black Wednesday' in September 1992 (Sanders 1996; Whiteley 1997). Moreover, Labour actually lost ground in the opinion polls during the campaign, its lead slipping by seven points in the six weeks from announcement of the election in March to polling day on 1 May. This chapter examines the elements of a good campaign. First, this requires that some criteria are established for assessing a good campaign. Our criteria are based on three dimensions:

1. Party Strategy

A coherent and workable strategy is accepted by campaigners and scholars alike as the most important criterion of an effective campaign (Faucheux 1995; Harrop 1997; Scammell 1995; Thurber and Nelson 1995).

The strategy sets out party objectives, identifies target voters, establishes the battleground issues, and generally lays the framework within which campaign communications are constructed. We outline below the main elements of the strategies developed by each of the Conservative, Labour and Liberal Democrat parties as they entered the campaign.

2. Campaign Communications

Modern campaigns are fought overwhelmingly in the media. News in the media and advertising offer the main contact between politicians and voters, eclipsing the pre-TV era techniques of mobilization: mass door-to-door canvassing, leafleting and rallies. Election campaigns ignore TV at their peril, and as a consequence, have come to be designed for the cameras. Since the Conservatives' pioneering campaign in 1979, all parties have demonstrated heightened awareness of the particular demands of TV news: the importance of deadlines, news values, novelty, personality and appropriate pictures. It was a newsworthy event when the Conservatives hired a TV producer (Sir Gordon Reece) and a leading advertising agency (Saatchi & Saatchi) to orchestrate their 1979 campaign. It would now cause a minor sensation if a major party *did not* employ the professional services of advertisers, TV experts and 'spin doctors'.

The parties' media campaigns can be summed up in the phrase 'the battle of the agendas'. Each party attempts to raise the news profile of issues and themes it considers most favourable for itself and most damaging to rivals, in the belief that prominence in the news will translate into increased salience in voters' minds, and thus influence voting decisions. This campaigning logic is in line with agenda-setting theories of media effects, which state broadly that if the media do not quite tell us what to think, they tell us what to think about (McCombs and Shaw 1972). The tussle to influence TV news agendas is particularly marked in Britain for two main reasons. First, paid political advertising is prohibited on television, thus denying the parties the crucial 'unmediated' means of persuasion available to US candidates. Second, the particular electoral obligations and traditions of public service on British TV guarantee prominent and balanced coverage for each party (see Chapter 2). Parties can be sure of, and prepare for, greatly increased opportunities to influence the electoral news bulletins, compared to normal 'peace-time' coverage. Again, this is in marked contrast to the relatively unregulated free market of US television where network news is driven far more by the usual news values and less by abstract notions of public service (Semetko *et al.* 1991).

If television is the key battleground for the news agenda, the importance of newspapers cannot be underestimated in Britain. The vigorously partisan national press, especially the tabloid newspapers, have been shown to have a significant, albeit modest, direct impact on voting choice

(Curtice and Semetko 1994; Miller 1991), rather more than TV. Historically newspaper partisanship has favoured the Conservatives. During the Thatcher glory years the papers were overwhelmingly Conservative (Harrop and Scammell 1992; Linton 1995) and the Tories could rely on their tabloid supporters for character assassination of Labour's leaders (Seymour-Ure 1995). However, after the 1992 election the traditional Tory papers cooled significantly towards John Major (Scammell and Harrop 1997). Partly through changes in press ownership and partly through tabloid disenchantment with Major's European monetary policy, the distribution of tabloid favours was far less predictable in the run-up to 1997. The 'battle of the agendas', therefore, promised to be far more competitive than usual.

Elsewhere (Chapter 5) we compare the changing news agendas over the last three British elections. Curiously, however, there has been little research in Britain which has attempted to quantify the party agendas and compare them against news output. There is no British equivalent of the US research that has systematically analysed candidates' preferred themes and issues on the basis of their advertising messages (Just *et al.* 1996). Assessments of agenda-setting success in Britain have had to rely instead on the *claims* of party strategists and match these against the content of news agendas (Scammell 1995). Previous measurements therefore have been of the subjective claims of what parties did rather than objective content analysis of their messages. This chapter sets out to remedy this omission through analysis of the party agendas as evidenced by their manifestos, their press releases issued during the campaign and their party election broadcasts (PEBs). This will provide three ways of assessing which party waged the best campaign:

- It will allow us to judge the internal coherence of the party campaign. How closely did the communications match the overall objectives of strategy?
- It will allow us to measure agenda-setting success. Which party's preferred agenda featured most prominently in the news?
- It will provide the basis for comparing party agendas against changes in the salience of issues in the public agenda.

3. The Civic Dimension

Our third criterion of a 'good campaign' is concerned not with judgements of effectiveness in terms of winning and losing, but with the quality of political discourse. US research has shown trends to increasingly negative party campaigning and has linked these to evidence of declining citizen engagement with the democratic process and increasing voter apathy (Ansolabehere and Iyengar 1995; Cappella and Jamieson 1997). Our analysis will be able to examine the *type* of information parties were seeking to put in the public domain. To what extent was it about substantive policy issues, to what extent about image and character? Is there evidence that Britain, too, is 'going negative', and if so, what are the consequences for citizen engagement?

Party Strategies

The Conservative Party

As discussed in the introduction, some political scientists have argued that the Conservatives effectively lost the election on Black Wednesday, 16 September 1992, when Britain was ejected from the European Exchange Rate Mechanism (ERM). The party's reputation for economic competence was severely damaged in that moment and never recovered sufficiently (Sanders 1996). Conservative Party strategists did not appear to agree. In the three years prior to the 1997 election and going into the campaign itself, they continued to believe that the economy was their strongest suit, just as it had been for the previous four elections. The party's traditional lead over Labour in the opinion polls on economic competence provided its main strategic weapon, summed up in its campaign theme: 'Britain is booming. Don't let Labour blow it' (interview with Sir Tim Bell). The strategy was based partly on their tried and trusted experience of the 1992 campaign. The unremitting attacks on Labour's tax and spending plans in 1992 were widely regarded by both Labour and Tory strategists to have worked, producing the late swing to the Conservatives which won the election (Scammell 1995: 260–8). The Conservatives planned to repeat the dose in 1997, focusing on the 'black hole' in Labour's spending proposals, exposing the 'costs' of Labour, in higher inflation, mortgages, tax increases and job losses. At the same time, the Conservatives could stand by their economic record, pointing to low and declining inflation, income tax cuts, export-led recovery and improving employment figures in the years since 1994.

> We are saying that we manage the economy well and that we have spread prosperity throughout the country, and that we would like to continue to do so, spreading prosperity deeper, through a whole list of measures including more tax cuts and pensions reform. There is no need to change to Labour, because Labour will make a mess of it. (interview, Bell, 14 April 1997)

The broad strategic plan that underpinned the campaign had been in place since late 1995 (Butler and Kavanagh, 1997: 34–5). It had three parts: first, convince the electorate that life was better with the Conservatives; second warn against the dangers of a Labour government; third, counter Labour's appeal of 'time for a change' with a positive message for the future. The first part led overwhelmingly to the economic agenda. The second, suggested an aggressive campaign against Labour both on the economy and on questions of the identity and sovereignty of the British nation. The latter meant pressing Labour on European Union issues, where strategists felt that Labour policies were vague and that the electorate was broadly in sympathy with the Conservatives' resolute hostility to further European integration. It also led to a focus on constitutional issues. Labour's devolutionary policies for Scotland and Wales were to be portrayed as a threat to the entire union of the United Kingdom, proposed purely because Labour was scared of losing votes to the SNP in Scotland. The third part, the counter to the appeal of 'time for a change', was the most difficult strategically. As one Conservative campaign manager put it: 'We don't have a good answer for this' (interview). The *only* effective option available here was the negative campaign, in the hope that voters' fears of Labour would outweigh their boredom with the Conservatives.

It seems to have been accepted strategy by June 1996 that the Conservatives should concentrate their campaigning efforts on attacking Labour, rather than promoting their own record (Butler and Kavanagh 1997: 34). The precise tactics, however, continued to be disputed. The Tories' main problem here was how to deal with Tony Blair. A strategy document written as early as November 1994, only three months after Blair's election to the Labour leadership, warned that Blair was the main threat to the Conservatives: he was 'the only thing' Labour had going for it, besides the health service (Peston 1994). As Blair set about building 'New Labour', the Tories debated various and sometimes contradictory lines of attack: that Blair may have changed, but that his party had not, it was the same old Labour behind the painted smile; that Blair was a 'phoney'; that Labour had stolen so much of the Conservatives' policies and rhetoric, that they had become a pale imitation of the genuine item. The argument seemed to be settled in the summer of 1996 when the Tories launched their 'New Labour, New Danger' campaign, its underlying logic being that Blair's Labour had indeed changed and was now 'newly dangerous in new ways' (Butler and Kavanagh 1997: 35). A series of advertisements pursued the theme: 'New Labour, No Britain' (a white flag of surrender); 'New Labour, New Taxes' and finally a poster of Blair pictured with red eyes under the 'New Labour, New Danger' banner. The campaign and the 'New Danger' slogan were abandoned by February 1997 on the instructions of the party chairman, Brian Mawhinney. The advertisements, especially the Blair 'demon eyes', had attracted widespread public criticism and, crucially, had not seemed to make any difference to the opinion polls.

Thus, the Tories entered the 1997 campaign sure of their agenda territory (economy, Europe and the constitution) and convinced of the need for a negative campaign but less certain of the best means of carrying the attack to Blair. They settled for a deliberately presidential race of 'Major versus Blair'. In the words of one party strategist, 'Blair is their only weapon. . . . On the other hand, he is their greatest liability and politically, until now, he has had a very soft ride' (interview).

The Labour Party

Labour's landslide in 1997 was scarcely imaginable after their fourth successive defeat in 1992. Some commentators predicted a future of permanent Conservative rule (King 1993), that underlying changes in the bases of electoral support favoured the Tories (Kavanagh 1994) and that a pact with the Liberal Democrats was probably Labour's best hope of preventing a sixth consecutive Conservative triumph. However, within six months of the 1992 election, the shock of 'Black Wednesday' had transformed the parties' standing in the opinion polls. Such was the turnaround that by the time Blair inherited the leadership, following the death of John Smith, in July 1994, a strong current of opinion in the party maintained that it was firmly on course for victory, provided only that it stayed steady and united and avoided own goals (Butler and Kavanagh 1997: 46). This line of thinking, associated with Blair's predecessor, John Smith, came to be known as the 'one last heave' strategy. It was predicated broadly on the belief that Labour under Kinnock and Smith had already changed enough, was no longer distrusted by voters and that all that was necessary was to keep a steady nerve and the party would automatically benefit from increasing voter disenchantment with the government.

However, the so-called Labour 'modernizers', with whom Blair was associated, rejected this view. The lines of disagreement emerged in the post-1992 election struggle to re-shape Labour's identity. At that time the leading proponent of Labour modernization was, not Blair, but Peter Mandelson, former communications director at Labour headquarters, and the political strategist Philip Gould, head of the Shadow Communications Agency, which had directed Labour's communication campaigns in the 1987 and 1992 elections. The modernizers made plain their admiration of Bill Clinton's US strategy, esteeming especially his re-positioning as a New Democrat representing the 'working middle class', rather than the sectional labour and minority interests of the 'old' Democrats (Hewitt and Gould 1993). All the major strategic changes that Blair pushed through as leader were trailed in advance by Hewitt and Gould's reading of the 'Lessons from America' (Gould 1998b).

Most importantly the modernizers began with a clear rejection of the thesis that campaign errors had caused Labour's defeat in 1992 (Heffernan and Marqusee 1992). Instead, their explanations relied on opinion surveys and focus group studies of target voters that reported that Labour was not trusted to run the economy, was regarded as a party of the poor and disadvantaged and was out of step with the increasingly 'upmarket' aspirations of the employed working class. These were virtually identical problems to those facing Clinton and the Democrats after three terms of Republican presidency, and the modernizers set about adapting Clinton solutions. First, to establish a new identity for Labour and position it as the party of the 'majority rather than minorities' (Hewitt and Gould 1993: 51; Gould 1998b), which meant appealing to the aspirational working and middle classes. This in turn required steps to reassure the electorate that Labour was committed to the market economy, was no longer a 'tax-and-spend' party, nor vulnerable to the sectional interests of its trade union paymasters. Second, to convince voters that changes in the substance of policy detail mattered less than the 'big position' – essentially a 'statement of values' supported by 'symbolic policies which illustrated those values' (Hewitt and Gould 1993: 47). Changes would not be believed unless (a) they were to result from genuine engagement in debate, and (b) they were supported by policies that symbolized these changes. Implied here was a criticism of Kinnock's Labour, that changes in policy had not been accompanied by the necessary debate and symbols, and thus had failed to convince voters that Labour was *really* different. Third, Labour believed that style was as important as substance. Voters turned off by the typical adversary aggression of normal political rhetoric had warmed to the informal, personal, non-ideological 'commonsense' style of Clinton (Hewitt and Gould 1993: 49). The style that they advocated for Labour was a deliberately 'non-political' style of politics.

The contours of 'modernization', then, were well established before Blair stepped up to adopt the mantle of project leader. It can be seen that he vigorously pursued the project. His first conference speech as party leader (October 1994) announced 'New Labour' and set in train the internal party debate over its constitution, as symbolized by Clause Four. This was almost entirely a 'symbolic' debate, in Hewitt and Gould's terms. The Clause Four commitment to public ownership of industry had long since ceased to be party policy, but it remained a potent symbol of 'Old Labour'. The internal debate over Clause Four and the overwhelming party-wide vote to remove it at a special conference in April 1995 became equally potent symbols of Labour's commitment to real change.

The party Blair led to power in May 1997 was radically transformed in image. The Clause Four debate was just the start. Blair's mantra that the trade unions could only expect 'fairness not favours' from a Labour government was supported by active measures to reduce party reliance on union funds (Butler and Kavanagh 1997: 55). Blair expressed publicly his admiration of Margaret Thatcher, for so long such a hate-figure for the Labour left, and pledged that there would be no substantive repeal of Tory trade union legislation. Shadow chancellor Gordon Brown ruled out any increase in public borrowing to fund spending plans and Labour entered the 1997 campaign committed to honouring income tax cuts introduced by the Conservative government. Labour pursued, with considerable success, a policy of seeking endorsements from well-known public figures to add credibility to their image change. Most importantly, in this regard, Blair courted the proprietors and editors of the tabloid press. The Labour leadership generally had been convinced that the hostility of the tabloid press had proved damaging in 1992 (Scammell 1995: 267). Moreover, they were impressed with the analysis of Martin Linton, a journalist who became a Labour MP in 1997, which correlated the party's vote share with the partisanship of the press (Linton 1995). A Philip Gould strategy document for the party leaders following the 1992 defeat also cautioned that the press had contributed to Labour's negative image and had helped set an anti-Labour news agenda (Butler and Kavanagh 1997: 47).

Labour, then, looked and sounded a different party. The issue agenda it chose for the 1997 campaign was the most centrist that the party had ever adopted, flanked to the left by the Liberal Democrats and to the right by the Conservatives (Budge 1999). Labour's 'war-book' predicted accurately that the Conservatives would attack on economic competence, and its strategy was primarily a defensive one, to be prepared to fight on this terrain, to offer rebuttals, produce endorsements and to counter-attack with charges of broken Tory promises, especially the '22 tax rises'. But it was not yet confident enough of its reputation to list the economy as its preferred issue territory (interview). A similarly defensive strategy was suggested for Europe. With the exception of the Social Chapter, to which Labour long before Blair had been committed, its European policy was remarkably similar to Major's: essentially 'negotiate and decide' on the basis of national economic interest whether or not to enter the single currency.

Labour's general campaign theme was 'hope versus fear' (war-book). Labour had to counter the Conservatives' campaign of fear with a message of hope delivered in two main ways: firstly, with the vague but optimistic claim summed up in their campaign PEBs and their theme tune: 'Things can only can better'; secondly, with its incremental but specific pledges of improvements: cut class sizes for under seven-year-old children; fast-track punishment for persistent young offenders; cut NHS waiting lists; get 250,000 unemployed young people off benefit and into work; set tough rules for government borrowing to ensure low inflation. Labour, as the Conservatives, wanted a presidential contest. Blair rated highly in the opinion polls as a strong leader (Kellner 1997), personified New Labour and was regarded by campaign strategists as the best party salesman of the message of hope. The overarching strategic themes meant that Labour wanted to fight primarily a positive campaign (interview). However, a memo prepared by Philip Gould warned that:

> The only way that fear of us can be truly defeated is by voters having a greater fear of them. . . . Fear of a fifth [Conservative] term makes them the incumbents, not us: the issue becoming not the risk of a Labour government, but of another Tory government. This is an essential part of our strategy. (quoted in Butler and Kavanagh 1997: 78)

To this end, Labour borrowed the 1996 campaign slogan of the Australian Liberal Party, 'Enough is Enough', and ran a series of press conferences highlighting broken Tory promises.

The Liberal Democrats

The Liberal Democrats had been disappointed with the outcome of the 1992 general election. They had expected a close race, a hung parliament was a high possibility and thus they might have ended up holding the balance of power. In the event they gained only 18 per cent of the vote and 20 seats, lagging well behind their 1987 performance. They seemed, however, to be beneficiaries of the Tory opinion poll collapse in the aftermath of 'Black Wednesday', September 1992, winning a series of by-elections with stunning swings from the Conservatives (Berrington and Hague 1997). Renewed optimism did not last long. The turning point was the election of Blair as Labour leader. Liberal Democrat support, running at 22 per cent until the spring of 1994, dropped to 17 per cent in August, the month after Blair's election. Their rating slid to about 12 per cent in mid-1995 where it stayed until the election campaign began in March 1997.

It seemed, therefore, that Blair was as significant a problem for the Liberal Democrats as for the Conservatives. As Labour moved right-wards, adopting much of the Tories' tax and public spending agenda, so space opened up on the left for the third party to exploit. As Richard Newby, the party communications director, put it, Labour had 'deliberately spiked' its own biggest gun, the National Health Service, by refusing to increase public spending (interview, April 1997). Labour could not focus relentlessly on health, as it had in 1992, simply because every time it raised the issue it would face tough questions from journalists on how it intended to fund improvements.

The Liberal Democrat campaign strategy for 1997 was very different from 1992. In 1992 it had decided to campaign on its single most distinctive policy – electoral reform – running under the slogans 'Fair Votes" and 'My Vote'. Its main task then was to establish the party firmly as the third force in British politics, seeing off the various remnants and rumps which had objected to the merger of the former Liberal Party and the Social Democratic Party in 1988. In 1997 its main issue agenda was health, education and crime (Newby interview). The issues were chosen for two main reasons. First, these were issues with high salience for voters. Strategists were persuaded that there was little point pressing issues of importance to the party (proportional representation, environment, Europe) if they were not already high on the public agenda. As Newby put it bluntly: 'There are no votes in proportional representation.' Second, the aim was to capitalize on the ground vacated by New Labour. The Liberal Democrats were now the only major party willing to raise taxes to fund education and health policies. The party thus felt able both to offer a unique profile in the mainstream political spectrum *and* to campaign on issues of high public salience.

According to Newby, the Liberal Democrats, no less than Labour, had been influenced by the American lesson of the importance of staying 'on message'. Party communications was, he felt, significantly more professional than previously. This meant intensified focus on a smaller range of key issues, and not, as in previous campaigns, a dutiful parade through all the major policy commitments.

Campaign Communications: The Battle of the Agendas

We measured campaign agendas in three ways: the manifesto agenda, the agendas in the press statements, and the PEB agendas. The manifesto agenda may be considered the parties' ideal strategic agenda. 'Ideal' here means not that the agendas were the parties' preferred options for a perfect world. Manifestos, of course, are normally constrained by strategic electoral considerations. As one rather cynical Labour adviser put it: 'In the mass media age, policy is there to win elections' (Butler and Kavanagh 1997: 61). Rather, 'ideal' means that the parties are in sole control of the content of the manifestos. The manifestos, as statements of party programmes for government, traditionally launch the official campaigns and attract widespread news coverage.

The press statements may be considered 'tactical' agendas. In the course of a campaign, parties may raise issues for purely tactical reasons, or as is often the case, may be forced to respond to attacks from other parties or may respond to important news events. One would expect, therefore, some deviation from the ideal to the tactical agenda. One would also expect that the tactical agenda would be far more negative. Manifestos might be expected to be overwhelmingly positive as they are effectively advertisements for the parties' policies. The press releases, how-ever, reflect the campaign battle, with its strategic and tactical demands of defence and offence.

The PEB agendas fall somewhere between the other two. They are 'ideal' in the sense of being unmediated communications, but are apt to be scrapped or revised as the tactical needs of the campaign change. How-ever, previous analysis of the PEBs has found that they offer reasonably accurate guides to the parties' preferred issue agendas and to their electoral strategies (Scammell and Semetko 1995).

These content analyses cannot tell us about the effects of spin doctoring and politicians' 'off the record' briefings of journalists (Jones 1997). These may be more or less important in the establishment of media agenda but they are impossible to assess.

Table 4.1 shows the party agendas as set out in the manifestos. It is immediately striking how close they were to each other. Social welfare was easily the top issue for each party, at 30 per cent and over. Given the Conservatives' strategic priority of the economy it is interesting that social welfare was also their top manifesto issue. Less surprisingly, the Conservatives placed more emphasis on the economy than the other two parties, although in each case it was the number two issue. Education, Europe and the political system (constitutional reform) ranked three, four

TABLE 4.1: *Issues in Major Party Manifestos*, 1997

Subject	Total all Major Parties		Conservative		Labour		Lib Dem	
	N	%	N	%	N	%	N	%
Social welfare	875	32.3	361	33.1	253	30.5	261	32.5
Economy	630	23.2	304	27.9	173	20.8	153	19.0
Education and arts	266	9.8	107	9.8	80	9.6	79	9.8
Europe/Foreign	245	9.0	92	8.4	72	8.7	81	10.1
Constitutional reform	211	7.8	74	6.8	62	7.5	75	9.4
Infrastructure	143	5.3	52	4.8	63	7.6	28	3.5
Regions	134	4.9	51	4.7	51	6.1	32	4.0
Environment/energy	122	4.5	26	2.4	31	3.7	65	8.1
Defence	56	2.0	18	1.6	20	2.4	18	2.2
Parties	23	0.9	4	0.4	15	1.8	4	0.5
TOTAL	2705	100	1090	100	830	100	802	100

Note: The figures represent the number of paragraphs and the proportion of coverage of each issue in the party manifestos.

Source: 1997 Election Party and Media Agenda Content Analysis, Margaret Scammell and Holli A. Semetko.

and five respectively in each of the Conservative and Labour manifestos. The Liberal Democrat agenda ranked the same subjects in slightly different order: Europe, education and constitution.

The Conservative emphasis on social welfare was largely accounted for by the radical reforms of pensions policy and elderly health care, which the government announced on the eve of the election. There is no doubt that at the launch of the manifestos, John Major regarded pensions reform as one of their flagship policies, which he believed would prove both popular and proof that the government had not run out of steam. During the campaign, however, it provided ammunition for some of the most bitter Labour attacks as they claimed that the Tories planned to 'abolish' state pensions. The Tories' tactical wisdom of placing such weight on a complex and controversial policy came to be seen by some party strategists as an error (Saatchi 1997).

Table 4.2 compares the ideal and tactical agendas of the three parties. The differences between the two are most striking for the Conservatives. Social welfare, the top item in the manifesto agenda, dwindled from 33 to about 9 per cent in its press statement agenda. The prominence of the economy increased to 51 per cent of all subjects in Conservative press statements (up from 28 per cent in the manifesto). Europe, for all its significance in the campaign, increased only slightly in the press statement agenda compared to the manifesto. However, Europe offered the most striking difference in the Conservatives' press statement and PEB agendas. The prominence of Europe in the PEBs reflected the extent to which the Tories were losing control of the agenda, as, encouraged by the *Daily Mail*, the trickle of internal party dissent at Major's single currency policy transformed into a flood. They decided to scrap their planned fourth

TABLE 4.2: *Comparison of Party Agendas: Manifestos, Press Releases and Party Election Broadcasts, 1997 (%)*

Subject Heading	Conservative			Labour			Liberal Democrat		
	M'festo	Press releases	PEBs	M'festo	Press releases	PEBs	M'festo	Press releases	PEBs
Conduct of campaign									
Parties		4	3	2	4	7	1	7	12
Opinion polls		7	12		11	17		12	9
Party leaders			1		1	12	1	1	6
Campaign issues	1	3	1	1	8	2	1	3	3
SUBTOTAL CAMPAIGN	1	14	18	3	23	37	1	23	30
Social welfare	33	9	11	31	21	24	33	34	24
Economy	28	51	36	21	31	25	19	15	9
Education and arts	10	10	6	10	13	9	10	18	18
Foreign affairs	8	11	19	9	8	3	10	5	3
Constitutional reform	7	1	4	8	1	2	9	2	9
Infrastructure	5	2		8	1		4		
Regions	5	2	7	6	2		4	1	
Environment/energy	2	1		4	1		8	3	6
Defence	2	1		2	1		2	1	
SUBTOTAL ISSUES	99	86	82	97	76	63	99	77	70
TOTAL ALL	100	100	100	100	100	100	100	100	100

Note: Not all columns add to 100 per cent because of rounding.

Source: 1997 Election Party and Media Agenda Content Analysis, Margaret Scammell and Holli A. Semetko

broadcast, and instead John Major recorded a straight-to-camera piece explaining the logic of his 'negotiate and decide' policy.

The figures suggest that of all the parties, the Liberal Democrats kept most closely to their ideal agenda of social welfare subjects throughout the campaign. Social welfare topped all three manifesto, press release and PEB subject agendas. Labour's tactical agenda shows a significantly increased emphasis on the economy, up from 21 per cent in the manifesto, to 31 per cent and 25 per cent in the press release and PEB agendas. However, it maintained high prominence for its favoured social welfare subjects and managed considerably more consistency across its three agendas than was achieved by the Conservatives.

Using the data in Table 4.2 we can measure the internal coherence of each party's campaign messages by the correlation between priority given to topics in the manifesto, representing each party's preferred agenda at the start of the campaign, with the topics which feature in their press releases and party broadcasts. The results in Table 4.3 summarize the pattern we have already observed, namely the campaign messages from the Liberal Democrats were most closely associated with the contents of their manifesto. The Conservatives were most deflected from their preferred agenda, with the lowest correlations, while Labour was located in the middle of the spectrum.

Overall, then, we can state that the Liberal Democrats ran the most internally coherent campaign. It maintained consistency across our three agenda measurements *and* with the declared strategic intentions of its communications managers. The Conservatives showed the least coherence. This is reflected not just in the higher degree of variation between its subject agendas, but in the difference between declared strategic intent and those agendas. The overwhelming strategic importance of the economy was not reflected in its manifesto; the manifesto prominence of social welfare was not reflected in its tactical agendas; and the constitution, highlighted as a major battleground by its strategists, was barely visible in its press statements.

Of course, it should be recognized that it is far easier for the Liberal Democrats than the others to achieve consistency. They were, almost completely, ignored in the campaign cut and thrust between Labour and

TABLE 4.3: *The Internal Coherence of Party Campaigns, 1997*

	Conservative Manifesto	Labour Manifesto	Liberal Democrat Manifesto
Press Releases	.68**	.77**	.82**
Party Election Broadcasts	.67**	.68**	.72**

Note: The figures represent correlations between the priority given to subjects by each party in manifestos and in press releases and party election broadcasts. See Table 4.2 for details. ** = p.<.01

Source: 1997 Election Party and Media Agenda Content Analysis, Margaret Scammell and Holli A. Semetko.

Conservatives. This is confirmed by our analysis of the targets of party attacks in press statements and PEBs. Of all attacks launched by the Conservatives, 97 per cent were aimed at Labour and Blair and just 3 per cent at the Liberal Democrats. *All* Labour attacks were aimed at the Tories and Major. The Liberal Democrats, therefore, were scarcely forced on the defensive and were free to pursue their own agenda. Their difficulties stemmed not from the other parties, but from their struggle to gain news coverage, particularly in the press.

Party Communications and Civic Engagement

Party campaigners insisted on the strategic needs of a negative campaign. Table 4.4 shows how their intentions were borne out in their press communications.

We regarded material as negative only where it explicitly apportioned blame or criticized the policies, record, competence or credibility of a named rival party or politician. It can be seen that the Tories ran an overwhelmingly negative campaign, with 58 per cent negative and 23 per cent mixed negative/positive. Labour shows a fairly even balance between positive and negative, while the Liberal Democrats were the only party to wage a predominantly positive campaign.

There is no comparable analysis of 1992 press statements, but a reasonably comparable analysis of PEB content suggests that 1997 was significantly more negative for both Labour and the Conservatives (see Scammell and Semetko 1995). However, if this indicates that Britain may be going negative, the targets of attack remain predominantly the parties, not the leaders. Of all the Conservative attacks, 50 per cent were targeted at the Labour Party and 21 per cent at Blair personally. For Labour the figures were: 64 per cent targeted at the Conservative Party, 20 per cent at John Major.

TABLE 4.4: *Tone of Press Releases and Party Election Broadcasts by Party,* 1997.

| Tone | Conservative | | | | Labour | | | | Liberal Democrat | | | |
| | Press release | | PEB | | Press release | | PEB | | Press release | | PEB | |
	N	%	N	%	N	%	N	%	N	%	N	%
Positive	21	19	2	40	35	32	1	20	17	38	2	50
Mixed	25	22	1	20	42	38	3	60	14	31	2	50
Negative	64	58	2	40	33	30	1	20	13	29	0	0
Can't detect	1	1	0	0	0	0	0	0	1	2	0	0
Balance	**-43**	**-39**	**0**	**0**	**+2**	**+2**	**0**	**0**	**+4**	**+9**	**+2**	**+50**
Total:	111	100	5	100	110	100	5	100	45	100	4	100

Note: The balance is calculated as the proportion of positive minus the proportion of negative.

Source: 1997 Election Party and Media Agenda Content Analysis, Margaret Scammell and Holli A. Semetko.

Labour concentrated its negative campaign on the record and policy proposals of the Conservatives (66 per cent) with surprisingly little on sleaze (5 per cent) and 10 per cent on weak Tory leadership. The Conservatives focused more intently on the image dimensions: 23 per cent of their attacks concerning the trustworthiness of Labour, 52 per cent on Labour's record and policy proposals.

Generally, the campaign was severely criticized in the press (Scammell and Harrop 1997). The *Financial Times* called it 'the most dispiriting of campaigns' with the Tories relentlessly negative and Labour remorselessly defensive. The *Daily Mail* had rarely seen so much evasion and dishonesty. *The Guardian* columnist Hugo Young could not recall a campaign when so many questions were shamelessly evaded. Nonetheless, before one can pass a verdict that the campaigners failed the test of civic virtue, it must be noted that the parties, far more than the media, concentrated on the substantive issues. Moreover, as Jamieson has argued (1992) it is an entirely necessary part of the democratic process that parties scrutinize each others' policies and reputations. At this election, only the Conservatives came close to a high threshold of negative campaigning.

Conclusions: Staying on Message

In summary, therefore, successful strategic communications depends upon parties fighting professional campaigns with clear objectives which identify target voters, consistent themes and images which touch a chord with their supporters, and coordinated messages across all party publicity. Parties which achieve these aims can be assumed to stay 'on message', rather than being deflected by the attacks and counter-attacks of their opponents.

In the aftermath of the election it was commonly assumed that Labour's Millbank machine had run the most effective campaign. Yet based on this conceptualization of strategic communications we found that of all the major parties it was the Liberal Democrats who were the unexpected victors, with the most consistent and internally coherent campaign. The Liberal Democrats also ran by far the most positive campaign, sticking to their own policy agenda rather than attacking opponents. Labour fell in the middle of the political spectrum according to our evidence. And in contrast the Conservatives proved to have the least consistent and the most negative campaign, confirming the popular impression that they were frequently derailed and thrown off course during the course of the official campaign.

Of course, coherence and consistency are not the only, or perhaps even the principal, virtues in a campaign. If campaign ads or broadcasts are failing then it could be argued that it is better to jettison plans and adapt to circumstances. Flexibility in warfare can be a virtue. Nevertheless, strategic communications are based on the principle of planning for all eventualities, and using the techniques of market research to develop popular messages well in advance of the heat of the election. Tearing up a planned party broadcast to provide an impromptu appeal to the party over Europe, as John Major did, is the antithesis of strategic planning. And staying on message, as the Liberal Democrats did, seems most likely to maximize their impact. How these party strategies affected the agenda of the news media, and how they eventually influenced voters, will be examined in subsequent chapters.

5 The News Agenda

In this chapter we set out the theoretical context of agenda-setting and then analyse the contents of the news agenda in the national press and on television, focusing on two central issues. The first concerns the media agenda. What was the pattern of coverage in national newspapers and the main evening television news bulletins during the 1997 general election campaign? And how did this compare with the 1992 campaign? The second concerns the parties' efforts to get issues across in the news. How did the parties' agendas compare with the issue agendas in the news in 1997? Were the priorities of the parties reflected in the news? Chapter 9 goes on to consider the relationship between the issue agendas of the news media and the public to explore who leads, and who follows, in this process.

The Theory of Agenda-setting

The theory of news agenda-setting suggests that the media drives the public's issue concerns, and tells people not 'what to think' but 'what to think about'. This idea can be traced originally to Walter Lippmann's *Public Opinion* (1922), before first being tested systematically in the work of McCombs and Shaw (1972). Should we be worried about falling educational standards in schools, threats of cancer from power lines, bankrupt pension schemes, or how the Asian financial crisis will affect the stock market in Britain? This theory suggests that stories which get headlined in the news become the problems which the public regards as the nation's most important. Agenda-setting is about the transmission of salience, not the determination of opinions about an issue. In the process, the practices of the news media are believed to influence the prominence of that small number of issues which come to command public attention (McCombs and Estrada 1997; McCombs 1997).

The public agenda-setting process has been described as inherently 'a political process in which the mass media play a crucial role in enabling social problems to become acknowledged as public issues' (Dearing and Rogers 1996: 22). This process may have significant political implications if public concerns ultimately feed into government priorities, and thereby help drive the policy process. Who sets the news agenda is commonly regarded as a highly competitive game between journalists, politicians, and the public (Bennett 1996: 6). Moreover this is a zero-sum game: the newshole is limited and emphasis on one issue necessarily means that another issue is diminished. Since the 1970s an extensive literature has developed with over 200 separate studies exploring how the campaign agenda is set by a process of competition between journalists, politicians, and the public (for a review see Dearing and Rogers 1996).

As indicated in Figure 5.1, research has commonly analysed five components of this process, in sequential order:

- the *party agenda* (the contents of the manifestos)
- the *media agenda* (measured by content analysis of the priority of items in the news)
- the *public's agenda* (reflected in surveys monitoring perceptions of the most important problem facing the country)
- the *policy agenda* (gauged by the priority of issues in legislative debates or government spending programmes)
- *'real-world'* indicators of issue priorities (such as official rates of crime, unemployment or drug-use).

We focus on the first three steps in this process, and the relationship between the party, media and public agenda. Did these move together during the campaign, with the news media acting as an intermediary connecting party policies with citizens' preferences? Or did they remain worlds apart, as Miller (1990) found in the 1987 general election? And if they did move together, who led, and who followed? The model in Figure 5.1 assumes a sequential process whereas in practice we would expect

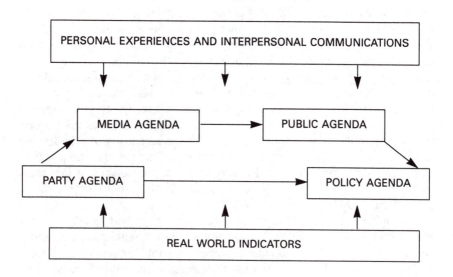

FIGURE 5.1: *The Main Components of the Agenda-setting Process.*
Source: Adapted from Dearing and Rogers (1996)

there to be fairly complex interactions; for example, public concerns may influence the priorities given to issues in party manifestos, as well as the stories blazed as headlines in the tabloid press.

Dearing and Rogers' (1996) summary of the literature found that many studies have documented how the public's issue agenda has been influenced by what they read or see in the news, in the United States and elsewhere. Despite this the available research in Britain has failed to establish this relationship within the context of election campaigns. The most thorough study by Miller (1991), based on comparing content analysis of newspapers and television with a panel study of voters in the 1987 election, found that there were significant differences in the issue agenda of the news media and the public, and there was no evidence that there was any closure during the course of the campaign:

> Television's issue agenda was very different from the public agenda. The public wanted a focus on social and economic issues not security issues. But television coverage in explicitly election news was balanced between social and security issues; while in its background news items television concentrated overwhelmingly on security issues. In the view of some political scientists this issue-emphasis constitutes a massive and consistent right-wing bias in the issue agenda. (Miller 1991: 231)

Accordingly as the first step we need to establish the contents of the media messages and what featured in the extensive election coverage on television and the press.

Content Analysis of the News Media[1]

This chapter analyses the contents of the evening news programmes on television and in a selection of national newspapers during the final month of the campaign (1–30 April 1997). The television programmes are BBC 1 and ITV's flagship news programmes, the *Nine O'Clock News* and ITN's *News at Ten*. We also content analysed the front pages of six national newspapers for the same period: the tabloids were *The Sun*, *The Mirror*, and *Daily Mail* and the broadsheets were *The Independent*, *The Guardian*, and *The Times*. These papers were chosen as mass circulation dailies providing comparison between tabloids and broadsheets, as well as reflecting different partisan leanings in the press. It was decided to prioritize in-depth analysis of a representative selection of papers, rather than covering all national and Sunday papers in less detail.

We classified all stories that mentioned 'politics' or 'politicians' in our selected media. This accounted for the vast majority of stories in the news during the election campaign. We identified the subjects of news stories to compare the emphasis on the campaign, the parties and their leaders, and policy issues. The electoral strategies and tactics of the parties are included in the 'conduct of campaign' category, the 'opinion polls' category refers to the reporting of polls or the horse race, and 'media treatment' refers to media attention to the media coverage. The 'parties' category refers to coverage about the party leader or key people in the party, or news about internal party politics. There are also 'campaign issues' which are specific to each election – in 1997 this was 'sleaze'. These types of news stories comprise the activities of the campaign with little or no emphasis on policy. We also identified coverage of policy issues in the news, and we present here nine major categories of policy issues. This includes, for example, constitutional reform, defence, and the economy. We classified the *primary* subject in the story, where the N. represents the actual number of *stories*. We classified the most important subject of the story, defined as the single most important theme, issue, or topic. Full details about the methodology are provided in the book's Technical Appendix.

What Was the Pattern of News Coverage in 1997?

Television

In comparison with other countries, British television news is remarkable for the sheer amount of attention it paid to the campaign. As discussed in Chapter 2, the election was covered heavily by the main TV channels with about ten hours of information per day about the campaign across all the major channels. All the main parties' manifestos, policies and campaigns were reported in detail. All the main channels devoted extra resources to the campaign. The BBC led the way, extending the *Nine O'Clock News* by 20 minutes every night throughout the campaign proper to 45 minutes, starting with the launch of the manifestos. The concentration on the campaign was evident across all channels. Election stories led the news on 38 of the 44 evenings between the announcement of the date of the election and polling day, on the BBC's main evening news programme, and 35 evenings on ITN's *News at Ten* (Harrison 1997). Sky tried to establish itself as the election news channel for the élite audience of the politically interested, offering live coverage of the morning press conferences, from the campaign trail, rallies and speeches and election news routinely dominated the first section of its hourly news broadcasts.

Overall about two-thirds of the coverage on television news in April was devoted to the campaign (60 per cent of BBC1's news and 66 per cent of ITN's) leaving the remainder for stories about substantive policy issues. Both television news programmes were similar in the rank order of the main subject of stories in the news – with the conduct of the campaign, the parties, and opinion polls as the most important topics (see Table 5.1).

One of the main conclusions to be drawn from the comparison of TV news agendas is that there was more similarity between BBC and ITN in 1997 than in 1992. One of the most notable changes in the television news agendas was the decline, on both BBC and ITN, in coverage of opinion polls. In 1992 there had been a significant difference between BBC and

TABLE 5.1:   *Change in the Main Subject of Political TV News Stories, 1992 and 1997*

	1992		1997	
	% BBC	% ITN	% BBC	% ITN
Conduct of campaign	6	15	24	29
Parties	13	8	17	17
Opinion polls	18	32	11	10
Party leaders	8	3	3	6
Campaign style/sleaze	5	4	5	3
Media treatment	0	1	2	1
[SUBTOTAL CAMPAIGN]	**[51]**	**[63]**	**[62]**	**[66]**
Social welfare	5	4	9	7
Regions/devolution	12	10	8	8
Economy	20	15	7	6
Foreign affairs	1		6	6
Education and arts	3	2	4	5
Constitutional reform	5	4	2	2
Infrastructure	2	1	1	1
Environment/energy	2	2	0	0
Defence	1	1	0	0
SUBTOTAL ISSUES	**[50]**	**[38]**	**[38]**	**[34]**
TOTAL ALL	100	100	100	100

Note: Not all columns add to 100 per cent because of rounding to integers. The content analysis is based on coding every news story on television during one month of the official campaign (1–30 April 1997) on BBC1 *Nine O'Clock News* and ITN *News at Ten.* The above figures are calculated as a percentage of all political stories during this month.

Source: 1997 Election Party and Media Agenda Content Analysis, Margaret Scammell and Holli A. Semetko.

ITN main evening news programmes in coverage of public opinion; ITN paid more attention to polls than the BBC at least in part because they used polls they had commissioned to study how electors were reacting to the campaign (Nossiter *et al.* 1995). In 1997, there was no significant difference between BBC and ITN in the amount of emphasis on this subject. Polls were far less often the main subject of news stories in 1997, declining on ITN from 32 per cent of stories in 1992 to 10 per cent in 1997. Polls also were less often mentioned as a subsequent subject in any story, falling on BBC from 15 per cent of stories in 1992 to 9 per cent in 1997. There are a number of reasons for this development. The flatness of the race in 1997 combined with Labour's comfortable lead meant that poll results were simply less newsworthy. In contrast in 1992 the closeness of the two-party lead in most polls, and anticipation of a hung parliament, lent the results more drama. There was also residual scepticism about the polls left over from the fiasco in 1992 (Crewe 1997). Moreover, at the BBC the new Birt regime sharply restricted use. The BBC *Producers' Guidelines* noted that even with polling conducted by reputable organizations great care was necessary in reporting results:

> Even in reporting polling conducted by reputable organizations according to the current best practice great caution is required. It will be appropriate,

especially in the run-up to a general election, for programmes to remind audiences of the poor performance of the polls in 1992. Until their track record for accuracy and reliability is established, the BBC should not give undue attention, weight or time to the findings of polls.

At the same time from 1992 to 1997 there was a significant rise in the proportion of stories on both channels described as the 'conduct of campaign' – dealing with the daily activities of leaders on the campaign trail, electoral strategy, and party tactics. This became the most common main subject of the news on both channels in 1997.

Television's Issue Agenda

The number of stories about substantive policy issues was slightly higher on the BBC (40 per cent of BBC's news stories and 36 per cent of ITN's), perhaps because of the larger news-hole to fill combined with the BBC's traditional public service culture during campaigns. Both channels agreed about the priority which should be given to substantive issues, with both covering social welfare, regions/devolution, the economy, foreign affairs (mainly about Europe), and education, in roughly similar proportions, with less than two per cent of stories on any other subject. The economy was also the most important substantive issue on Sky, which paid slightly more attention to this issue as a main subject in the news.

The Dynamics of the Issue Agenda

Generally, the pattern of coverage every week followed similar trends across BBC and ITN. In the first week, with the launch of the manifestos, the economy was the main substantive subject with social welfare issues, particularly education and health, fairly close behind. Sleaze (listed in the tables under 'campaign issues') dominated the month of March with stories about the financial affairs of Neil Hamilton and the sexual affairs of Piers Merchant leading the pack (Harrison 1997; Norris 1997a). Sleaze continued to have some prominence in the first week of the campaign proper, but dwindled to virtually nothing shortly afterwards. Across the entire month of April, sleaze took only about two per cent of all subjects in the news. This issue remained a kind of 'structuring absence' in other stories related to campaign conduct, but as a subject in its own right, it disappeared. This could only partly be accounted for by the restrictions of the Representation of the People Act which inhibits coverage of individual constituency candidates. A similar trend was evident in the press, which was not subject to the same constraints.

Social welfare issues featured prominently in the overall agenda, primarily education, pensions, and health, in that order. The week-by-week pattern showed social welfare was first or second in importance throughout April. In the last days of the campaign social welfare even rose in priority, a pattern evident across all channels but most marked on ITN.

This was due to the bitter exchange about pensions between Major and Blair, after Labour claimed that the Conservatives planned to abolish the state old-age pension. The pensions row effectively displaced Europe on the agenda.

Europe, commonly seen as the defining issue of the campaign, made little impact on the agenda in the early stages. A trickle of stories about Conservative dissidents' opposition to the European single currency emerged in the second week. In the third, Europe dominated the lead stories in the news, as John Major used a press conference to urge his own party not to 'bind my hands' in negotiations. The story peaked in the course of the third week, with 13 per cent of all stories in the news and 15 per cent of all subjects of stories. Europe dominated the top of the bulletins for the third week and going into the fourth, as well as the front pages of the newspapers (Scammell and Harrop 1997).

Europe fuelled many of television's 'conduct of campaign' stories that were not about the issue of Europe or monetary union proper, but rather about party strategies, tactics and prospects. The subject of Europe was important not so much because of the intrinsic news value of the EMU but because of the subject's power to provoke turmoil within the Conservative Party and its significance for their party image and post-election prospects. Over the entire campaign, Europe was the single most time-consuming policy issue; in the tables it is classified within the category of 'foreign affairs'. In 1997 it dominated this category whereas in 1992 it accounted for less than a handful of stories. Although the 'economy' represented a higher proportion of stories than 'foreign affairs', this general category encompasses a wide range of sub-topics including inflation, unemployment, taxes, and budgetary policies.

In general we can conclude that on TV news the proportion of stories with a substantive policy focus as the main subject fell from 1992 to 1997, particularly on the BBC. Nevertheless, in the 1997 campaign just over a third of all TV news stories continued to cover public policy issues such as health, education and the economy, although in 1997 such issues were more often discussed within the context of the 'party strategy', perhaps reflecting the greater focus on strategic campaigning adopted by the parties themselves.

The Press

Did newspapers follow a similar agenda? Taking the main subject of each story, the coverage in newspapers focused on, respectively: the conduct of the campaign, the parties, polls, foreign affairs, economy, social welfare, media treatment and campaign issues, party leaders, education and the arts, with other topics accounting for less than one per cent of stories (see Table 5.2 and 5.3). The most important substantive issue was Europe (coded as 'foreign affairs') on the front pages across all the newspapers taken together, when we consider the main subject, though there were significant differences between the newspapers. It was the most important substantive issue on the front page of *The Guardian*, *The Times*, and *The Sun*, and the second most important substantive issue in *The Independent* and the *Daily Mail*, while it came after the economy, social welfare, education and the arts in *The Mirror*.

The *Mail*'s agenda stood apart. It pursued its own anti-Europe agenda and under the banner 'The Battle of Britain'; it saluted the Conservative Party's EMU dissidents and ran a crusade encouraging them into public rebellion. This was reflected not only in its Europe focus but also in the fact that the *Mail* devoted more attention proportionately to the parties and their internal politics than the other newspapers. The *Mail* also frequently covered the economy, with a steady diet of attacks on Labour, especially U-turns on privatization and links with 'job destroying' union 'bully boys'. Generally, the anti-European newspapers (*Mail*, *Sun*, and *Times*) paid more attention to Europe than did the pro-European press. Europe featured more prominently in the newspaper agenda than on television, largely because of the anti-single currency press.

TABLE 5.2: *Main Subject of Front-Page Broadsheet Newspaper Stories, 1997*

	% Guardian	% Independent	% Times
Conduct of campaign	41	25	31
Parties	12	15	21
Opinion polls	15	18	9
Party leaders	3	2	6
Campaign style/sleaze	5	7	3
Media treatment	3	2	4
[SUBTOTAL CAMPAIGN]	**[79]**	**[68]**	**[74]**
Social welfare	5	10	1
Regions/devolution			
Economy	5	7	9
Foreign affairs	11	9	13
Education and arts	2	3	3
Constitutional reform			1
Infrastructure			
Environment/energy		2	
Defence		2	
SUBTOTAL ISSUES	**[21]**	**[32]**	**[27]**
TOTAL ALL	100	100	100

Note: Not all columns add to 100 per cent because of rounding. The content analysis is based on coding every front-page news story in six newspapers during one month of the official campaign (1-30 April 1997). The above figures are calculated as a percentage of all political stories during this month.

Source: 1997 Election Party and Media Agenda Content Analysis, Margaret Scammell and Holli A. Semetko.

TABLE 5.3: Main Subject of Front-Page Tabloid Newspaper Stories, 1997

	% Mail	% Mirror	% Sun
Conduct of campaign	9	19	14
Parties	4	10	21
Opinion polls	13	5	21
Party leaders			7
Campaign style/sleaze	9	10	
Media treatment		19	29
[SUBTOTAL CAMPAIGN]	**[35]**	**[62]**	**[93]**
Social welfare	4	10	
Regions/devolution			
Economy	35	14	
Foreign affairs/EU	27	5	7
Education & arts		10	
Constitutional reform			
Infrastructure			
Environment/energy			
Defence			
SUBTOTAL ISSUES	**[65]**	**[38]**	**[7]**
TOTAL ALL	100	100	100

Note: Not all columns add to 100 per cent because of rounding to integers. The content analysis is based on coding every front-page news story in six newspapers during one month of the official campaign (1–30 April 1997). The above figures are calculated as a percentage of all political stories during this month.

Source: 1997 Election Party and Media Agenda Content Analysis, Margaret Scammell and

The question of Europe directly and indirectly dominated the front-page leads, but nearly half of the stories were concerned with the Conservative Party's division on the issue. Of the 37 front-page leads devoted to Europe in all newspapers (and not just the six analysed here), seventeen concerned Conservative divisions, ten were about the European Union, nine focused on the EMU and one was on European fisheries policy. As expected, the tabloids in 1997 featured front-page news about the election considerably less often than the broadsheet papers.

As discussed in Chapter 2, the 1997 election was the first time Labour held more press endorsements than the Conservatives. Six of ten national newspapers backed Labour, including the highest circulation tabloid *The Sun*. Of the six newspapers analysed here, three in 1992 had supported the Tories (*Sun, Mail, Times*), two Labour (*Guardian, Mirror*) and *The Independent* offered no endorsement. In 1997 all but the *Mail* and *The Times* preferred a Labour victory and only the *Mail* advocated a Conservative vote, while the *The Times* urged readers to support their local Eurosceptic candidate, regardless of party. As argued in Chapter 2, the shifting allegiances of the press can more plausibly be seen as dealigning rather than realigning, because support for new Labour remains weaker and more contingent than during the Thatcher era.

Most newspapers reduced the overall priority which they gave to the

1997 election (see Table 5.4). If we consider the number of front-page lead stories and editorials, only 42 per cent of all editorials focused on the campaign compared with 62 per cent in 1992, and front-page interest also dropped off steeply in the tabloids (Scammell and Harrop 1997). It was generally a quieter, less strident press, with Europe virtually the only issue capable of igniting the newspapers' passions.

The front pages of the national newspapers saw a decline in the emphasis on opinion polls as the main subject of a news story between 1992 and 1997, just as on television, and, with the exception of *The Sun*, polls were also mentioned less often as a subsequent subject on front-page stories. The increase in the attention given to the 'conduct of campaign' in the news was substantial on the front pages of *The Guardian* and *The Times*, but the changes were hardly apparent in the other newspapers. The substantive issues presented on the front pages of the newspapers varied, but from 1992 to 1997 the economy became less important while social welfare issues rose in salience, particularly in the *Guardian*, *The Independent*, and *Daily Mail*.

TABLE 5.4: *Main Subject of Front-Page Newspaper Stories,* 1992–97

	All Newspapers 1992	All Newspapers 1997	Change 1992-97
Conduct of campaign	20	28	+8
Parties	2	15	+13
Opinion polls	23	13	−10
Party leaders	5	3	−2
Campaign issues/sleaze	7	5	−2
Media treatment	3	5	−2
[SUBTOTAL CAMPAIGN]	**[61]**	**[70]**	**[+9]**
Social welfare	5	5	
Regions/devolution	1	0	−1
Economy	26	10	−16
Foreign affairs	0	12	+12
Education and arts	3	3	
Constitutional reform	2	0	−2
Infrastructure	0	0	
Environment/energy	0	0	
Defence	1	0	−1
SUBTOTAL ISSUES	**[39]**	**[30]**	**[−9]**
TOTAL ALL	100	100	100

Note: Not all columns add to 100 per cent because of rounding to integers. The content analysis is based on coding every front-page news story in six newspapers during one month of the official campaign (1–30 April 1997). The above figures are calculated as a percentage of all political stories during this month.

Source: 1997 Election Party and Media Agenda Content Analysis, Margaret Scammell and Holli A. Semetko.

Party Agendas and Media Agendas

The key question to assess the success of each party's strategic communications is how far the messages which the parties attempted to disseminate were actually picked up by the news media. As discussed in the introduction to the book, did Labour manage to 'set the news agenda' during the campaign, as the conventional wisdom often assumes? If parties are becoming more successful in using professional strategic communications to control the campaign agenda, then we might expect that the news would follow the party lead. On the other hand, if we are experiencing the rise of a more autonomous and dealigned media, as suggested by Swanson and Mancini (1996), then we would expect to find considerable contrasts between the party and news agendas. As discussed in the previous chapter, the party agendas have been ascertained from different sources – the manifestos, the press releases, the party election broadcasts. In this chapter we compare the contents of the party press releases with the agenda in the news, because the press releases are an indication of the tactical day-to-day activities of the parties in fighting the campaign.

The results in Table 5.5 show stark contrasts between the focus of the parties and the media. While all the major parties wanted to talk about substantive policy issues, notably the economy, welfare and education, the news media focused overwhelmingly on the campaign. Party press releases did give some attention to what we have called campaign issues. In 1997 these were primarily sleaze and sex in the Tory Party, and also the activities of the parties and conduct of the campaign. Taken together, these campaign-related subjects amounted to about one-quarter of the subjects in Labour and Liberal Democrat press releases, and approximately 14 per cent of those issued by the Conservatives. But overall 80 per cent of party press releases were about the problems of substantive policy issues such as jobs and pensions, compared with one-third of the election coverage in the news. Television and the press devoted two-thirds of all stories to campaign-related subjects compared with one-fifth of the party press releases.

If we turn to just the substantive issue coverage we find that party agendas were dominated by the economy (32 per cent), social welfare (21 per cent), education (13 per cent), and Europe (8 per cent), with all other topics receiving only marginal attention in press releases. In contrast the press devoted most issue space to Europe, followed by the economy and welfare, with almost no attention to education. Television gave a more even and balanced spread to different issues, leading with social welfare, regions, the economy, Europe and education, in that order. Some minor but still important manifesto issues, notably constitutional reform (other than devolution), which can be regarded as the defining feature of the new Blair government, were scarcely visible in the news or party agenda.

We can examine this pattern more systematically by looking at the correlations (Spearman's Rhos) between party agendas and media agendas, presented in Table 5.6. When we compare the entire list of subjects presented in the news the correlations between media and party agendas were consistently insignificant, confirming the pattern we have already observed. Journalists and politicians were marching to different beats in the election and there is no evidence here that parties led the media, or vice versa.

The pattern also demonstrates how close BBC and ITN were to each other in their news priorities, with a correlation of .97, and indeed how close television and the press were to each other. There was considerable consensus among the news media about the major headlines in the campaign, and they were not those which the politicians preferred. Far from presenting a diverse range of stories in a competitive news environment, this suggests that many journalists shared similar priorities.

If we compare only the issue agendas, that is the priority given to various substantive policy areas, we find a closer correspondence between party and press agendas. The range of correlations between party agendas and the press all proved significant, although the relationship was slightly stronger for the Conservatives than for the Liberal Democrats. The correlations between party issue agendas and individual newspaper issue agendas ranged from .14 to .87. Moreover, there was also a significant correlation between the issue agenda at the BBC and that of the Conservative Party, although none of the other television–party correlations proved statistically significant.

Lastly, we should note that this comparison of agendas is concerned only with the *priorities given to various subjects* on the front pages of newspapers or in the main evening news programmes, and *not with the tone* of the story towards a political party. The theory of agenda-setting is only concerned with salience, not direction. A high correlation between party and media agendas means that the issue priorities were similar, but the tone of the story might have not been what the party wanted. For example, the agenda of the front page of *The Sun*, which supported Labour in 1997, was more closely correlated with the Conservatives' agenda (.34) than with Labour's (.10). The press and the Conservative Party both gave a lot of attention to Europe, but the image of a deeply divided leadership battling over Conservative policy towards EMU, and even arguing over their own advertising on this issue, probably proved deeply damaging for party morale and for public perceptions of the government. The theory that parties have 'issue-ownership' suggests that parties are trying to steer the electoral battle towards the issues where they enjoy a decisive advantage (Budge and Farlie 1983). The Conservatives clearly thought that the economy in 1997 was their strong card ('Britain is Booming') and hence half their press releases were on this topic. But less than one in ten front-page stories focused on this issue. In contrast, Labour and the Liberal Democrats wanted to fight the election more on their home turf of social welfare, but again the press and

TABLE 5.5: *Party Press Releases and News Agendas, 1997 (percentages)*

Subject	Con	Labour	Lib Dem	Total	TV	Press
Conduct of campaign	4	4	7	5	26	28
Parties	7	11	12	10	17	15
Opinion polls		1	1		11	13
Party leaders			1		4	3
Media treatment					1	5
Campaign issues	3	8	3	4	4	5
SUBTOTAL CAMPAIGN	**[14]**	**[24]**	**[23]**	**[20]**	**[63]**	**[69]**
Social welfare	9	21	34	21	8	5
Regions	2	1	1	1	8	0
Economy	51	31	15	32	7	10
Europe/foreign	11	9	5	8	6	12
Education and arts	10	13	18	13	5	3
Constitutional reform	1		2	1	2	0
Infrastructure	2	1		1	1	0
Environment/energy	1	2	3	2	0	0
Defence		1	1	1	0	0
SUBTOTAL ISSUES	**[86]**	**[77]**	**[77]**	**[80]**	**[37]**	**[31]**
TOTAL	**100**	**100**	**100**	**100**	**100**	**100**

Note: Not all columns add to 100 per cent because of rounding. The content analysis is based on coding every front-page news story in six newspapers during one month of the official campaign (1–30 April 1997). The above figures are calculated as a percentage of all political stories during this month.

Source: 1997 Election Party and Media Agenda Content Analysis, Margaret Scammell and Holli A. Semetko.

TV news largely failed to follow their lead. The Liberal Democrats may have run the most effective campaign in terms of staying most consistently on message in their own communication strategy, but they proved the least successful of the three parties in getting their message heard on television or in the press.

To put these figures in a long-term context, it is worth returning to the findings of a study comparing party and media agendas in the British 1983 and US 1984 general election campaigns. That comparison of party agendas and television news agendas found that in Britain the correlations ranged from .38 to .83 (a perfect correlation would be 1.0), whereas those in the United States ranged from .14 to .37. The correlations between the party and newspaper agendas in Britain ranged from .52 to .77, whereas those in the United Stated ranged from .03 to .19 (Semetko *et al.* 1991: 141, 168). The conclusion of that study was that American reporters exercised greater discretion in taking up and reporting the subjects put forward by candidates, whereas in Britain it appeared that political parties had greater potential to shape the campaign agenda. We believe that this conclusion still remains valid today. The range of correlations between party and media agendas in 1997 on all subjects did not reach the levels found in 1983 in Britain, there has been some press–party

TABLE 5.6: *Correlations between Party Press Releases and News Agendas, 1997*

ALL SUBJECTS	BBC	ITN	All Press
Conservatives	.38	.31	.40
Labour	.37	.27	.45
Liberal Democrats	.41	.34	.44
BBC		.97***	.80***
ITV			.72**

SUBSTANTIVE ISSUES	BBC	ITN	All Press
Conservatives	.67*	.64	.88**
Labour	.51	.42	.82**
Liberal Democrats	.53	.41	.75*
BBC		.98***	.59
ITV			.53

Note: These are Spearman's Rho rank order correlation coefficients.
*** p < .001, ** p < .01, * p < .05
All subjects (N = 15) as presented in Tables 5.2–5.4.

Source: 1997 Election Party and Media Agenda Content Analysis, Margaret Scammell and Holli A. Semetko.

dealignment, but at the same time they did not approach the low levels that were found in the United States in 1984.[2] (See Table 5.7.)

Conclusions

Agenda-setting theory suggests that one of the critical battles during the campaign is the attempt by parties to set the news headlines, and thereby influence public priorities about the most important problems facing the country. Theories of issue ownership suggest that it is very difficult for parties to gain electoral advantage on issues which they do not 'own' (Budge and Farlie 1983). Labour, for example, usually has an historic advantage in terms of public perceptions about the best party for managing the National Health Service, while the Conservatives have usually been regarded as the strongest party on defence. Images of party competence on particular issues are seen as fairly persistent and deep-rooted, although not unchangeable. If issue ownership is difficult to alter, then the essential battleground in election campaigns concerns which issues are prioritized. If the welfare state is seen as under threat, then Labour is believed to have a long-standing advantage in the eyes of the electorate whereas if the most important problem is high taxation then we would expect the Conservatives to benefit. Hence Miller (1991) concluded that agenda bias, notably the predominance of defence and foreign policy in the 1987 news headlines, largely served to benefit the Thatcher government.

What can we conclude from the analysis of the party and news agendas a decade later? First, that if the press once followed the party lead more

TABLE 5.7: *Correlations between Party Press Releases and Newspaper Agendas, 1997*

ALL SUBJECTS	Guardian	Independent	Times	Mail	Mirror	Sun	All Press
Conservatives	.30	.34	.39	.37	.51*	.34	.40
Labour	.32	.50	.38	.37	.62**	.10	.45
Liberal							
Democrats	.36	.51*	.40	.28	.58*	.09	.44
BBC	.81***	.77***	.72**	.67**	.54*	.41	.80***
ITV	.75***	.68**	.71**	.56*	.39	.44	.72**

ISSUES ONLY	Guardian	Independent	Times	Mail	Mirror	Sun	All Press
Conservatives	.86**	.63	.90***	.78**	.86**	.41	.40
Labour	.81**	.87**	.80**	.75	.92***	.14	.45
Liberal							
Democrats	.77*	.85**	.73*	.59	.86**	.14	.44
BBC	.61	.45	.51	.59	.61	.14	.80***
ITV	.54	.34	.47	.51	.50	.21	.72**

Note: These are Spearman's Rho rank order correlation coefficients.
*** p < .001, ** p < .01, * p < .05
All subjects (N=15) as presented in Tables 5.2–5.4.
Source: 1997 Election Party and Media Agenda Content Analysis, Margaret Scammell and Holli A. Semetko.

closely, today the news media is fairly autonomous in its news priorities, following its own 'media logic' rather than the priorities of any party. The evidence on the issue agenda confirms the argument in Chapter 2 that the 1997 election saw a further step in press dealignment, or a weakening of the press–party ties. The top three subjects on television news and in the press were the conduct of the campaign, the parties, and opinion polls. These speak to a strategic focus of the news, rather than a policy focus. In comparison with the 1992 election, the dynamics of the campaign continued to predominate in coverage. But within this category of stories there was considerably less attention to the horse race in 1997, perhaps because the results were so flat and unchanging (Crewe 1997), and instead journalists devoted more attention to the day-to-day activities of politicians on the campaign trail, and the strategies and tactics of the parties. British political parties may have become far more professional and polished in waging campaigns in the past decade or so but our comparison of party and media agendas in 1997 shows that this did not result in anything like a perfect correlation between them. The analogy is like running up the down escalator: parties today are trying ever harder, but failing more often, to set the issue agenda. Occasionally a headline splash can be seen as picking up a party lead, whether the 'Unions' conspiracy of silence' in the *Daily Mail* (3 April), or 'Tories admit job figure lies' in *The Mirror* (16 April). On the issue agenda alone, both *The Mirror* and the *Mail* were close to the issue priorities of the parties each paper supports, with strong and significant correlation. But increasingly the press, driven by the need for readers, is following its own priorities, more 'Hamster eats through car' (*The Sun* 12 April) and Spice Girls (*Daily Star* 1, 3, 10, 11, 14, 19 and 28 April), than constitutional reform, the Common Agricultural Policy or a minimum wage.

The results of this analysis speak to a general concern that the news during election campaigns has become more strategy oriented or preoccupied with the daily events of the campaign at the expense of serious policy debate. This claim is heard most often in the United States where the criticisms have been the strongest (Patterson 1993; Fallows 1996). This process has gone less far in Britain, given the public service ethos which still predominates on British television. Indeed journalists could well argue in their defence that by the time of the official campaign the public had already heard all that it needed to know about policy debates, and that in a (relatively) long, flat and uneventful campaign yet more attention to issues like nursery education, transportation policies, or youth training would have simply turned off voters even more. In a more fragmented media environment, with more choices available at a click of the remote, public loyalty towards particular media outlets has eroded. But to do more than simply speculate about the consequences of this coverage we need to go on in the next chapter to examine the public's reaction to the campaign, how much attention they gave to the news coverage, and how it affected them during the long and short campaign.

Notes

1. The content analysis is based on variables developed in Semetko *et al.* (1991). See the Technical Appendix for details.
2. Semetko *et al.* (1991) used the opening statements made by the parties at the daily morning press conferences as the basis for establishing the party agendas in 1983, whereas in 1997 we use the press releases provided by the parties each day. *The Independent* was not included in the 1983 study. It is worth noting that the range of correlations between party and television news agendas in 1983 in the UK, when only the substantive issues were considered, was from .30 to .90, whereas in 1997 this was from .41 to .67. The comparable figures for the newspaper agendas in 1983 were .40 to 1.0, whereas in 1997 they were from .14 to .90.

6 The Public's Reaction

Given this news environment, how did viewers react to the campaign coverage and, in particular, did they reach for their remotes to turn off, or turn over, from news and current affairs on television? Who proved attentive to the news media? And did the public feel that the election coverage was interesting, informative and fair?

Before we can assess the strength of any effects of the news media we need to establish their reach in terms of the audience. Seminal studies of American campaigns by Lazarsfeld and colleagues laid the foundations for the conventional wisdom about who is most attentive in elections (Lazarsfeld *et al.* 1944; Berelson *et al.* 1963). The Columbia studies established that because of selective exposure and attention the public who tuned into candidate speeches on the wireless, followed the campaign in newspapers, and discussed politics with friends, were the most committed partisans who were unlikely to change their minds. Campaign propaganda largely preached to the converted. In contrast the genuine 'waverers' or 'floaters' who were undecided about which side to support proved least attentive, interested, and informed about the electoral choices before them. Party propaganda thereby failed to reach the undecided whom candidates most wanted to contact.

If this pattern continues to hold half a century later, there are important implications for democratic theory: floating voters, who may play a disproportionate role in determining the outcome of an election, may do so more from indifference than from reasoned choice. If the role of the media is largely limited to reinforcement not conversion, this also has significant consequences for the study of campaign effects. The Columbia view was subsequently confirmed by the earliest studies of voting behaviour in Britain (Butler and Stokes 1974; Milne and Mackenzie 1954, 1958; Trenaman and McQuail 1961; Blumler and McQuail 1968).

To explore these issues this chapter examines the audience for campaign news based on the Broadcasters Audience Research Board (BARB) data, surveys in *Television: The Public's View* (ITC), and evidence from the 1997 British Election Campaign panel study. We analyse who usually reads, listens to and watches political news, and public reactions to the coverage, to see what we know about 'the attentive public' in British election campaigns.

The Size of the Audience for Television News

To monitor the size of the audience for television news during the campaign we can draw on the most comprehensive and reliable information on viewership figures using data supplied by the Broadcasters Audience Research Board. BARB provides the industry-standard measure of viewing behaviour from a panel sample of over 4,000 monitored households which uses electronic feedback to monitor whether the television is switched on in the household, which channel is being watched, and how many people are viewing the programme.

The main evening news and current affairs programmes on British television continue to reach a mass audience, but the availability of alternative channels has slightly eroded their market share. Commentators noted that BBC1's *Nine O'Clock News* suffered particularly sharply from a fall in viewership after it was specially extended with campaign news to 50 minutes after Easter. The BARB figures confirm that this programme lost one-third of its viewers, down from 5.8 million in the first week to 4 million thereafter (see Figure 6.1). This figure was also well down from the equivalent audience during the spring 1992 campaign, when about 6.3 million viewers tuned into BBC1's main evening news. But what commentators failed to notice was that ITN's *News at Ten*, with its regular 30-minute slot, also steadily lost some of its audience during the campaign, down from 6 million in the first week to 5.6 million in the last. *Channel 4 News* at 7pm (with 0.6 million viewers), ITV's *Early Evening News* at 5.45pm (with 4 million) and BBC1's *Six O'Clock News* (with 5.8 million)

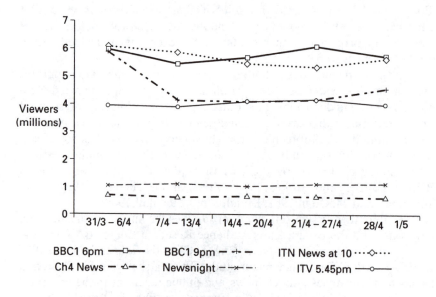

FIGURE 6.1   *Audience for Evening News (31 March – 1 May 1997)*
Source: BARB

remained popular and relatively stable, subject only to the natural trendless fluctuations caused by the television schedules.

Current affairs programmes also experienced fluctuations in their audiences (see Figure 6.2). The sharpest fall was registered by BBC1's *Panorama* which carried interviews with all the major party leaders (with an average viewership of 2.8 million throughout the campaign), although they also picked up towards the end of the campaign. A similar pattern was registered with *Question Time* (2.8 million), while BBC1's *On the Record* (1.5 million) managed a modest and steady rise during the campaign. Among the special programmes the BBC's 9am *Election Call* gathered about 0.6 million television viewers, but more listened via Radio 4, and the programme maintaining high standards of public service broadcasting. ITN's *People's Election*, with a live studio audience of 500, attracted a stable viewership of about 2.8 million. On Channel 4 Vincent Hanna's *A Week in Politics* (0.8 million) and *Midnight Special* (0.2 million) retained a loyal, if modest, audience of political aficionados throughout the campaign.

As discussed in Chapter 2, the party election broadcasts (PEBs) allocated in the 1997 campaign followed the 5:5:4 ratio, with five for Labour, five for the Conservatives, four for the Liberal Democrats and one each for minor parties who mustered a minimum of 50 candidates, including the Greens, the Natural Law Party and the British National Party. Special regulations governed the regions (for details see Chapter 11; Scammell and Semetko 1995; Harrison 1997). Although the major

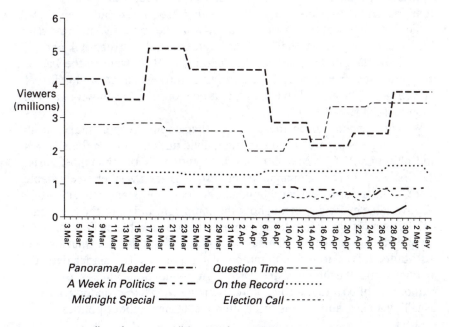

FIGURE 6.2   *Audience for Current Affairs (March – April 1997)*
    Source: BARB

parties are given ten minutes air time per PEB they have tended to use less than their allocation, and 1997 proved no exception. Recently there have been proposals by the broadcasting authorities to reduce the number and length of party broadcasts, although the Neill Report (1998) does not support this idea. PEBs have often suffered an audience drop-off during the first few minutes, as viewers reach for their remotes, although the overall level of audience penetration may be substantial and depends more on their position in the evening line-up, and whether they followed or preceded popular programmes. In the 1997 campaign the Labour and Conservative parties showed five election broadcasts, which attracted an average audience of about 11.2 million per broadcast across all channels, while the four Liberal Democrat broadcasts were seen by 10.6 million per broadcast, and minor parties were watched by about 10.1 million (see Table 6.1). None proved particularly memorable, though some aroused minor controversy (such as Labour's use of Fitz the bulldog, traditionally seen as a symbol of the far right BNP, and a Pro-Life film featuring graphic footage of abortions). The ratings were well down on 1992, when PEBs averaged about 13 million viewers.

Public interest may have flagged during the long, uneventful and flat campaign but it revived on polling day. On election night, at its peak (at 10.45pm) 12.7 million people tuned into the election specials, or almost one-third of the electorate (see Figure 6.3). While the news of Labour's landslide started to sink in across the nation, the BBC experienced an equivalent landslide of viewers against ITV, by a ratio of about 7:3. The numbers gradually subsided as the evening progressed but even so 5.2 million remained glued to the set at 1.45 in the morning, as Tory after Tory faced the end of their political careers, and between 1.4 and 6.3 million watched bleary-eyed all the next day as Blair went to the Palace, then emerged triumphant to enthusiastic throngs in Downing Street. Indeed the night proved so exciting that one journalist even wrote a book about it (Cathcart 1997).

We can conclude from these figures that popular commentary during the campaign exaggerated how far the public turned off from the election, and, although BBC1's *Nine O'Clock News* suffered more than most during the first week of the campaign, the pattern after then was relatively stable. Since, as mentioned earlier, about ten hours of news and current affairs was available every day throughout the campaign, and since the horse race was flat almost throughout, this represents a remarkable achievement for television broadcasters. But how widely did this information get distributed? Was it just committed voters, or did the undecided, the apathetic and the uninterested also learn about the campaign from this outpouring of coverage? To explore this issue we need to understand who usually watches, and who is most attentive, to news about politics.

TABLE 6.1: *The Audience for Party Election Broadcasts, 1997*

Date April 1997		Party	Min	BBC1 Cons 000s 1997	BBC1 Cons Share 1997	BBC2 Cons 000s 1997	BBC2 Cons Share 1997	ITV Cons 000s 1997	ITV Cons Share 1997	Ch4 Cons 000s 1997	Ch4 Cons Share 1997	Ch5 Cons 000s 1997	Ch5 Cons Share 1997
9	Wed	Con 1	6	2,272	9	886	5	6,012	37	650	3	277	1.0
16	Wed	Con 2	6	2,607	11	837	4	6,785	39	699	6	69	0.0
22	Tues	Con 3	6	3,415	15	993	6	7,673	44	1,130	5	138	1.0
25	Fri	Con 4	6	3,300	15	858	5	5,086		421	3	242	1.0
29	Tues	Con 5	5	3,327	14	822	5	6,480	35	1,117	5	217	1.0
10	Thur	Lab 1	6	3,016	15	1,097	7	6,430	39	727	10	141	1.0
15	Tues	Lab 2	6	3,000	13	877	7	7,018	42	619	4	264	1.0
21	Mon	Lab 3	6	3,055	13	1,105	6	6,039		652	6	145	1.0
24	Thur	Lab 4	10	3,400	17	1,099	7	5,382		930	7	216	1.0
28	Mon	Lab 5	5	2,834	11	850	4	5,587	28	1,338	12	295	1.0
11	Fri	LDem 1	7	3,653	17	954	5	4,789	27	832	9	145	1.0
22	Tues	LDem 2	5	4,349	24	618	8	4,337	27	—	—	66	0.0
23	Wed	LDem 3	7	3,300	16	848	5	6,436	37	729	8	349	2.0
27	Sun	LDem 4											
25	Fri	BNP 1	6	5,593	30	635	6	4,190	24			254	2.0
18	Fri	NLaw 1	5	4,828	27	614	6	3,989	25	377	4	160	1.0
24	Thur	ProLife	7	4,231	21	814	11	4,121	29			80	2.0
15	Tues	Ref 1	5	4,837	28	603	7	3,583	21	924	4	40	0.0
23	Wed	SNP 1	5	340		59						74	1.0
28	Mon	SNP 2	4	737		49		391				88	1.0
26	Sat	SocLab	6	4,341		1,330	6			417	8	96	1.0
		Mean		3,322	17	797	6	5,240	32	771	6	168	1.0

Source: BARB.

Note: Cons 000s = Consolidated number of viewers including live and VCR.

Cons share = Consolidated share of all viewers (see BARB definitions and measures). SNP only broadcast in Scotland.

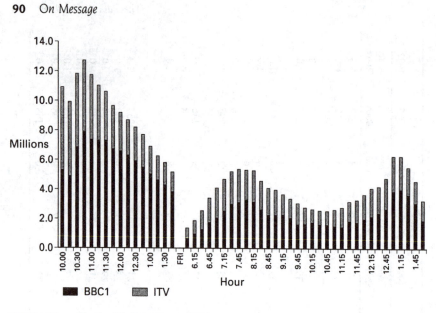

FIGURE 6.3   *Election Night Audience,* 1997

Who Watches Television News?

Attention to political news can be conceptualized as a form of civic engagement, representing the first step in the ladder of political participation. Milbrath (1965) suggests that during campaigns most citizens are like attentive spectators at a sports event, following their side but not becoming more active in more demanding ways. The process of following the news facilitates other forms of participation, ranging from political conversations to voting, displaying party posters, attending local public meetings, and becoming active in constituency parties. Understood in this way, the standard social and political variables explaining civic activity could also help predict attention to campaign news. This includes the usual social factors (class, education, age, and gender), along with political attitudes (interest and strength of partisan identification) (Parry *et al.* 1992; Verba *et al.* 1995). Earlier studies found that age and education commonly proved important predictors of news use (Miller 1991; see also Milne and Mackenzie 1958: 94; Gunter *et al.* 1994; McQuail 1992: 238).

Exposure to Campaign News

Most people in Britain spend far longer viewing television than any other leisure activity. On average most people devoted over 25 hours per week to television, in addition to 16 hours listening to the radio, and 3 hours a week reading newspapers, not including time spent using more specialized media such as magazines, films or the internet. In total, most people usually spend just over six hours a day exposed to the mass media, at least as routine background activity, almost as much time as they spend at work or sleeping (*Social Trends* 1997: 216). The British Election Campaign panel study monitored regular viewers of general television (defined as those who reported watching six or more days a week); regular users of TV news (defined according to whether respondents said that they watched the news 'yesterday' in each of the successive waves A, B and C during the long and short campaign); and regular users of newspapers (defined by the same criteria as TV news).

The results in Table 6.2 show that age proved a strong predictor of media use: the elderly were far more likely to be regular consumers of TV news and newspapers. One explanation is that the older group, often confined to the home, usually watched far more television in general, such

TABLE 6.2: *Social Characteristics of the News Audience*, 1997

	Regular TV Viewer	Regular Viewer TV News	Regular Newspaper Reader
All	63	32	31
Salariat	65	36	40
Routine NM	55	33	22
Petty bourgeoisie	60	45	38
Manual foremen	64	35	29
Working class	57	24	28
Men	63	38	41
Women	56	27	22
17–24	34	19	14
25–34	41	21	18
35–44	52	26	24
45–54	63	33	38
55–59	78	46	42
60–64	78	45	46
65+	84	48	48
Paid work	51	27	29
Unemployed	77	32	25
Retired	83	48	48
Looking after home	54	25	22
Graduate	57	31	34
O level equiv.	55	30	28
No qualification	68	29	31

Notes: Only respondents in all waves (ABCD) are included (N.1422).

Regular TV Viewer watches television 6 or more days per week.

TV News Regular User: respondent reported having watched a television news broadcast yesterday in each of waves A, B and C.

Newspaper Regular Reader: respondent reported having read a newspaper yesterday in each of waves A, B and C.

Source: 1997 British Election Campaign panel study.

as light entertainment, sports and films. While 84 per cent of the elderly watched television six days a week or more, this was only true of one-third of the under-24s. In this sense exposure to news could be attributed to leisure patterns more than deliberate choice. Yet this was only part of the answer; for example, the unemployed were almost equally heavy viewers of television but they were far less likely than the retired to watch TV news or read newspapers. Patterns of media consumption by social class (using the Goldthorpe-Heath five-fold class schema) show that there were few class differences in terms of regular viewing of any television, but class did influence regular use of TV news and newspapers, with the working class least likely to be exposed to these media. There was also a modest gender gap across all three indicators of media habits, with women particularly less likely to be regular newspaper readers. As market research has often shown (Seymour-Ure 1995) there are fewer female readers of the two largest circulation daily tabloids, *The Sun* and *The Mirror*.

What were the political characteristics of the attentive public?

TABLE 6.3: *Political Characteristics of the News Audience*, 1997

	Regular TV Viewer	Regular Viewer TV News	Regular Newspaper Reader
All	63	32	31
Vote 1997			
Cons Voter	62	36	35
Labour Voter	62	32	30
LibDem Voter	66	35	30
Other Voter	50	38	39
Decided how to vote			
Decided End-Apr	63	34	32
Undecided End-Apr	49	28	26
Party Id/Direction			
Con	62	33	35
Lab	63	32	33
Ldem	68	41	29
Other	46	38	39
None	39	22	19
Party Id/Strength			
Very strong	75	40	43
Fairly strong	67	39	33
Not very strong	57	29	30
Attentive to political news			
'A great deal'	53	61	44

Notes: Only respondents in all waves (ABCD) are included (N.1422).

Regular TV Viewer watches television 6 or more days per week.

TV News Regular User: respondent reported having watched a television news broadcast yesterday in each of waves A, B and C.

Newspaper Regular Reader: respondent reported having read a newspaper yesterday in each of waves A, B and C.

Source: 1997 British Election Campaign panel study.

Lazarsfeld suggested that people most exposed to news during campaigns were the most partisan who had already made up their minds how to vote, whereas waverers most in need of information proved least attentive. As shown in Table 6.3 this pattern was strikingly confirmed in our data. Those who remained undecided how to vote in the last two weeks of the election campaign (mid to late April) were less likely to be heavy television viewers or regular consumers of news on TV or in the press. Those who lacked a party identification, or had only a weak one, were also less likely to be exposed to campaign news than strong partisans. Yet the evidence also suggests that exposure to news was fairly uniform across all parties, whether measured by vote cast in 1997 or the direction of partisan identi-fication. There was a tendency for Labour supporters to be less exposed to news sources than Conservatives, but the difference was only modest.

Did partisans tune in most to information about the party they supported, as Lazarsfeld suggests? Because we cannot identify a strong directional bias in television news we cannot examine this through the panel survey on TV news. But we can look at who was most attentive to the party election broadcasts. The pattern in Table 6.4 tends to confirm the Lazarsfeld thesis: although all types of voters tuned into each of the party broadcasts, nevertheless there was a modest tendency for Labour and Liberal Democrat voters to prove the strongest viewers of their own party's PEBs. This does suggest that parties should not just target their own supporters in PEBs, but broadcasts do function to help reinforce their own voters.

The Public's Reaction to Campaign News

For more information about viewers' reactions to the election we can turn to data from the four-wave panel survey, *Television: The Public's View*, with 15,356 viewers conducted before, during and after the 1997 campaign by RSL for the Independent Television Commission. The public were asked to evaluate a range of factors in television's coverage of the campaign.

As shown in Table 6.5, the results confirm that in the 1997 election the public felt there was far too much coverage of the campaign, as popular

TABLE 6.4: *The Audience for Party Election Broadcasts by Vote, 1977*

	Conservative vote	Labour vote	Liberal Democrat vote
Watched Conservative PEB	**21**	18	21
Watched Labour PEB	21	**26**	24
Watched Liberal Democrat PEB	17	21	**27**

Note: Wave C (mid to late April) Q: *'Have you watched all or part of any party election broadcast on television during the last 7 days?'* IF YES: *'Which party's?'* PROBE. *'Any others?'* CODE ALL THAT APPLY.

Source: British Election Campaign panel study 1997.

TABLE 6.5: *Public Evaluation of Television Coverage, 1977*

Coverage of Election	Far too Much	Too Much	About Right	Too Little	Far too Little	Net PDI#
COVERAGE OF ELECTION	41	19	11	14	15	33
COVERAGE BY CHANNEL:						
Sky News	72	21	7	0	0	92
ITV	57	19	19	5	0	71
Ch4	35	35	26	2	1	66
BBC1	35	22	42	1	0	57
BBC2	25	26	45	4	1	46
Ch5	7	14	67	10	2	10
COVERAGE OF TOPICS:						
Opinion polls	41	36	22	1	0	76
By outside experts	63	15	18	4	1	73
Party leaders	12	53	34	1	0	64
Press conferences	31	28	28	3	1	56
By TV's correspondents	39	22	33	6	0	54
Party policies	23	30	42	3	2	48
COVERAGE OF PARTIES:						
Conservatives	28	39	31	1	0	66
Liberal Democrats	41	13	33	7	6	41
Labour	22	39	17	22	0	38
Referendum	43	9	29	12	7	34
Green	37	14	27	11	9	31
COVERAGE OF ISSUES:						
European issues	25	29	37	5	5	45
Economy	41	13	33	7	6	41
Foreign affairs	37	14	28	12	9	31
Social policy	43	9	29	12	7	34
Constitutional issues	17	22	45	10	6	24
Environment	15	20	42	13	10	13

Note: Q: 'Thinking about television news during the campaign, what did you feel about coverage of. . .'
The Net Percentage Difference Index (PDI) is the proportion who think there is too much minus the proportion who think there is not enough.

Source: ITC (N. 15,356).

commentators often suggested. Nevertheless, while a clear majority (60 per cent) agreed that there had been far too much about the campaign on television, about a quarter of the public thought that there had been too little, and few felt that broadcasters had got the balance right. This pattern may have important implications for future elections as British broadcasting moves into a more diverse digital media environment. A multiplicity of channels will make it far easier for some to tune out from politics, while other political junkies will be able to watch 24-hour news.

If we turn to coverage by different channels, contrary to the conventional wisdom, Sky News (with Adam Boulton's rolling live campaign) and

ITV were most widely criticized for providing too much coverage, while the public seemed more satisfied by the BBC scheduling. Despite the decline in coverage of opinion polls noted earlier, the public still felt that there was far too much attention to the horse race on television. Outside pundits were also unpopular and viewers seemed happier with television's own correspondents. Reflecting the government's unpopularity in the polls, the public thought there was too much coverage of the Conservative Party in television news, while in contrast a fifth of all viewers would have liked more about the Labour Party, and also the minor parties like the Greens who rarely featured in the news. As we have seen, Europe received extensive attention in the press, but the public felt that the amount of news about this topic was excessive, along with the level of attention given to foreign policy more generally.

Lastly, the public were also asked to evaluate the standards of television news, whether it met the requirements of public service broadcasting by being accurate, informative, balanced and interesting. Here viewers expressed largely positive reaction to news programmes on British television (see Table 6.6). Channel 4's *Seven O'Clock News* anchored by Jon Snow came out particularly well from this evaluation, especially in terms of accuracy and balance, perhaps because the distinctively longer format allows more opportunity to present all points of view. The general picture which emerges from this survey during the campaign confirms once more that British television news is widely held in high regard for providing a broadly impartial source of information, across all the major channels.

Conclusions: Preaching to the Converted?

Based on this analysis we can conclude that the available evidence does tend to support Lazarsfeld's theory of the attentive public. The overall audience for political news clearly was large, even if the long and uneventful campaign produced a drop in viewers for television news. Those who tuned into the campaign news were already those who were most attentive to politics, whereas the undecideds who remained unsure

TABLE 6.6:   *Public Evaluation of Standards of Television News, 1997*

% Positive	BBC1	BBC2	ITV	Ch 4	Ch 5
Accurate	56	73	51	87	64
Interesting	35	71	51	54	56
Informative	46	59	65	60	50
Balanced	31	48	49	89	41

Note: Q: "To what extent do you think that news programmes on . . . are . . . .'
Percentage positive represents those who responded 'just about always' or 'most of the time' as opposed to those who responded 'some of the time' or 'hardly ever'.

Source: ITC (N.15,356) Campaign Poll April 1997.

which party to support as polling day approached were also least likely to be heavy viewers of television news or regular readers of the press. It seems plausible that in the short term those with the greatest political interest, civic engagement and strong partisanship are most likely to switch on the news, although in the long term we might expect a virtuous cycle as those who regularly keep up with current affairs will be more likely to be interested and knowledgeable. Although this proposition seems plausible, the evidence in this chapter cannot tell us what effects exposure and attention to the news media had on the public during the campaign. To explore this issue we need to move beyond understanding the audience as a cross-section of the electorate and explore the dynamics of the campaign, looking at changes in media habits, or political attitudes, or both. Accordingly in the next chapter we go on to examine the effects of the media on civic engagement to understand changes in political knowledge and mobilization.

PART III

IMPACT

7 The Impact On Civic Engagement

It has long been argued in Britain that the role of the media is to serve the 'public interest'. In Lord Reith's classic phrase, the guiding mission of the BBC since 1922 has been to 'educate, inform and [not just] entertain'. The public service tradition in British broadcasting emphasizes the provision of news and current affairs to enhance the quality of political debate (Blumler and Gurevitch 1995; Humphreys 1996). Yet critics charge that the news media fell far short of these standards in their coverage of the 1997 British general election. Far from informing and mobilizing the public, commentators claim that news coverage encouraged public cynicism and political apathy.

To examine this issue we start by summarizing the debate about the effects of the media during campaigns, contrasting video-malaise, mobilization and minimal effect theories. Subsequent sections use the 1997 British Election Campaign panel survey to analyse what the public learnt about party policies from watching and reading about the campaign; whether the news affected public trust and cynicism; and whether the media influenced political participation. The conclusion considers the implications of the findings for theories about media effects and more generally for our expectations about the role of the news media in a democracy.

The Debate about Cognitive and Mobilization Effects

Video-malaise Theories

In recent years many have emphasized the negative impact of the media. Popular criticism of the press has been common in the United States but in recent years the trickle of complaint has become an onslaught. 'Video-malaise' theories argue that the dominant values and structural biases of the news media produce campaign coverage dominated by the poll-led horse race, personal scandal, and cynical insider strategy, at the expense of detailed and informed debate about serious policy problems (Robinson 1976; Postman 1985; Patterson 1993; Fallows 1996; Schudson 1995). Blumler (1997) suggests that a 'crisis' of civic communications has afflicted Britain as well as the United States.

Support for the video-malaise thesis has been documented in studies of American newspapers (Miller *et al.* 1979), television documentaries (Robinson 1976), and TV campaign news (Chan 1997). Gerbner (1980) argued that watching television produced a 'mean-world' effect. The most convincing and thorough experimental study (Ansolabehere and Iyengar 1995) demonstrated that watching negative television advertising suppressed American voter participation. Experiments by Cappella and Jamieson found network news guilty of sensationalizing and over-simplifying complex issues like health care, producing a 'spiral of cynicism' among the public (Cappella and Jamieson 1997). Local television news, in particular – the main source of news for most Americans – is accused of allowing trivial 'infotainment', crime and sports to drive out serious coverage of public affairs in the State House or Capitol Hill (Klite, Bardwell, and Salzman 1997). Putnam indicts television for the dramatic erosion of civic engagement and social capital in America (Putnam 1996). The industry perennially debates the virtues of a range of panaceas to answer their critics, including civic journalism (Jay Rosen), free television time for candidates (Paul Taylor), and revised codes of professional practice (Tom Rosensteil).

Yet generalizations about the impact of the American news media may not necessarily apply in the European context given different media structures, journalistic cultures and political systems. Political communications operates within an institutional environment. The effects of repeated 30-second attack ads shaping candidate images during the lengthy primary process, for example, may well differ significantly from the influence of single-shot five-minute party political broadcasts during the shorter British campaign. Important transatlantic contrasts include the public service ethos which permeates British television versus commercial considerations driving American network and local news; the predominance of a highly competitive national press in the UK compared with regional papers dominating local markets in the United States; and significant differences in journalistic cultures including more overt newspaper partisanship in Britain (Patterson and Donsbach 1996).

The debate about media coverage of politics has been more muted in Europe but nevertheless similar concerns have been aired. Cultural theorists claim that growing 'tabloidization' has undermined the audience's ability to make sense of public affairs and, echoing Habermas, there is widespread concern about the decline of the public sphere (Dahlgren 1995; Dahlgren and Sparks 1997; Langer 1998; Lull and Hinerman 1997). In Germany and Sweden studies have demonstrated that macro-level trends towards increased coverage of scandals and negative news have been accompanied by declining confidence in political leaders

(Friedrichsen 1996; Westerstahl and Johansson 1986). Nevertheless, it is not possible to draw a clear causal link between these developments since changes in news content may influence, or only reflect, an erosion of public confidence in government.

In Britain, although there is little direct evidence, much of the post-election commentary echoed the video-malaise thesis. Many complained that the campaign was flat, dull and uneventful and the media was commonly blamed for overkill, saturation and boredom (Harrison 1997). The fact that in the last election turnout fell to 71.6 per cent, its lowest level since 1935, caused considerable concern (Heath and Taylor 1999). Observers believed people were turned off by overloaded media coverage (Denver and Hands 1997b; Scammell and Harrop 1997), especially the focus on negative stories about 'sleaze' (sexual and financial) which dominated the early weeks of the campaign (Norris 1997a; Seymour-Ure 1997). Blumler (1997) points to various developments which may have encouraged political cynicism: the period of campaigning has lengthened, attack campaigning has become more common, journalistic criticism of national political institutions has increased, and a media-led personalization of political conflict has grown. Circumstantial evidence therefore seems to bolster the claim that media coverage of the British campaign may have discouraged civic engagement.

Mobilization Theories

Yet this view is challenged by mobilization theories which suggest that the modern mass media have a significant impact on the public, but in a positive direction which functions to sustain and promote democratic participation (Newton 1997). This view stresses the wide availability of a diverse range of news media providing a rich information environment in advanced industrialized societies. Higher levels of literacy and education have increased the cognitive skills which allow citizens to make use of this environment. In many western democracies these developments, some suggest, have produced an electorate better informed, more engaged and more sophisticated about public affairs than ever before (Dalton 1996; Inglehart 1997).

Rather than a blanket critique of 'the media', mobilization theories emphasize that we need carefully to disentangle the positive and negative effects of different media, messages, audiences and effects. In Britain and America heavy users of television have been found to be less participatory than average. Nevertheless, regular consumers of television news and regular readers of broadsheet newspapers have been found to be more likely than average to be informed, interested and engaged in political life (Newton 1997, 1999; Norris 1996, 2000).

> Those who read a tabloid regularly, and who watch a lot of television in general, are most likely to show signs of political malaise. In comparison those who watch a lot of television news, and particularly those who read a broadsheet,

show stronger signs of political mobilization and fewer signs of malaise. (Newton 1997: 160)

The most extensive study using panel surveys and content analysis to examine the effects of the media on the British electorate, by Miller (1991), concluded that television largely succeeded in informing the electorate during the 1987 campaign, particularly as polling day approached, while the press functioned to mobilize voters and reinforce partisanship.

Minimal Effects Theories

Lastly, as discussed earlier, in the minimal effects perspective the effects of the media during the campaign are largely to reinforce, but not to change, public opinion in either a positive or negative direction (Lazarsfeld *et al.* 1944; Berelson *et al* 1954). Because of selective exposure and attention, Lazarsfeld concluded, the public who tuned into candidate speeches on the wireless, followed the campaign in newspapers, and discussed politics with friends, were the most committed partisans who were unlikely to change their minds. Campaign propaganda largely preached to the converted. In contrast the genuine 'waverers' or 'floaters', who were undecided about which side to support, proved least attentive to the news, and therefore absorbed little new information about the electoral choices before them. The 'reinforcement not change' thesis was subsequently confirmed by the earliest studies of voting behaviour in Britain (Butler and Stokes 1974; Milne and Mackenzie 1954; Trenaman and McQuail 1961). More recent studies in Britain have emphasized the limited effects model, particularly in terms of the power of the press to influence short-term vote switching during the election campaign (Curtice and Semetko 1994).

Evidence for the Media's Role in Civic Engagement

Previous studies have come up with different answers about whether campaign coverage by the news media has the capacity to encourage or discourage civic engagement, or alternatively whether it simply passed by the electorate. In this chapter to explore this issue we draw mainly on the British Election Campaign panel survey outlined in Chapter 3. The design allows us to monitor whether use and attention to the media was associated with changes in political knowledge (including information about party policies); changes in political efficacy; and changes in political participation. To supplement this source we also draw on the 1997 BES for alternative measures of political knowledge. To increase the reliability of the analysis we used a range of survey questions, forming scales of political knowledge, efficacy, and participation. Theoretically, we would expect that these attitudes would be interrelated (for example, that political efficacy might be associated with voting turnout) although we treat this as an empirical question which will be explored later in the multivariate analysis.

On the basis of the previous literature we also hypothesize that patterns of civic engagement would be associated with different types of media use, as summarized in Figure 7.1. The survey allows us to distinguish between types of audiences. When asked about their most important source of political information people usually nominate television news (Gunter *et al.* 1994). Based on previous studies (Miller 1991) we hypothesize that use of, and attention to, television news, as a more neutral medium, would be likely to have the strongest impact on changes in political knowledge. In contrast, we expect that use of, and attention to, broadsheet and tabloid newspapers would probably have the strongest effect on mobilizing turnout, through reinforcing partisanship.

In monitoring media effects, as discussed in the introduction, we draw a distinction between long-term (cumulative) and short-term (campaign-specific) effects. Long-term media effects are analysed in terms of absolute differences between groups of media users; for example, whether regular broadsheet readers are better informed than tabloid readers. We cannot prove that any persistent differences are a result of patterns of media attention *per se*, but nevertheless this seems like a plausible assumption. While the more educated and more informed may well possess the cognitive skills which make it easier for them to read newspapers, nevertheless reading newspapers can also be expected to make people more informed.

Media effects within the campaign are measured by comparing changes in knowledge, trust and participation among the most and least regular and attentive users of newspaper and television. The measurement of changes in the dependent variables, using the natural time-line of the campaign, provides a more convincing and thorough test of short-term media effects. Relative change allows us to control for stable factors which commonly distinguish both the characteristics of media use and political

High use/attention	Increases in		
	Knowledge	**Trust**	**Participation**
Television news	Moderate	Moderate	Low
Television no news	Low	Low	Low
Broadsheet newspapers	High	High	Moderate
Tabloid newspapers	Moderate	Moderate	Moderate
No newspapers	Low	Low	Low

FIGURE 7.1:   *Core Hypotheses about Civic Engagement*

attitudes, such as higher levels of education among regular readers of broadsheet papers.

Political Knowledge

What do people learn from the campaign? This can depend upon what criteria are used (Price and Zaller 1993; Chaffee and Kanihan 1997). Political knowledge has different dimensions, whether learning about the main policies in party programmes, general information about 'civics', or about the background of local parliamentary candidates. One common measure is accurate information about issue differences between the major parties since this is the basis for rational voting. To test this the panel survey used a six-point scale based on answers to the following questions:

- *Which party would you say is most in favour of proportional representation?* (Correct answer: Liberal Democrats)
- *Which party would you say is most in favour of reducing government spending in order to cut taxes?* (Correct answer: Conservatives)
- *Which party would you say is most in favour of local authority control of schools?* (Correct answer: Labour)
- *Which party would you say is most in favour of independence for Scotland?* (Correct answer: SNP)
- *Which party would you say is most in favour of letting private industry run the railways?* (Correct answer: Conservatives)
- *Which party would you say is most in favour of setting a minimum wage level, below which no one can be paid?* (Correct answer: Labour)

The knowledge scales were first tested in Wave A (May 1996) then repeated towards the end of the campaign in Wave C (April 1997). Items were recoded into correct and incorrect answers then summed into a six-point scale. These scales proved to be reliable when tested (Cronbach's Alpha=.75) with a normal distribution of responses.

While other knowledge scales have focused more generally on 'civics', these items were designed to tap awareness of party policies which might be expected to rise as politicians debate the issues during the long and short campaign. Note that our choice of items is not based on any claim that these were the issues that received most attention during the campaign. Indeed, during the election few of these specific issues achieved the prominence of Europe or sleaze. Rather we would suggest that these were amongst the issues on which the differences between the parties were most significant, knowledge of which would be a prerequisite for the voter to make an informed choice at the polling station. In short, it matters just as much if the electorate failed to learn about these differences simply because the media failed to address them as it does that they failed to acquire knowledge because the media coverage of the issues was ineffective.

TABLE 7.1: *Changes in Knowledge of Party Policies*

	Political Knowledge		
	Wave A May 96	Wave C April 97	Change A:C
Correct answer Which party most favours...			
Private railways (Con)	81	78	–3
Minimum wage (Lab)	75	77	2
LA control of schools (Lab)	56	53	–3
Tax/spending cuts (Con)	49	47	–3
Proportional representation(LD)	40	45	5
Scottish independence (SNP)	32	35	3
None correct	8	6	–2
One to three correct	43	47	4
Three to five correct	38	34	–3
All items correct	11	12	2
Mean score out of six	3.3	3.3	.0

Note: Only respondents in all waves (ABCD) are included (N.1422).

Source: British Election Campaign panel survey 1997.

Looking first at the distribution of knowledge, the results in Table 7.1 show considerable variations in how far the public could correctly identify which party was most closely associated with each policy, even at the end of a lengthy and exhaustive election campaign. Over three-quarters of the public knew that rail privatization was most strongly advocated by the Conservatives and that support for a minimum wage was proposed by Labour. Even if people had not read or heard anything about these policies a general understanding about party differences across the left–right spectrum could provide information short-cuts to help guess the correct position of the major parties on these items.

Nevertheless, only about half could correctly identify that Labour proposed maintaining local authority control of schools and that the Conservatives were the party most in favour of cuts in taxation and spending. Lastly there was widespread confusion about two policies most closely associated with minor parties. Less than half identified the Liberal Democrats as most in favour of proportional representation while only a third recognized the Scottish National Party as favouring Scottish independence. Indeed more people admitted that they didn't know than gave a correct answer to this question. The distribution of scores confirmed the differences in political knowledge found elsewhere (Delli Carpini and Keeter 1996; Zaller 1993). In Britain there is a highly informed and attentive minority: about one in ten got all items correct. At the other end of the spectrum is a small group of people who possess almost no current information about party politics, with no correct answers. Most people fall between these extremes by paying enough attention to party politics to get at least some of the answers right. The score for the average citizen was about three correct answers out of six.

If we examine how patterns of media use and attention relate to knowledge, the results in Table 7.2 demonstrate significant differences between groups. Those who are most regular users of television news, and the most attentive, are more knowledgeable about party policies than average. Moreover, readers of broadsheet papers proved the most aware of party policies, scoring almost five out of six. In contrast there was no significant difference in knowledge between regular readers of tabloids and those who did not regularly read a paper, each group getting about half the answers right. This confirms the pattern found in earlier studies which suggests that newspapers and television news are highly informative about public affairs (Norris 1997b; Newton 1997; Chaffee and Kanihan 1997). Despite the problems of disentangling the causality in this relationship, this pattern can be read as broadly indicative of a long-term or cumulative effect of media use on our store of political awareness. Yet we wanted to see whether the background of readers and viewers influenced their patterns of news use and their political knowledge. As we have seen in Chapter 6 the most important factors which might be expected to

TABLE 7.2: *Changes in Knowledge of Party Policies by Patterns of Media Use and Attention*

Media Use/Attention	Political Knowledge			
	Wave A Spr 96	Wave C April 97	Change A:C	N.
ALL	3.3	3.3	+.0	1422
USE OF TV NEWS				
Regular user	3.8	3.8	+.0	455
Not a regular user	3.1	3.1	+.0	967
ATTENTION TO TV NEWS				
Attentive to political news	4.1	4.1	+.0	266
Not attentive	3.1	3.2	+.1	1156
USE OF NEWSPAPERS				
Regular reder of any paper	**3.8**	**3.7**	–.1	440
Not a regular reader	3.1	3.2	+.1	982
TYPE OF NEWSPAPER				
Broadsheet reader	4.8	4.7	–.1	152
Tabloid reader	3.2	3.1	–.1	492
ATTENTION TO NEWS IN PAPER				
Attentive to political news	4.4	4.3	–.1	145
Not attentive	3.2	3.2	+.0	1277

Notes: Cell entries are mean scale scores. The scale ranges from 1 to 6.
TV News regular user: respondent reported having watched a television news broadcast yesterday in each of waves A, B and C.
Newspaper regular reader: respondent reported having read a newspaper yesterday in each of waves A, B and C.
Attentive to political news: respondent claimed in wave B to pay 'quite a bit' or 'a great deal' of attention to stories about politics in the TV news/newspaper they read yesterday.
Broadsheet reader: respondent reported at wave B reading *Financial Times, The Guardian The Independent, Daily Telegraph, The Times, The Scotsman* or the *Herald* yesterday.
Tabloid reader: respondent reported at wave B reading *The Express, Daily Mail, The Mirror, Daily Record, Daily Star* or *The Sun* yesterday.
Only respondents in all waves (ABCD) are included (N.1422).

Source: British Election Campaign panel survey 1997.

influence reading a newspaper or turning on the television news are age, gender and education (a scale of the respondent's highest educational qualification). We therefore entered these factors into an OLS regression model with the six-point knowledge of party policy scale as the dependent variable. The results in Table 7.3 show that once we introduced social controls, attention to politics in the news media remained significant, but use of the news media failed to be significant.

If we turn to knowledge gain over time, as Tables 7.1 and 7.2 demonstrate, most strikingly, there was no significant change in the public's level of awareness of these party policies as a result of the long and short campaign. Nor is there any evidence that the most regular and attentive users of the media became more informed about these party policies during the campaign. Despite the heated political battle to dominate the airwaves, despite extensive television coverage with up to ten hours each day devoted to news and current affairs on all channels, despite all the areas of newsprint devoted to election supplements, knowledge of party policies remained unchanged.

To test whether this was an artefact of the measure of knowledge about party politics which we used in the campaign panel, we replicated the approach using the six-point 'civics quiz' included in the cross-sectional 1997 British Election Study. This asks people to identify whether a series of statements are true or false, as follows:

Here is a quick quiz. For each thing I say, tell me if it is true or false. If you don't know, just say so and we will skip to the next one. . .

- The number of Members of Parliament is about 100? (false)
- The longest time allowed between general elections is four years? (false)
- Britain's electoral system is based on proportional representation? (false)
- MPs from different parties are on parliamentary committees? (true)
- Britain has separate elections for the European Parliament and the British Parliament? (true)
- No one may stand for Parliament unless they pay a deposit. (true)

TABLE 7.3: *Regression Models of Knowledge of Party Policy Scale by Patterns of Media Use, with Social Controls*

	Beta	Sig
Regular use of TV News	.01	
Attentive to political news on TV	.09	*
Regular use of newspaper	−.04	
Attentive to political news in paper	.06	
Age	.16	**
Gender	−.34	**
Education	.46	**
Adjusted R2	.35	
Std. Error	1.41	

Note: OLS regression model with knowledge of party politics at wave C (on a six-point scale) as the dependent variable.

Source: British Election Campaign panel survey 1997.

Perhaps even if people do not learn much about more technical and detailed aspects of party policies, as a result of news and current affairs they may acquire general information about the political system? The results of the comparison of regular and attentive readers of newspapers and viewers of television news on the civics quiz (Table 7.4) confirms the pattern we found earlier in terms of knowledge of party policy: those who were more attentive to politics in the news were significantly better informed than those who were not. Again this remained significant after testing in regression models (not reproduced here) controlling for age, education and gender.

Yet it can be argued that knowledge of civics is fairly abstract and, although generally useful, not necessarily critical to the electoral choices facing voters. Also it can be suggested that closed-ended (true/false) tests are far removed from any real understanding of political processes (Graber 1994). An alternative open-ended indicator in the 1997 BES taps knowledge about the candidates standing in the voter's constituency, an important indicator of awareness about local electoral choices, using the following question:

TABLE 7.4: *Knowledge of Civics by Patterns of Media Use and Attention*

	Mean Score Civics Quiz out of 6	Eta (Sig.)	N.
All	4.08		2863
USE OF TV NEWS			
Regular	4.22		2326
Not regular	3.54		399
Difference	0.68	.14***	
ATTENTION TO TV NEWS			
Attentive to political news	4.81		1082
Not attentive	3.79		1442
Difference	1.02	.30***	
USE OF NEWSPAPERS			
Regular	4.30		1708
Not regular	3.75		1155
Difference	0.55	.16***	
ATTENTION TO NEWSPAPERS			
Attentive to political news	5.10		540
Not attentive	4.11		982
Difference	0.99	.30***	

Notes: Cell entries are mean scale scores. The scale ranges from 1 to 6. The significance of the mean difference between groups was measured by ANOVA. For the items in the quiz see text.

TV News regular user: respondent reported watched a national news programme on any television channel at least 3 days per week.

Newspaper regular reader: respondent reported regularly reading one or more daily newspaper.

Attentive to political news: respondent claimed to pay 'quite a bit' or 'a great deal' of attention to stories about politics in the TV news/newspaper they read yesterday.

Source: BES 1997 (cross-sectional).

TABLE 7.5: *Knowledge of Candidates by Patterns of Media Use and Attention*

	Ability to Indentify Parliamentary Candidates	Eta (Sig.)	N.
All	.85		2863
USE OF TV NEWS			
Regular	.89		2355
Not regular	.62		404
Difference	.27	.09***	
ATTENTION TO TV NEWS			
Attentive to political news	1.06		1091
Not attentive	.77		1455
Difference	.29	.13***	
USE OF NEWSPAPERS			
Regular	.92		1718
Not regular	.72		1187
Difference	.20	.09***	
ATTENTION TO NEWSPAPERS			
Attentive to political news	1.18		542
Not attentive	.86		986
Difference	.32	.13***	

Notes: Cell entries are mean scores for the number of local candidates correctly identified. The significance of the mean difference between groups was measured by ANOVA. For the question see text.

TV News regular user: respondent reported watched a national news programme on any television channel at least 3 days per week.

Newspaper regular reader: respondent reported regularly reading one or more daily newspaper.

Attentive to political news: respondent claimed to pay 'quite a bit' or 'a great deal' of attention to stories about politics in the TV news/newspaper they read yesterday.

Source: BES 1997 (cross-sectional).

Do you happen to remember the names of any candidates who stood in your constituency in the general election this year?

Respondents could identify up to six different candidates in their seat. The results showed that half the electorate (50.5 per cent) could not name a single candidate correctly, just over one-quarter (26.7 per cent) could name one candidate, 15 per cent could name two, and 8.3 per cent could identify three or more. If we look at the pattern of media use in Table 7.5, again those who were the heaviest news consumers were significantly more likely to score well on candidate name recognition, confirming the general pattern which we have established. Clearly there may well be interaction effects, as people who are knowledgeable about politics may be more inclined to switch on or read about the news. Nevertheless, we would argue that the most plausible interpretation is that in the long term those who pay attention to politics in the news learn about party programmes, just as they improve their general knowledge about the British political system and about the electoral choice of candidates in their seat.

Political Trust and Efficacy

The issue of declining trust and confidence in government has aroused considerable concern in many democracies (Nye *et al.* 1997; Norris 1999a). This can be gauged in many ways, including the belief that the system of government is unresponsive to the grievances of the public, which can be termed 'system efficacy'. To examine the media's impact on system efficacy the British Election Campaign panel survey measured agreement with the following statements:

- Generally speaking those we elect as MPs soon lose touch with people pretty quickly.
- Parties are only interested in people's votes, not in their opinions.
- It doesn't really matter which party is in power, in the end things go on much the same.

A comparison of trends over time, documented elsewhere (Curtice and Jowell 1997), shows that system efficacy remained fairly stable from 1974 to 1991, but from 1991 to 1996 government was increasingly seen as out of touch with the needs of the electorate.

How far does responsibility for this phenomenon lie in political coverage by the news media? Table 7.6 establishes the mean system efficacy scores, based on summing the above three items into a single scale ranging from 1 to 15. The results show that system efficacy did increase modestly during the campaign: as polling day approached more people

TABLE 7.6:   *Changes in Political Efficacy by Patterns of Media Use and Attention*

Media Use/Attention	Political Efficacy			
	Wave A Spr 96	Wave B April 97	Wave D May 97	A:D Change
ALL	6.8	7.4	8.3	1.5
USE OF TV NEWS				
Regular user	6.8	7.6	8.5	1.7
Not a regular user	6.8	7.3	8.2	1.4
ATTENTION TO TV NEWS				
Attentive to political news	7.5	8.5	9.3	1.8
Not attentive	6.9	7.4	8.3	1.4
USE OF NEWSPAPERS				
Regular reader of paper	6.7	7.4	8.3	1.6
Not a regular reader	6.4	7.1	8.0	1.6
TYPE OF NEWSPAPER				
Broadsheet reader	8.2	8.5	9.2	1.0
Tabloid reader	6.4	7.1	8.0	1.6
ATTENTION TO NEWS IN PAPER				
Attentive to political news	7.8	8.5	9.2	1.4
Not attentive	6.7	7.3	8.2	1.5

Notes: Cell entries are mean scale scores. The scale ranges from 1 to 15. Only respondents in all waves (ABCD) are included (N.1422).

Questions on political efficacy were only asked of one-third of sample at wave A.

Source: British Election Campaign panel survey 1997.

came to believe that they could influence the outcome. Nevertheless, the change in political attitudes was similar across all groups of media users. Contrary to both the video-malaise and mobilization schools of thought, there is no evidence here that short-term changes in political cynicism or trust are associated with the media. Nevertheless, as with political knowledge, attention to politics on television and in the press was positively associated with higher levels of political efficacy, suggesting the long-term influence of the media in a positive direction.

Political Participation

Lastly does news coverage encourage or discourage political engagement? This is the heart of the video-malaise thesis charging that television creates civic couch potatoes. We can examine the probability to vote during the campaign based on a 10-point scale using the following question:

> Talking to people about the general election, we have found that a lot of people are not likely to vote. How about you? If nought means there is absolutely no chance that you will vote in the general election and ten means that you will definitely vote in the election, what mark out of ten best describes how likely you are to vote?

Moreover, we can compare the average score given by respondents before the election with the proportion within each of our media groups who reported after polling day that they had actually voted.

As shown by Table 7.7, the official campaign did have a modest mobilizing effect, as might be expected: the average score reported by respondents increased from 8.0 to 8.3 between the beginning and end of April, while in the event as many as 85 per cent of respondents reported having voted. Moreover, regular and attentive viewers and readers were more likely to say they had turned out. This confirms previous studies which found that television use of the news was one of the strongest predictors of political participation (Norris 1997a).

Still, when we look at the trend in the table across the course of the campaign there does appear to be some evidence which is consistent with the video-malaise thesis. Comparing their actual turnout with their reported propensity to turn out at the beginning of the campaign, we find that regular watchers of television news and those attentive to the news in any form were less successfully mobilized during the campaign. However, we should also bear in mind that regular readers of a newspaper were more successfully mobilized than non-readers. And that readers of the supposedly trivial tabloid press were more likely to be mobilised than readers of the more serious broadsheet press. Moreover, much of the pattern we see in Table 7.7 appears to reflect a propensity amongst those who pay most attention to politics in election campaigns to overestimate their likelihood of actually voting on the day. If we compare the trends

TABLE 7.7:   *Changes in Political Participation by Patterns of Media Use and Attention*

Media Use/Attention	Probability to Vote		Reported Vote	
	Wave B Early Apr	Wave C Late Apr	Wave D May 97	B:D Change
ALL	8.1	8.4	8.5	+0.4
USE OF TV NEWS				
Regular user	8.7	9.0	8.9	+0.2
Not a regular user	7.8	8.0	8.3	+0.5
ATTENTION TO TV NEWS				
Attentive to political news	9.2	9.4	9.1	-0.1
Not attentive	7.8	8.1	8.3	+0.5
USE OF NEWSPAPERS				
Regular reader of paper	8.3	8.7	8.9	+0.6
Not a regular reader	7.9	8.2	8.3	+0.4
TYPE OF NEWSPAPER				
Broadsheet reader	9.1	9.3	9.1	+0.0
Tabloid reader	7.8	8.1	8.4	+0.6
ATTENTION TO NEWS IN PAPER				
Attentive to political news	9.2	9.4	9.1	-0.1
Not attentive	7.9	8.2	8.4	+0.5

Notes: Only respondents in all waves (ABCD) are included (N.1422).

Probability to vote: mean mark out of 10 respondent gave to indicate the probability they would vote.

Reported vote: per cent reporting having voted/10.

Source: British Election Campaign panel survey 1997.

amongst the various media groups between waves B and C of our survey, we see little association at all.

Our results are further supported by the evidence of our experiments with television news (see Chapter 3). True, after taking part those who participated in the experiments were on average more likely to say that they would vote. Doubtless, participation in the experiment itself heightened their interest in the election. But if the video-malaise school is correct, those who were exposed to predominantly negative news (whether it be about Labour or the Conservatives) should have been less likely to have reported an increase in their propensity to vote than those who were not so exposed. In fact the participation scores (using the same score as in Table 7.7) of the two groups both rose by 0.2. Equally if the mobilization thesis is correct, those who were exposed to positive news might have been expected to be more likely to report an increased propensity to vote than those who were not. But again the changes in participation score for the two groups are identical to each other. More elaborate multivariate analysis confirms the absence of any association.

The Dynamics of Media Use

There is, however, an important objection that might be made to what we have done so far. *Inter alia*, we have examined the apparent impact of the media on the electorate's engagement in the political process by comparing those who regularly watched television news or read a newspaper throughout the campaign. In effect we have assumed that the greater the degree of exposure to the media, the more its impact on engagement should be apparent. But perhaps this is to miss the point. If indeed the media's coverage of politics discourages involvement in the political process, then surely it might be expected to discourage people from watching or reading about politics as well? In short, perhaps those whom the media are turning off politics are turning off media coverage of politics as well?

After all, newspaper circulation in Britain is in long-term decline. And in 1997, as in previous elections, the viewership of the major evening television news programmes dropped during the campaign (see Chapter 6). Our evidence is certainly consistent with the picture of a diminishing audience for political coverage as the campaign progressed. Table 7.8 shows a six-point drop in the proportion of people saying that they had read a newspaper yesterday between spring 1996 and the last fortnight of the election campaign. Meanwhile, the drop in reported television viewership is even more dramatic – no less than 20 points – though there is reason to believe that this may in part reflect differences in the context in which the question was asked in the two waves. In the spring 1996 survey respondents were asked whether they had watched the television news yesterday after they had been asked whether they had watched any television over the previous week. In contrast in the two campaign waves respondents were simply asked whether they had watched television news yesterday. It may be that the former procedure meant that people were reluctant to admit they had not watched the news yesterday once they had claimed to have watched it on some occasion during the last week.

But do we find evidence of disengagement amongst those who stopped watching or reading the news? Table 7.9 examines what happened amongst those who stopped watching. It compares the change in our knowledge, efficacy and probability of voting scores amongst those who stayed tuned into the television news and those who by the end of the campaign had turned off. And here we do indeed find some difference.

TABLE 7.8:   *Trends in Reported Patterns of Media Use*

	Wave A Spr. 96 %	Wave B Early Apr %	Wave C Late Apr %
Watched TV news yesterday	70	53	50
Read newspaper yesterday	52	48	46

Note: Only respondents in all waves (ABCD) are included (N.1422).

Source: British Election Campaign panel survey 1997.

TABLE 7.9: *Changes in Knowledge, Efficacy and Probability of Voting by Change in TV News Use*

Mean Change In:	TV News Behaviour		
	Turned Off	Stayed Off	Stayed On
Knowledge score	−0.1	+0.2	+0.0
Efficacy score	+0.9	+1.7	+1.6
Probability voting	+0.3	+0.4	+0.3
N.	397	304	587

Note: Respondents who did not report at wave A having watched TV news yesterday but who did so at wave C are excluded.
Turned Off: respondent reported at wave A having watched TV news yesterday but did not do so at wave C.
Stayed Off: respondent did not report at either wave A or wave C having watched TV news yesterday.
Stayed On: respondent reported at both wave A and wave C having watched TV news yesterday.
Change in knowledge score: mean change in score on Knowledge Scale between waves A and C.
Change in efficacy score: change in mean score on Efficacy Scale between waves A and D.
Change in probability voting: mean change in reported probability of voting between waves B and C.

Source: British Election Campaign panel survey 1997.

Those who had turned off the television news were less likely to have felt more efficacious by the campaign, or to have felt more motivated to go out and vote. Indeed, the increase in the scores amongst those who had turned off was even lower than amongst those who had not tuned into the media in the first place.

So perhaps we have found some evidence to support the 'video-malaise' thesis at last. Yet we should be careful. After all, the argument of this thesis is that people are put off politics because the media's coverage is too trivial. Yet the constant complaint of the British public at election times – when coverage of the campaign is significantly more intense than it is in the United States – is that there is too much coverage of politics, not too little (Norris, 1997a). In contrast to the video-malaise thesis perhaps what we are finding is that television news coverage of the election was not too trivial but too heavy.

Distinguishing between these two interpretations is undoubtedly difficult. But evidence which is at least consistent with the interpretation that television news lost its audience because its coverage was too heavy is reported in Table 7.10. For if this interpretation is correct we would expect to find that those who were most likely to stop watching television news were those who at the beginning of the campaign were also less likely to be interested in politics. And this is precisely what we find.

TABLE 7.10: *Who Turned Off?*

Change in % who:	Political Interest	
	High	Low
Watched TV news yesterday	–17	–22
Read newspaper yesterday	–5	–8
N	466	515

Note: Only respondents in all waves (ABCD) are included (N.1422).
Political Interest - High: respondents who said at wave A that they had a 'a great deal' or 'quite a bit' of interest in politics.
Political Interest - Low: respondents who said at wave A that they had a 'little' or no interest at all in politics.
Table excludes those who said they had 'some' interest in politics.
Source: British Election Campaign panel survey 1997.

Conclusions: Shooting the Messenger

This chapter has considered evidence from panel surveys for the video-malaise, mobilization and 'minimal effects' theories about the role of the media in civic engagement. The most plausible conclusions from this analysis are that in the long term levels of political knowledge and partic-ipation are significantly associated with patterns of media consumption. Those most attentive to news on television and in the press, and regular viewers and readers, were significantly more knowledgeable than the average citizen about party policies, civics and the parliamentary candidates standing in their constituency. They were also more likely to turn out. If these differences most plausibly represent the effects of cumulative patterns of media habits then this supports the mobilization thesis. Far from producing cynicism and turning-off voters, as critics charge, this evidence suggests that the British media largely succeed in their public service role.

Nevertheless, the test of short-term media effects based on the evidence of change in knowledge and attitudes during the long and short campaign shows a different pattern. The most plausible conclusion from this analysis is that patterns of media use and attention had little significant impact, positive or negative, on *changes* in levels of political knowledge, efficacy, and participation during the 1997 election. This suggests that news media influence voters as a result of long-term habits, where regular attention mobilizes civic engagement, just as traditional patterns of socialization influence people within the family, school and workplace. The body of evidence in Britain and in other industrialized societies suggests that although many commonly blame the news media for all the pervasive sins of the body politic – notably low turnout, political cynicism and lack of awareness of the issues – we should probably stop shooting the messenger and look elsewhere for the causes of these civic ills.

8 The Impact on the Public's Agenda

Previous chapters have outlined the theory of media agenda-setting which suggests that the news drives the public's issue concerns, and analysed news coverage on television and in the national press during the course of the campaign. This chapter focuses on understanding how far news headlines influence public opinion. Cross-sectional designs have been common, looking at the relationship between content analysis of the news agenda and public concerns about 'the most important issues' facing the country, as well as longitudinal designs looking at trends over time. Yet both these approaches suffer from serious limitations in establishing critical tests of cause and effect. In the first section we draw on the experimental research design by manipulating television stories in a controlled setting to see whether news priorities can potentially influence the problems which viewers regard as the nation's most serious. In the second section we then examine the case-study of Europe, which came to dominate the headlines during the middle of April, using the panel study to see whether the change in coverage during the campaign actually influenced the public's priorities.

Most studies in the United States, although not all, have generally confirmed that the amount of news coverage of issues influences the public's priorities, and indeed that the media's role is more important in this regard than real world indicators (McCombs and Shaw 1972; Protess and McCombs 1991; Dearing and Rogers 1996; McCombs 1997). Studies suggest that the concerns of the American public are shaped more by news headlines than, for example, by actual rates of AIDS, violent crime or use of crack-cocaine. The strength of the effect of media agenda-setting depends upon a variety of conditions, including the campaign context, the type of media source, the length of time being considered, the nature of the media coverage, the type of issue and the information environment. Research has also examined media agenda-setting effects in many other countries including Germany (Brosius and Kepplinger 1990; Schoenbach and Semetko 1992), France (Sawicki and Leland 1991), Australia (Gadir 1982), Canada (Johnston et al. 1992), Japan (Takeshita 1993; Takeshita and Mikami 1995), and Scandinavia (Asp 1983; Esaiasson and Holmberg 1996). It should be noted that the agenda-setting theory suggests that it is only the *priority* of issues in the news, not their tone or content, which affects the public's issue concerns.

Yet despite the accumulated body of work, and the weight of conventional wisdom, previous research has found no evidence that television sets the public agenda in Britain. The idea was first raised by Trenaman and McQuail (1961) but only tested systematically when Miller and his colleagues carried out a detailed panel survey of public opinion during the 1987 British election campaign, accompanied by content analysis of television and the press (Miller 1990; Miller 1991). The study found that the issue agenda dominating television differed significantly from that of the general public. During the campaign, television news focused heavily on security and defence issues (notably Labour's policy on unilateral nuclear disarmament and visits by party leaders to Moscow and Washington, DC), but this produced only a modest rise in public concern. Viewers gave greater priority to the economic agenda, particularly unemployment, although this hardly featured on television news. During the course of the campaign, the public remained concerned about health, education and social services, but there is no evidence that the public followed the television agenda on these issues: 'The agenda set by television was miles away from the agenda of issues that the electorate rated important and wanted discussed' (Miller 1990: 62).

Others have proved equally sceptical about media agenda-setting effects in the British context. Norris (1997a) found that the public's issue agenda shifted from the 1987 to the 1992 election, as public concern about defence subsided while, in contrast, health and taxation rose in importance. This broadly reflected the change in the amount of media coverage devoted to these issues during these campaigns. But from the available survey evidence, at only two points in time, it was impossible to establish whether the media led, or simply followed, public opinion. The shift in the issue agenda was similar among viewers most, and least, attentive to television news. Curtice (1996) concluded that there was little evidence that the issue priorities of the electorate shifted much at all between elections, still less that any change depended on their pattern of media usage. During the 1997 campaign MORI also concluded that the media followed its own agenda and that many of the issues that the media addresses at length in the campaign were not of primary concern to voters. In particular the press focused too much on the economy, foreign affairs and Europe while the public expressed most concern about health, education, jobs, law and order and social security (http://www.MORI.COM/ pubinfo/trfollow.htm).

Therefore despite the conventional wisdom among broadcasters, commentators and politicians, and the weight of research elsewhere, previous studies in Britain have failed to detect direct evidence that television coverage affects voters' policy priorities. This suggests one of two possible interpretations. On the one hand, the particular context of UK campaigns may limit the agenda-setting role of British television. This includes the legal regulations controlling political broadcasting, particularly concepts of 'political balance' in the Representation of the People Act, which are central to the way that British elections are reported (discussed in Chapter 2). If every story about pensions or jobs or the environment has to contain party charge and counter-charge, this mixed message may negate any agenda-setting role (a Punch and Judy 'the jobless figures are down' 'No, the real jobless figures are up'). The partisanship of the British press may also limit their agenda-setting role, since journalists may prefer to follow the party lead, compared with a more 'objective' tradition of journalism in the United States (see Chapter 5).

An alternative interpretation is that the UK news may influence viewers, but previous British studies may have been unable to capture these effects. Aggregate time-series data, and cross-sectional surveys, are clumsy instruments to monitor media effects on particular voters. We usually do not know exactly what messages people have received, only self-reported patterns of general media use and attention. If we establish a significant association between the media's agenda and the public's priorities, we cannot tell from cross-sectional surveys whether this is because the media leads, or follows, or both. Cross-sectional surveys are often like sledgehammers when we need fine scalpels. To disentangle the agenda-setting process further in this chapter we first use the experimental designs to test for the potential impact of media messages, we then focus on a case-study of Europe which combines content analysis of the news media with the rolling panel survey monitoring public concerns during the campaign.

The Agenda-setting Video Experiments

The Selection of Stories

The basic methodology of the experimental design was outlined in Chapter 3 so here we will focus upon the particular compilation of stories chosen to test issue salience. The video format consisted of a sandwich, with ten minutes of standard footage at the top and bottom of the programme, and one of sixteen different experimental video stimuli in the core. Respondents were not told which video was being shown to which group. To test for the effects of agenda-setting, we monitored the reaction of 474 participants who were divided at random into seven treatment groups. The control group viewed a non-political core compilation, and six other groups were each shown a core compilation focusing for ten minutes on one of the following issues: taxation, unemployment, health, pensions, Europe, and aid to developing countries (see the Technical Appendix for details). Following the conventions of British campaign coverage, all the issue items we selected were relatively balanced in terms of the direction of coverage of party policies, with critical comments from one spokesperson interspersed by positive remarks by another.

Measures of Issue Salience

We designed the research to achieve conceptual replication, that is, tests were repeated with conceptually identical but empirically different measures of the variables under scrutiny. To monitor the effects of the experiments we included two alternative measures of issue salience in the pre- and the post-test questionnaires. First, we asked respondents the open-ended question:

Which two issues mattered most to you in deciding how to vote in the general election?

These were subsequently coded into 73 minor categories, then collapsed into five major issue categories. Second, we also asked respondents:

Below is a list of issues that some people think the government ought to tackle. Please indicate how you would rate the importance of each issue where '0' means not very important and '10' means very important.

People were asked to rank 13 issues, from 'Britain's role in Europe' to 'sleaze'. The results are analysed by measuring the change over time recorded in pre- and post-test questionnaires for each experimental group, compared with the change over time for the control group (defined as the rest of the respondents who were not subject to that particular experimental stimuli). The significance of mean differences between the experimental and control groups were measured by Analysis of Variance (ANOVA). This built in another check: even if the experimental group differed from the other participants at the outset, we are only relying upon the *relative* change over time within each group, not the absolute levels of issue salience. We anticipated that any effects as a result of this process would be relatively modest, since we only used a 'single-shot' design. The cumulative effect of repeated experimental stimuli, such as exposure to newspaper, radio and television stories about Conservative sleaze every night on the news for weeks, would be more likely to influence public concern about this issue. Indeed, if we found major effects as the result of a single short-term experiment, we would become concerned about the stability of the responses we were monitoring.

Hypotheses

In the light of the literature we developed four core hypotheses about media agenda-setting. The most straightforward test is that the amount of issue coverage on British television news should influence the public's concerns about the major problems facing the country. In particular, we expected that:

More time devoted to different topics on the evening news – whether taxation, unemployment, pensions, health or Europe – would increase the priority of these issues among viewers (H#1).

Agenda-setting theory suggests that the number of news stories is what counts, not their tone or contents.

Moreover, the literature suggests that the effects of agenda-setting might well vary among different types of *issues*. In particular, we anticipated that:

> The impact of the media agenda would be more influential over foreign policy than over domestic issues (H#2).

The reasoning is that most people have direct personal experience of issues like jobs, prices and interest rates which could be used to counter media information. But on issues like the potential effects of Britain's membership of the European Monetary Union, poverty in Haiti, or the problem of civil war in Bosnia, we are heavily dependent upon the news.

Thirdly, we also anticipated that:

> The impact of agenda-setting would vary according to the initial salience of a problem (H#3).

Our reasoning was that the media could be expected to have more influence over issues which were initially low on the public's radar rather than those which were already well-established matters of public concern. By reminding people about certain issues which they had not previously considered – for example, the Ethiopian famine or the problems of mad cow disease – the news could raise the priority of these issues.

Lastly, the literature also suggests that:

> The impact of the media agenda would vary among different types of viewers (H#4).

Iyengar and Kinder (1987: 59) found that those with little formal schooling were influenced more than the well-educated; independents more than partisans; and the apathetic more than the politically active. Accordingly we examined media agenda-setting effects controlling for differences in social characteristics, television attention and use, and political knowledge.

The Impact of the News Agenda on the Public's Concerns

The first hypothesis was that greater exposure to issues in the news would produce a modest increase in public concern about that problem. Starting with simple bivariate relationships, Table 8.1 summarizes the mean issue salience for each group using the scale measures in the pre-test, the post-test, and the difference over time. The pattern shows modest confirmation of the media agenda-setting thesis: on the issues of taxation, pensions, Europe and the developing world, the groups subjected to the relevant news stories slightly increased their ratings of the importance of these problems. In contrast the groups who did not see these stories decreased their rating of the importance of these issues.

Nevertheless the modest confirmation of agenda-setting effects needs certain important qualifications. First, the only results which proved statistically significant and in the expected direction concerned the issues of European Monetary Union and the problems facing the developing world. In both cases, exposure to coverage of foreign affairs modestly increased concern, while these issues dropped in importance for the control groups.

Equally important, not all results of the other tests pointed in a consistent direction. Despite being shown a third of the news on the problems of unemployment and health, the importance of these issues dropped from the pre- to the post-test among the experimental group. Ratings of issue salience for the problem of unemployment fell even more sharply among the control group. Overall these findings remain counter to the basic media agenda-setting thesis that the *amount* (not the type) of coverage should boost public concern.

There are two ways to interpret the initial findings about the impact of the media on the issues of Europe and the developing world. Perhaps, as Cohen suggested (1963), foreign policy is the area where the media has most influence in telling the public, not what to think, but what to think about. The lack of alternative information about the consequences of Britain's entry to the EMU, or the problems of starvation and poverty in Haiti, or the politics of Zaire, may mean that we are particularly dependent upon the news media for our information about these concerns (H#2). Alternatively, it may be that these issues proved to be the ones where the public was initially least concerned, whereas on the well-worn themes of health and unemployment there might be some 'ceiling' effects: the public was already worried about these issues so concern could not

TABLE 8.1: *Agenda-Setting Effects by Type of Issue*

Video	Pre	Post	Mean Issue Salience Diff.	Eta	Sig.	N.
ECONOMIC POLICY						
Tax	7.46	7.55	.03			72
No tax	7.80	7.54	−.25	.06	.24	392
Jobs	8.69	8.52	−.10			63
No Jobs	8.51	8.09	−.38	.06	.19	404
SOCIAL POLICY						
Health	8.21	7.93	−.21			62
No health	8.83	8.77	−.05	.04	.36	409
Pensions	8.28	8.31	.03			67
No pensions	7.74	7.55	−.17	.05	.29	406
FOREIGN POLICY						
Europe	6.73	6.84	.18			56
No Europe	7.53	7.15	−.31	.12	.00	418
3rd World	6.17	6.31	.16			76
No 3rd World	6.34	5.88	−.49	.13	.00	393

Note: The figures represent the mean position on a scale from 0 (not very important) to 10 (very important).
ANOVA was used to estimate the coefficient of association (Eta) and significance.

Source: Television news experiments (N. 476).

rise much further (H#3). Subsequent multivariate analysis discussed later, which controls for the initial salience of issues, lends greater weight to this second interpretation.

An alternative way to measure issue importance came from the open-ended questions in the experiments when people were asked to indicate the 'two issues which mattered most to you when deciding how to vote'. The list of responses was classified into 73 minor categories, and these were recategorized into the major categories of public policy. The results in Table 8.2 confirm that overall social policy was regarded as by far the most important group of issues, mentioned by more than half (55 per cent) of all participants. This was followed by economic policy (mentioned by 21 per cent), and foreign policy (13 per cent). If we compare the results in the post-test measure, according to experimental groups, it is apparent that those who saw the video stimuli about unemployment were twice as likely to regard economic issues as important compared with the control group, and they were far more likely to mention the economy compared with all other groups. In terms of foreign affairs, those in the European stimuli group were also most likely out of all groups to prioritize foreign affairs. Nevertheless, the pattern in terms of the other issues is less clear cut; for example social policy was seen as almost equally important across all treatment groups.

Multivariate Controls

To see whether the bivariate relationships hold up when multivariate controls are applied we used ordinary least squared regression analysis. We tested for five types of theoretically relevant control variables. We included social characteristics which have commonly been found to be associated with political attitudes, coded as dummy variables, including gender, age, race, education, work status, and housing tenure. We controlled for media attention, measured by interest in political news and current affairs, on the grounds that we expected more attentive people should be less likely to change their views. Political knowledge was also

TABLE 8.2:   Issue Salience (Open-Ended Measures)

Group	Most imortant policy issue						
	Foreign	Economic	Social	Const.	Other	%	N.
Control	15	16	58	2	10	100	62
Jobs	12	33	41		15	100	61
Tax	11	21	55		14	100	66
Health	10	20	58	5	7	100	59
Pensions	17	17	59	3	5	100	66
Europe	20	18	56		7	100	45
3rd World	7	24	60		9	100	68

Note: Post-test 'Which two issues mattered most to you in deciding how to vote in the general election?' (1st mention only).

Source: The Study of Television News, 1997.

included, for similar reasons, assessed by a five-point true/false quiz, while television use was measured by the average number of hours watched per week. Lastly we controlled for the respondent's pre-test salience score on the agenda item that is being tested. Here we expected to find significant and negative coefficients on the grounds that people who already gave high priority to an issue would be less likely to increase their estimate than those who initially gave an issue low priority.

The results in Table 8.3 give one example of the multivariate model, in this case for the effects of watching the taxation video, including a pre-test priority term. This specification does not include the effects of exposure to the other agenda videos, which are all estimated in separate equations. In this example, watching the tax video increased viewers' ratings of the tax issue salience although this failed to be statistically significant. Out of all the controls, only attention to current affairs (which was positive) and the pre-test measure of issue salience (which was negative) proved to be more strongly related to the change in issue salience.

Using similar OLS regression equations, Table 8.4 reports the coefficients for video exposure for each issue. In line with our earlier results,

TABLE 8.3: *Effects of Exposure to Taxation Video on Issue Salience*

	Change in issue salience of taxation pre and post-test		
	b	se	Coding
SOCIO-DEMOGRAPHIC FACTORS			
Housing tenure	.20	.18	Owner occupier/Not
Education	–.15	.19	Graduate/Not
Race	–.13	.20	White/Not
Gender	–.05	.17	Male/Not
Unemployed	–.05	.34	Unemployed/Not
Work status	.04	.26	Paid employment/not
Student	–.02	.32	FT student/Not
Class	.01	.19	Non-manual/Not
Age	.01	.01	Years
INTEREST, KNOWLEDGE AND TV USE			
Interest in current affairs	.45***	.19	Interest in current affairs/not
Interest in news	.05	.18	Interest in news/not
Political knowledge	–.10	.06	0–5 quiz scale
TV use	.00	.01	Hours per week watched
VIDEO EXPOSURE AND PRIOR SALIENCE			
Exposure to tax video	.28	.22	Yes/No
Pre-test priority of tax issue	-.29***	.03	10-point scale
Corrected R2		.14	
N		440.00	
se		1.68	

Note: The figures are beta coefficients from ordinary least squared regression analysis with change in issue salience from the pre-test to post-test as the dependent variable.

Source: The Study of Television News, 1997.

TABLE 8.4: *Effects of Video Exposure on Issue Salience*

	Video Exposure			Pre-test Priority		
	b	se	sig	b	se	sig
Tax	.28	.22		−.29	.03**	
Unemployment	.31	.20		−.20	.03**	
Health	−.19	.16		−.26	.03**	
Pensions	.25	.17		−.18	.03**	
Europe	.37	.20*		−.17	.03**	
Developing world	.52	.22*		−.23	.03**	

Note: The figures are beta coefficients from ordinary least
squared regression analysis with change in issue salience from the
pre-test to post-test as the dependent variable.
Only exposure and pre-test priority coefficients are reported.
See previous table for the full multivariate model.

Source: The Study of Television News, 1997.

the multivariate analysis confirms that only the videos on Europe and the developing world have a statistically significant effect, although the coefficients from all videos, apart from health, indicate that salience increased with exposure to each agenda video in the expected direction.

Corrected Models

As the last step we conducted difference of means tests for the treatment and control groups using 'corrected' measures of agenda priorities. To get rid of some random noise, these controlled for how far participants were likely to change their issue priorities in general or how far they were usually stable. First we calculated how far each respondent changed his or her pre-test to post-test priority on each issue. We then calculated the average change score across all agenda items. For each respondent the corrected measure for each issue was calculated by the pre-test to post-test change in the salience of a particular issue (e.g. jobs), minus the average change in issue salience across all issues. The results in Table 8.5 and 8.6, using the corrected measures, slightly strengthen the previous findings. They confirm that showing people the videos about Europe and the developing world produced a significant effect on their issue priorities, and after correction the tax issue also emerged as statistically significant.

The Impact of Europe on Public Concerns

The results of the experiments therefore suggest that exposure to television news has the potential capacity to influence the public's issue agenda, but (i) the effects of a single exposure design remain modest, and (ii) the impact varies according to the initial salience of the issue. News stories about funding the NHS and unemployment in the North East failed to influence the public's concern, because the public already

TABLE 8.5:   *Difference of Mean Change in Issue Priority: Corrected Measures*

Video	Mean Change	Sig.	N.
ECONOMIC POLICY			
Tax	.34		66
No tax	−.04	.05	330
Jobs	.10		54
No Jobs	−.11	.12	342
SOCIAL POLICY			
Health	.23		54
No health	.17	.75	342
Pensions	.09		51
No pensions	.05	.81	345
FOREIGN POLICY			
Europe	.26		44
No Europe	−.13	.07	352
3rd World	.48		67
No 3rd World	−.21	.00	329

Note: The figures represent the pre- to post-test change in the mean position on a saliency scale ranging from 0 (not very important) to 10 (very important).

The 'corrected' measure controls for the stability or changeability of respondent's issue priorities. See text for details.

Source: The Study of Television News, 1997.

regarded these issues as important problems facing the country. Further coverage may have reinforced, but it did not alter, public concerns. In contrast news about foreign affairs did significantly increase issue salience. The most plausible reason is that problems such as poverty and health care in Haiti, human rights in East Timor, and political instability in Zaire, were already low on the public's radar so news coverage increased concern. This is consistent with research in the United States which found that the media's agenda-setting role was greatest on 'unobtrusive' issues rather than those which have a daily impact on people's lives like jobs, education and health care (Zucker 1978).

What are the implications of these results for understanding the actual role of the media during the April 1997 British campaign? The experimental design allows us to consider what the impact might be *if* television news focused on the issues we selected. The effects are therefore conditional and one-directional. We need to turn to other components in the research design to relate these findings to the real world of what messages were actually headlined in campaign news and how the electorate reacted to this coverage.

In examining the potential impact of media agenda-setting during the campaign we are looking for issues which suddenly become important in the news. During general elections certain topics may suddenly grab the headlines, create a feeding frenzy among journalists, and deflect both major parties from their planned agenda: examples include the row over miners' pay in February 1974, Labour splits about Polaris in 1983, and the

TABLE 8.6:   *Effects of Video Exposure on Issue Salience: Corrected Measures*

	Video Exposure			Pre-test Priority		
	b	se	sig	b	se	sig
Tax	.32	.19		−.22	.03**	
Unemployment	.25	.18		−.16	.03**	
Health	−.02	.13		−.20	.03**	
Pensions	.07	.16		−.10	.02**	
Europe	.41	.19*		−.09	.02**	
Developing world	.56	.19**		−.16	.02**	

Note: The figures are beta coefficients from ordinary least squared regression analysis with change in issue salience from the pre-test to post-test as the dependent variable. Only exposure and pre-test priority coefficients are reported.
See Table 8.3 for the full multivariate model.
The 'corrected' measure controls for the stability or changeability of respondent's issue priorities. See text for details.

Source: The Study of Television News, 1997.

'war of Jennifer's ear' in 1992. During the 1997 British general election the issue of Britain's role in the European Union provides the best case-study to examine the short-term agenda-setting effects of the media. Admittedly the issue of Europe was hardly new: throughout the 1992–97 Parliament it was a continuing source of headlines over controversies such as the Exchange Rate Mechanism, the Maastrict Treaty, mad cow disease and beef export restrictions, and quota-hopping. Nevertheless, this issue provides a suitable case-study because Europe burst into public view again during the middle of the campaign, with public leadership splits within the Conservative Party dominating the headlines. The question here is whether the news headlines actually changed public priorities.

To analyse the dynamics of issue coverage we turn to content analysis of the national press conducted by CARMA, which provides a large number of stories throughout the official campaign facilitating reliable trend analysis. CARMA monitored 6,072 articles in the national daily and Sunday newspapers for six weeks from the announcement of the election (18 March) until polling day (1 May). The study analysed whether the article featured the Conservative Party (4,827 articles), Labour (4,536), the Liberal Democrats (1,390) or the Referendum Party (319), then for each party classified the major topic of these articles using 150 coding categories (such as inflation, education and trade unions). CARMA counted the number of articles (although not the length) which mentioned each topic every day, as well as estimating the favourability or unfavourability of each story.[1]

The CARMA data suggest that, overall, almost half of all the press coverage (45 per cent) discussed policy issues. About one-quarter of this coverage (27 per cent) focused on problems of domestic social policy, (particularly education, the National Health Service, pensions and crime). The economy absorbed another quarter of the coverage (particularly taxation, trade unions (for Labour), unemployment and privatization, in that order). In most elections foreign policy rarely surfaces as a major issue, unless the country is at war or there is major international conflict abroad. During the 1992 campaign, for example, although Labour's defence policy was highlighted by Tory posters, foreign affairs occupied a mere one per cent of front page news.[2] Yet in 1997, despite an era of peace and prosperity, at a time when the West had won the Cold War, a remarkable 17 per cent of all issue coverage in the press focused on foreign policy, nearly all concerning Britain's role within the European Union. The press headlined Conservative splits over Europe: almost a fifth of the coverage of Conservative issues (19 per cent) focused on Europe. The dynamic of the issue coverage is shown in Figure 8.1 notably the dramatic rise in coverage of foreign policy (principally Europe) from early to mid-April.

Bubbling fissions within the Conservative Party over Europe were dramatically highlighted by the press following BBC *Newsnight* on Friday 11 April when it was revealed that Angela Browning, a junior minister in Agriculture, had come out against a single European currency in her election address, apparently breaking the official party line of 'wait and see'. This was sufficient to spark the conflagration that was waiting to happen. The next week other senior Conservatives, including John Horam and James Paice, were identified as also against the Euro in their election addresses. *The Independent* headlined the rift: TORIES DEFY MAJOR:

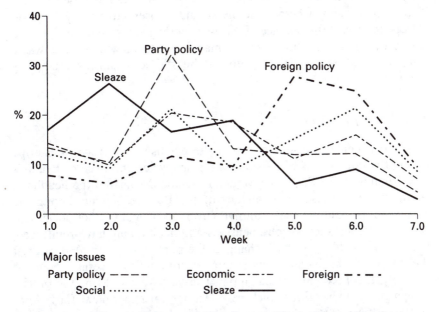

FIGURE 8.1   *The British Campaign Agenda, 1997 (% of All Issue Stories in the National Press)*
Source: CARMA *Content Analysis* (N.6072 *articles*) 18 Mar - 1 May 1997

NO EURO SURRENDER (11 April 1997). The once-faithful Tory press proved most troublesome for John Major. The *Daily Mail* splashed THE BATTLE FOR BRITAIN across its front page (15 April), claiming that politicians for the major parties had refused to debate the fundamental issue of ERM: 'There is a deafening silence at the heart of this election and its name is Europe.' For the *Daily Express*, Major's 'wait and see' policy was a feeble battle cry: 'Who goes over the top shouting "wait and see?".' The Conservative Party was forced to respond, and thereby reinforce, the media's agenda. To try to dampen down the row, John Major tore up the intended presentation on education at the morning press conference, and scrapped the planned election broadcast on 17 April, to launch a bare-bones impromptu personal appeal for unity within the party over Europe. This was quickly sabotaged by the party advertisement published the next day depicting Blair as a puppet on Kohl's lap, producing public rebuke of Conservative Central Office from leading Europhiles including Edward Heath and Kenneth Clarke, as well as the German government. The headlines and editorials during the period from 12 to 22 April were dominated by Tory divisions over Europe. The *Mail, Star, Telegraph, Express, Sun* and *Times*, with a total circulation of 9.7 million (or 71 per cent of readers) backed the Eurosceptic camp (Seymour-Ure 1997: 597). Long lists of Eurosceptics were published by many papers, and subsequently *The Times* (29 April 1997) officially endorsed Eurosceptic candidates from all parties. The importance of this issue to the press was overwhelming: 'Overall, Europe was editorially the prime issue of the campaign' (Seymour-Ure 1997: 598). The central question raised by this blanket coverage is whether the media and Conservative Party focus on Europe increased the salience of this issue among voters and damaged the Conservatives in the short term, as many assume, or whether this was a campaign controversy which reinforced, but did not change, voters' party preferences.

The Public's Agenda

Our experiment results suggest that the extensive coverage of Europe during the later stages of the 1997 campaign, when the issue of Britain's membership of the European Monetary Union dominated the headlines, should have increased the saliency of the European issue among the electorate. In contrast the extensive coverage of many other social and economic issues, such as jobs, pensions and health, may have reinforced, but seems less likely to have changed, the public's concerns. We can test these propositions by analysing the pattern of public concerns monitored in the British Election Campaign panel survey. We can divide the official campaign into two periods which provide a 'natural' experiment. Early April (from 1–10 April) was a period dominated in the media by stories of sleaze and the official launch of the party manifestos, before Europe rose on the campaign news agenda. This period can be compared with mid-April when Europe burst into the news and dominated the headlines (from 11–17 April). Given the different news coverage within these periods, if the media produces a short-term effect on the public, this should be apparent by a 'before' and 'after' paired comparison. Clustering responses into these two periods is more reliable than looking at changes in public reactions on a daily basis, since this reduces random noise from each day's sample. To analyse how the public reacted to this coverage we can examine the salience of issues, which was measured in the British Election Campaign panel survey by asking people: 'Which two issues matter most to you in deciding how to

TABLE 8.7: *The Public's Campaign Agenda*

Issue	Early April	Mid-April	Change
SOCIAL POLICY			
Health	25.9	28.6	2.7
Education	23.2	28.8	5.6
Law and order/crime/police	5.1	5.2	.1
Pensions/care for elderly	3.2	2.5	−.7
Welfare State/benefits	3.1	2.1	−1
Environment	2.2	2.3	.1
Housing/homelessness	1.6	1.3	−.3
Equality/social justice	.6	.3	−.3
Racism/ethnic minorities/immigration	.3	.3	0
Transport	.5	.8	.3
Family values/CSA/single parents	.2	.4	.2
Scotland/Wales/devolution	.2	.1	−.1
Other constitutional issues	.2	.3	.1
ECONOMY			
Employment/unemployment	6.4	6.0	−.4
Macro-economic issues	5.7	4.1	−1.6
Taxation	4.5	3.7	−.8
Inflation/wages/standard of living	2.3	1.1	−1.2
Other economic	.7	.5	−.2
Interest rates/mortgages	.4	.3	−.1
Nationalization/privatization	.4	.0	−.4
Industry/business	0	.1	.1
FOREIGN POLICY			
European Union	2.8	3.1	.3
Defence	.2	.1	−.1
Foreign affairs	.2	.0	−.2
Overseas aid	.1	.0	−.1
OTHER			
Conservative Party	.1	.1	0
Labour Party	.1	.3	.2
Sleaze/mistrust politicians	.5	.1	−.4
Gun control/hunting	.3	.1	−.2
Other specific	1.4	1.2	−.2
Uncodable	1.9	.7	−1.2
Don't know	3.1	3.2	.1
Refusal/no answer	2.4	2.1	−.3
TOTAL	100	100.0	

Source: British Election Campaign panel survey 1997.

vote in the election?' (coding an open-ended, unprompted response). This item was asked during the second and third waves, and the responses were coded into 40 major issue categories.

The results in Table 8.7 show that overall the social agenda of health and education dominated, with more than half the public nominating these issues as most important. This was followed a long way behind by the economic agenda, including jobs, taxation, and the macro-economy. In contrast, the foreign policy agenda was mentioned by relatively few voters, and only 2.9 per cent said the European Union was the most important issue when deciding how to vote. Moreover, if we look at the changes from early to mid-April, the most striking finding is that both education and health increased slightly in importance during this period. Despite the barrage of news coverage those who mentioned the EU rose from 2.8 to only 3.1 per cent. The clear conclusion from this measure of issue salience is that despite all the commentary, headlines and editorials devoted to Europe in the news, and the forced shift in Conservative Party strategy, the public remained indifferent to this issue. All the banging of the anti-European drum in the news headlines seems to have washed over the public who remained worried about the basic problems of health care, education and jobs. Another illustration of the apparent failure of media agenda-setting is given by 'sleaze', an issue which dominated coverage in the opening weeks of the campaign, yet it was mentioned as important when deciding how to vote by less than one per cent of the public.

Conclusions: The Public Followed its Own Agenda

The analysis therefore suggests that despite extensive coverage in the news headlines the issue of Britain's role within Europe, a matter of heated passion to editorial writers, and a matter which publicly split the Conservative leadership, did not rise on the public's agenda during the official campaign. Like the earlier Miller study (1990), the public and media agendas diverged widely in the election. Yet in the experiments we found that concern about foreign affairs *did* increase significantly when people were shown television news stories about Europe and developing countries. How therefore do we account for the difference between the experimental and the panel survey results? There may be a number of reasons why findings may differ.

First, in the agenda-setting experiments we selected stories about the problems facing the developing world, such as those in East Timor, the WHO in Haiti, and Zaire, which may well have been fairly new and unfamiliar to our audience. The issue of aid for developing countries was certainly low on the list of concerns of our respondents prior to showing the video. Moreover, the issue of overseas development was not one which was closely associated with party politics. In contrast the constant barrage of stories about Conservative splits over Europe during the British campaign followed a series of similar headlines ever since at least the Maastricht Treaty in 1989, if not earlier. Like the months and months of headlines about the Lewinsky affair in the United States, the public's reaction may well have been: 'enough, already'. In this regard the challenge for agenda-setting studies is to explore the conditionality of effects, namely when stories may influence the public's concerns and shape perceptions of party leaders, as Zaller (1998) notes. There are certain cases where we commonly assume that news headlines did have an immediate effect on the public; for example, the impact of Chernobyl on fears of nuclear accidents, the influence of the initial warnings about mad cow disease on public worries about food safety, or the footage of the Ethiopian famine which led to an outpouring of Band Aid. There are other cases where, despite wall-to-wall news coverage, public opinion seems to remain largely untouched. In the short period of the official election campaign in Britain, with parties seeking to remain in control, there was remarkably little which was dramatically new in March and April which might have disturbed public priorities. The most effective way to test this further would be to conduct other 'events-analysis' case-studies, where we measure the pattern coverage over time in the news media and public priorities with a series of different issues.

An alternative explanation is that we found different results because these are the product of our methodologies. Experiments provide a more satisfactory way to examine the short-term impact of media messages, since they are sensitive to even modest changes over time. Experiments tell us what happens conditionally if people watch news which contains many stories about international news. In contrast, many different factors other than the news media could influence public concerns monitored by the campaign panel survey, and these could produce cross-cutting eddies which cancel each other out. We go on in the next chapter to consider whether any agenda-setting effects influenced party preferences and to examine other ways in which the contents of television news can potentially influence voters.

Notes

1. The newspapers included the *Daily/Sunday Telegraph, The Times/Sunday Times, The Independent/Independent on Sunday, The Guardian/The Observer*, the *Financial Times*, the *Daily Mail/Mail on Sunday, The Express/Express on Sunday, The Sun/News of the World, The Mirror/Sunday Mirror*, the *Daily Star* and *The People*. Articles relevant to the general election were selected from all major sections of the paper, excluding cartoons and events listings.

   Details of the methodology were kindly provided by Peter Christopherson at CARMA International, Godalming, Surrey. The results are available in 'Media content analysis of national press' CARMA International Ltd (http://www.carma.com), May 1997.

2. See Holli Semetko, Margaret Scammell and Tom Nossiter, 'The media's coverage of the campaign' in Anthony Heath, Roger Jowell, and John Curtice *Labour's Last Chance?* (Aldershot, Dartmouth, 1994).

9 The Effects of Television News on Party Preferences

Many observers believe that television has increased its role in the postmodern election so that what is on television news *is* the campaign (Kavanagh 1995). But in what regard can media coverage be expected to influence public opinion? In principle, there are three main ways in which the contents of the news might be expected to affect voters' party preferences: (1) *directional coverage* concerns how far television presents distinctively favourable or unfavourable messages about a party; (2) *stop-watch coverage* concerns how much coverage is devoted to a party; and lastly (3) *agenda coverage* concerns how far coverage focuses on issues that favour the party's position.

The strong tradition in British public service broadcasting has been to aim for neutrality in all three of these respects – even though, as noted in Chapter 5, strict neutrality has not always been achieved. In relation to directional coverage, participant observation studies of British newsrooms during election campaigns have found that editors and producers commonly stress the need for equidistant coverage of the main political parties, balancing favourable and unfavourable stories about each party, as well as even-handedness in commentary, interviews with party leaders, and reports from the campaign trail (Blumler and Gurevitch 1995; Semetko 1996b). The typical story in most British election campaign broadcasts tends to present one party's policy proposals or record, followed by a rebuttal from opponents, in a familiar 'on the one hand and on the other' sort of format, rather like watching the ball at Wimbledon. Similar news values have been found in other countries: a five-nation survey by Patterson (1998) found that balance, or 'expressing fairly the position on both sides of a dispute', was one of the commonest ways for journalists to understand objectivity, especially in the United States and Britain.

With regard to stop-watch balance, British broadcasters assiduously apply 'stop-watch' calculations to ensure that the major parties are given more or less equal air-time during election campaigns. Traditionally, a ratio of 5:5:4 (Conservative: Labour: Liberal Democrat) has been used, though there is some evidence to suggest that the ratio has not always been put into effect evenly. For example, in the 1987 British election Miller and colleagues added up the total hours of coverage of each party on television and concluded that there was a 'massive imbalance' which was overwhelmingly right-wing: 'The parties did not receive equal treatment. ... The Conservative government got two bites of the television cherry: once as a party, once as a government' (Miller *et al.* 1989; Miller 1991: 77; for a critique of this approach see Harrison 1989).

Finally, in relation to the *agenda balance*, it has often been suggested that by focusing election coverage disproportionately on one set of issues, such as problems of inner city poverty or immigration, broadcasters activate conventional party stereotypes and can therefore unintentionally skew their coverage in a partisan direction. The idea of agenda balance is based on the premise of 'issue ownership', with right-wing parties usually regarded as stronger on defence, crime and inflation while left-wing parties are seen as stronger on welfare, education and unemployment (Budge and Farlie 1983). Based on this assumption Miller *et al.*, for example, argued that the media focus on international security issues in the 1987 British election campaign constituted a 'massive and consistent right-wing bias in the issue agenda' which favoured the Thatcher government (Miller *et al.* 1989: 650).

Core Hypotheses

In this chapter we assess how far each of these potential sorts of effect – directional, stop-watch, and agenda balance – had the potential to affect voter preferences during the 1997 campaign. The model that we employ makes two core assumptions: that television news is an important source of political information for voters; and that voters modify their political attitudes and preferences in the light of messages they receive about political parties. We assume further that, although significant and permanent changes in perceptions are likely to occur only after repeated exposure to new and potentially challenging information, small (and possibly ephemeral) changes in perceptions are likely to result from quite limited exposure to TV news. We also assume that some voter-types are more likely to change their perceptions than others. Based on these assumptions, our first major *directional* hypothesis (H1a) is that, *ceteris paribus*:

> *'Positive' television news coverage of a particular party, in comparison with 'neutral' coverage, will tend to increase support for that party among voters; 'negative' coverage will tend to reduce support.*

By 'positive' news, we mean items that present the party in question in a favourable light, such as reports that stress its unity, morale or success. By 'negative' items, we mean reports that portray a party in an unfavourable light, stressing its embarrassment, disunity, failure or disarray. The specific videos used in these experiments are described in the Technical Appendix. Party support is measured on a 10-point scale as described below. An obvious corollary to this directional hypothesis derives from the potentially 'zero sum' character of party politics. If positive coverage of one party increases that party's ratings, it may serve to reduce the ratings of others – to inflict *collateral damage* on them. This produces H1b:

> *'Positive' television news coverage of a particular party, in comparison with 'neutral' coverage, will tend to reduce support for the other main parties; 'negative' coverage will tend to increase support for the other main parties.*

Our second major hypothesis relates to the concept of *stop-watch balance*. Here, again, our expectation is simple. Other things being equal, more coverage should be good for a party's electoral fortunes and less coverage should be bad. Specifically (H2):

> *Greater exposure for a party will tend to increase support for that party; less exposure will tend to reduce its support.*

Finally, we hypothesize that exposure to certain *issue-agendas* – of the sort described in Chapter 8 – should work to the advantage of the party that 'owns' the issue, regardless of the way that these items are presented, and should therefore be associated with distinctive changes in party support patterns. Given the characteristic positions of British parties along the ideological spectrum, we would expect (H3a) that:

> *News items focused on taxation serve to boost Conservative support, whereas items about social policy (such as jobs, health and pensions) are more likely to increase Labour support.*

The impact of foreign policy issues is more complex to predict. However, given the type of coverage during the 1997 campaign, the well-publicized splits within the Conservative Party on the European issue, and Labour's higher profile on 'Third World' issues, we would anticipate *a priori* (H3b) that:

> *News items focused on Europe serve to disadvantage the Conservatives, whereas news about overseas aid for developing countries slightly benefits Labour.*

Mediating Variables

These simple hypotheses, however, say nothing of the different tendencies of various sorts of voter to shift their party-support perceptions. In line with evidence reported by Iyengar and Kinder (1987), we might well expect that the effects of media exposure on party preferences would not be uniform across the electorate but would vary in systematic and predictable ways according to voters' prior political predispositions, television habits and social background. Many studies, starting with Lazarsfeld *et al.* (1944), have suggested that the groups most susceptible to influence by the media during the campaign are the waverers who have yet to make up their minds even late in the campaign. Specifically, we would therefore expect strong partisans, the politically well-informed and those who are interested in politics and current affairs to be less likely to change their pre-test to post-test responses than their respective comparator groups, the less partisan, the ill-informed and uninterested. The partisan, the informed and the interested are all likely to have thought seriously about political matters prior to being exposed to our experimental manipulations. They are more likely to hold stable political views than others. This in turn implies that we should observe smaller differences in their pre- and post-test party-image responses.

The effects of partisanship, knowledge and interest do not necessarily stop here, however. In addition to being less likely to change their party-image responses, it can be argued on *a priori* grounds that these groups are also less likely to be affected by exposure to television news; that is to say they are less likely than their comparators to be affected by our positive and negative experimental manipulations. The partisan, the informed and the interested are all less likely to be influenced by what they see and hear about party images in our video experiments – either because they have already made up their minds (the partisan) or because on many previous occasions they have been exposed to, and have taken note of, similar messages (the knowledgeable and the informed). Technically, these expectations imply that there should be interaction effects between partisanship, knowledge and interest, on the one hand, and video exposure, on the other: any observed effects of positive or negative video exposure should be weaker for the partisan, the knowledgeable and the interested than they are for comparator groups.

Two other sets of potential effects on voters' changing perceptions need to be considered. In addition to the purely experimental controls that we apply in H1–H3, given the information that we obtained from our pre-test and post-test questionnaires, we are also in a position to apply non-experimental controls both for (a) the standard set of socio-demographic variables (age, gender, class and so on) that are normally found to exert significant effects on voters' political preferences and perceptions and (b) respondents' television-watching habits. As a result of our experimental design, however, our hypotheses in both of these contexts favour the null. The experimental approach is predicated on the random assignment of subjects to test and control groups. If the stimulus (video exposure) genuinely affects the response (a shift in the respondents' party image), the group effect should be observable regardless of respondents' socio-demographic characteristics or television-habits because the test and control groups should contain roughly equal proportions drawn from all groups. At the individual level, we could, of course, simply assume that socio-demographic and television-habit effects do not confound any bivariate statistical relationships that we might observe between video exposure and changing party-images. We prefer, however, to conduct formal tests for any such possible effects. Specifically, we hypothesize that the observed relationship between positive/negative video exposure and pre- to post-test changes in party-image will not be confounded by the application of statistical controls for the effects of (a) the standard battery of socio-demographic variables or (b) respondents' television-watching habits.

Operational Measures

Measures of changes in party support. We designed the research to achieve conceptual replication of responses, that is, tests were repeated with conceptually similar but empirically different measures of the variables under scrutiny. This was particularly important given that this was the first time that British voters' party preferences had been measured in an experimental context. We included nine related, BES-based, measures of party support in both the pre-test and the post-test. For each of the three major parties, we asked respondents to assess, on 0–10 scales, (a) how likely it was that they would vote for the party, (b) how much they liked the party, and (c) how highly they rated the (named) party leader. Tests proved that these items were strongly inter-correlated and formed reliable scales (the Cronbach Alpha was, respectively, .90 for the Conservative index, .89 for the Labour index, and .82 for the Liberal Democrat index). For each party, and for both the pre-test and the post-test measures, the three scales were averaged to produce a single party-support index where a 0 score meant a respondent had a very poor image of the party and 10 meant a very good image. Calculating each respondent's 'change in party support' score was simply a matter of subtracting the pre-test score from the post-test score: a positive (negative) change indicated that a respondent had a more (less) favourable view of the party in question after the experimental manipulation than before it. We assume that our composite support scores, precisely because they are based on three different response items, more accurately measure each respondent's party preference than any single party-response item considered in isolation.

Measures of exposure to television news. To test for the effects of *favourable and unfavourable* news, we conducted four 'directional' experiments involving 258 respondents who were divided at random into four treatment groups. Members of each group were shown a video compilation representing, in a 12-minute 'middle' segment, consistently Positive Conservative, Positive Labour, Negative Conservative or Negative Labour news items. As noted in Chapter 2, we were unable to compile equivalent Positive and Negative videos for the Liberal Democrats because of the dearth of unfavourable items about the party in the six-month period prior to the beginning of the campaign. All four Positive and Negative videos contained similar proportions of 'talking heads', reporter commentary and location shots. Each of the Positive videos contained a brief extract of an interview with the party leader, while the two Negative videos focused on more general stories about the relevant party's image. All four videos, however, contained similar numbers of references to the party leaders, to personalities within the respective parties, and to party policy. Details of the contents of each video are described in the Appendix.

To test for the effects of *stop-watch* balance on party preferences, we monitored the reactions of 261 participants who were divided at random into three treatment groups. Members of these groups were shown, respectively, a 20-minute core of Conservative coverage (CON20), 20 minutes of Labour coverage (LAB20), and 20 minutes of Liberal Democrat coverage (LIB20). Most importantly, the stories selected for the composite news bulletins were judged to be 'internally balanced' or neutral overall. Each story usually opened with the proponent's case and then presented a rebuttal by opponents. A claim that, for example, taxes had been cut under the Conservatives would be followed by counterclaims by Labour and Liberal Democrat spokespersons, with equally pro and con comments from vox pop and outside experts. We recognize the difficulty of objectively determining whether or not the content of a particular video selection is genuinely 'internally balanced'. Our decision rule as to what constituted positive, negative and neutral news coverage was that an item had to be coded as such by two independent coders. We have every confidence, however, that similar codings would have been produced by other researchers. Full transcriptions of the content of the videos concerned are available from the authors.

To test for *issue agenda and ownership* effects, we randomly assigned 484 respondents into six groups, as outlined in Chapter 8. Each group was shown a distinctive 12-minute middle core which focused on a particular policy issue (unemployment, taxation, pensions, health, Europe and aid to the Third World). As with the stop-watch test videos, each compilation contained items that had been coded as 'party neutral' by two independent coders.

Finally, in addition to the three sets of treatment groups, we also monitored the reactions of an explicit control group of 110 participants. The middle segment of the video shown to this group contained a series of items on sport. Overall, the control video followed the broadcasters' standard ratio of 5:5:4 stop-watch party balance. Our simple expectation is that subjects in this control group did not significantly change their preferences for the major parties between the pre- and the post-test whereas subjects in the test groups did. For the multivariate analysis, in order to compare the relative effects of the stop-watch, directional and agenda balance experiments, we recoded all the 14 groups into dummy variables (excluding the control group), comparing the effects of those who received one treatment against all the other participants.

Measures of partisanship, political knowledge and political interest. For each party, the respondent's partisan commitment was measured using the pre-test score on the aggregate 'probability of supporting the party' scale referred to above: it was assumed that a higher pre-test score reflected a greater degree of commitment to the party; a lower score, a weaker degree of commitment. Political knowledge was measured from the responses to a five-item political quiz that had been included in the post-test question-naire. Political interest was measured according to whether or not respondents expressed a strong interest either in current affairs or in political items of television news.

Measures of socio-demographic characteristics and television-watching habits. Previous research has shown that voting preferences (though not necessarily *changes* in preference) are linked to a range of socio-demographic and attitudinal characteristics (Butler and Stokes 1974; Särlvik and Crewe 1983; Heath *et al.* 1985, 1991, 1994). During the 1980s and early 1990s – though not, perhaps, in 1997 – Conservative support tended to be weakest, and Labour support strongest, among men, younger voters, manual workers, the unemployed, students, non-home-owners, non-graduates and voters from ethnic minorities (Brynin and Sanders 1997; Norris 1997a). With the exception of age, which was measured as a continuous variable, these various characteristics were all measured as dummy variables so that they could be entered as independent variables in OLS regression equations. Finally, television-watching habits were measured as the average number of hours per week that the respondent watched television.

The Impact of TV News

First, what changed in the main dependent variables of our study? Table 9.1 reports the average change between the pre- and post-test measurements. All the scales, including the three party-support indices, range from zero to ten. The overall pattern of pre-test and post-test averages shows that Labour was the most popular party (post-test average index score = 5.34) and the Conservatives the least popular (index score = 3.44). This pattern increases our confidence in our results, since it is broadly in line with the substantial Labour victory that occurred on polling day, two weeks after our experiments were conducted. The average *change* scores in Table 9.1 indicate that the Conservatives and the Liberal Democrats were both viewed marginally more favourably after our experimental manipulations than before them: the 'probability of voting' scores, the 'liking' scores and the 'party-support' indices all increased for both parties. Tony Blair's ratings also increased marginally, though this tendency was counteracted by small reductions in our respondents' 'liking' and 'probability of voting' for Labour: as a result, Labour's average party-support index score remained more or less constant. For the remainder of this chapter, we concentrate on changes in the *party-support indices.* This emphasis reflects our conviction that, because these indices are based on three different measures of party support, they are more likely to capture genuine pre-test to post-test movements in respondents' preferences than any single measure considered in isolation.

There are two obvious explanations for the general increase in

TABLE 9.1: *Average Ratings on Party Preferences*

	Pre-test Mean	Post-test Mean	Mean Change	N for Mean Change
Probability of voting Conservative	2.82	3.01	+0.21	945
Liking of Conservatives	3.19	3.32	+0.14	1082
Liking of Major	3.86	3.84	−0.02	1084
Conservative Party preferences	3.33	3.44	+0.11	916
Probability of voting Labour	5.67	5.50	−0.09	1003
Liking of Labour	5.30	5.29	−0.03	1085
Liking of Blair	4.94	5.08	+0.13	1089
Labour Party preferences	5.40	5.34	+0.01	969
Probability of voting Lib-Dem	3.25	3.43	+0.20	889
Liking of Liberal Democrats	4.46	4.64	+0.13	1053
Liking of Ashdown	4.69	4.76	+0.04	1068
Liberal Democrat Party preferences	4.13	4.30	+0.10	859

Note: All measures based on 0–10 scales. The index score for party preferences is the arithmetic average of the three other scores in each party grouping. It is only measured for respondents who answered all three component questions. The average change figures are calculated only from those respondents who answered both pre-test and post-test questions.

Source: Experimental Study of Television News, 1997.

Conservative and Liberal Democrat ratings shown in Table 9.1. One is that this increased sympathy was somehow triggered by our participants' being reminded of the election campaign: all our videos began with the opening item from BBC1's *Nine O'Clock News* on the day that John Major called the election. Another possibility is that what we thought was generally neutral coverage in the common 'top' and 'bottom' of each video 'sandwich' was not in fact neutral but slightly pro-Conservative and pro-Liberal Democrat. We are not in a position to determine which, if either, of these explanations is correct (though we would prefer to believe the first). However, the fact that there is a slight 'inflation' of Conservative and Liberal Democrat scores does not in any sense damage either the character or the purpose of our experiments. *What matters is whether there are any treatment differences in the average change scores; whether or not subjects who watched our test videos exhibit a different change profile from those subjects who watched a control.*

The Effects of Positive and Negative News

Table 9.2 allows us to explore this question in relation to the Positive and Negative news videos. It compares the average changes in our aggregate measures of party support across five groups of respondents: the control group (who were shown neutral coverage); and those who were exposed to Positive Conservative, Negative Conservative, Positive Labour and Negative Labour coverage. The first point to note about the table is that, for the control group, all three party-support index scores show only small pre-test to post-test differences (+.05 for the Conservatives, –.02 for Labour and +.04 for the Liberal Democrats). This suggests, notwithstanding our previous comments about Table 9.1, that the overall coverage in the control videos *was* broadly politically neutral.

The crucial feature of Table 9.2, however, is that only two of the test video groups yield mean changes that are significantly different from those of the control group. Respondents shown the Positive Conservative video increased their support for the Conservatives by an average of .50, compared with .05 in the control group. Those shown the Positive Labour video increased their support on average by .40, compared with a .02 reduction among the control group. In contrast, respondents shown the Negative videos were *not* significantly different from the control group. This suggests a marked asymmetry in the effects of positive and negative news, only partially confirming H1a. Although positive coverage clearly improves a party's image among voters, negative news appears not to damage it. The other non-significant results in the table also imply a rejection of H1b: favourable (unfavourable) news about one party does *not* seem to inflict collateral damage (benefit) on others.

This conclusion is strongly reinforced by the results shown in Table 9.3. The table outlines three more fully specified models of preference change, one for each of the party-support index measures. The effects of type of news coverage are measured using dummy variable predictors reflecting respondents' exposure (or not) to each of our four (positive and negative) experimental manipulations. The base category is the control group who

TABLE 9.2: *Mean Changes in Party Preferences by Positive/Negative News*

Video News	Change in Party Preferences					
	Conservative		Labour		LibDem	
Control	0.05	(501)	–0.02	(534)	0.04	(476)
Positive						
Conservative coverage	0.50**	(55)	–0.18	(54)	0.07	(52)
Negative						
Conservative coverage	0.14	(63)	0.20	(53)	0.19	(52)
Positive						
Labour coverage	0.20	(.53)	0.40**	(59)	0.17	(51)
Negative						
Labour coverage	0.20	(42)	0.07	(54)	0.23	(42)

Note: Figures in parentheses indicate the number of cases in the mean calculation.
*denotes ANOVA difference of means test significant at p<.05; ** denotes p <.01.

In addition to the four treatment groups, we monitored the reactions of two control groups. The first was an *explicit* control group of 110 participants – referred to in the text – who were shown a non-political video 'core'. The second was an *implicit* control group whose 700 members were shown 'politically neutral' video footage relating to the other experiments that we conducted. Given the similarities in the responses of these two preliminary control groups, the results reported here combine them into a single, larger, control group. We continue with this practice in subsequent tables in the chapter.

Source: Experimental Study of Television News, 1997.

were exposed to politically neutral coverage only. The models all apply controls for the standard battery of socio-demographic characteristics and for the respondents' television-watching habits, as well as for partisanship, knowledge and interest.[1]

Two main conclusions are suggested by the table. First, the inclusion of a battery of additional control variables does not in any way perturb the strong effects of exposure to the Positive Conservative and Positive Labour videos: the estimated coefficients on these variables are large, significant and positive while the coefficients on the remaining exposure

TABLE 9.3:   *Direct Effects of Positive and Negative News on Party Preferences*

| | Change in Party Preferences | | | | | |
| | Conservative | | Labour | | Liberal Democrat | |
	b	se	b	se	b	se
Exposure to POSCON coverage	.36**	.13	−.22	.15	.04	.16
Exposure to NEGCON coverage	.09	.12	.19	.15	.16	.16
Exposure to POSLAB coverage	.13	.13	.48**	.14	.09	.16
Exposure to NEGLAB coverage	.10	.14	−.01	.15	.18	.18
Male/not	−.05	.06	−.08	.07	−.04	.08
Age (years)	.001	.002	.003	.002	.004	.003
Ethnic minority/not	−.06	.08	.08	.08	.02	.10
Graduate/not	−.15*	.07	−.01	.07	−.02	.08
Owner occupier/not	−.09	.07	−.06	.07	−.32***	.08
Unemployed/not	−.01	.09	.04	.10	−.27*	.12
Interested in current affairs/not	−.08	.07	.05	.08	.16	.09
Interested in political news/not	−.10	.07	.09	.08	.02	.09
Hours per week watch television	.00	.00	−.005	.003	−.004	.003
Political Knowledge (0–5 scale)	.01	.02	.00	.07	−.03	.03
Pre-test Conservative support	−.00	.01				
Pre-test Labour support			−.07***	.01		
Pre-test Lib Democrat support					.08***	−.02
Constant	.14	.12	.42	.15	.62	.16
Corrected. R^2	.01		.04		.04	
N	900		947		843	
Standard error of estimate	.91		1.04		1.11	

Note: * denotes coefficient significant at $p<.05$; **$p<.01$; ***$p<.001$.
Estimation by OLS. The dependent variable in each model is a pre-test to post-test change in party-support measure. With panel data, it is standard practice to use a lagged endogenous variable (LEV) specification in which the current level of the dependent variable (at time t) is on the left-hand side of the equation and the previous level (at t-1) is on the right-hand side. We use a change specification, with the pre-test party-support level on the right-hand side, for three reasons. First, from a theoretical viewpoint, the measured dependent variable – change – corresponds exactly to the 'test effect' that we are seeking to measure. Second, the r2 values reported in our specification are meaningful, whereas those in the LEV specification are not. Third – and most important – the coefficients on the pre-test party-support indices in our specification have a far clearer theoretical interpretation than in LEV. In our specification, these coefficients represent the extent to which prior partisanship inhibits the tendency of respondents to shift their party allegiances as a result of their exposure to our experimental manipulations.

Source: Experimental Study of Television News, 1997.

measures are, as in the bivariate relationships shown in Table 9.2, clearly non-significant. Second, the socio-demographic and television-watching variables fail to demonstrate any consistent pattern of effect on the change indices. The model for Conservative support suggests that graduates are significantly less likely to change their overall view of the Conservatives (b = −.14), but this finding has no confirming counterpart in either the Labour or the Liberal Democrat equation. The crucial point is that the socio-demographic and television-habit variables simply do not affect respondents' propensities to change their images of the three main parties. Indeed, the critical driving factor that influenced our subjects' tendencies either to change their party support patterns or to retain them was whether or not they were exposed to our experimental manipulations. And what mattered, in particular, were the two manipulations that featured positive images of the Conservative and Labour parties.[2]

An obvious question follows from the somewhat asymmetrical empirical findings that we have reported. Why should positive news have exerted such clear and consistent effects on our respondents' party-support perceptions while negative news appears to have had so little impact? Although we cannot answer this question definitively, we can explore the possible reasons for this asymmetry. One possibility relates to the timing of our experiments. Our fieldwork was conducted after a long period – covering most of the 1992 Parliament – in which the two major parties had focused a significant part of their campaigning efforts on attacking their opponents. This in turn could have inured voters to the effects of negative political images to such an extent that they failed to respond to the negative images to which we exposed them: they would have needed a much more powerful negative stimulus to have produced a measurable response. If this were indeed the case, it would imply that negative campaigning perhaps contains within it the seeds of its own long-term failure: the more that voters are exposed to it, the less they are affected by it.

A second possibility is that British voters are more susceptible to positive news images precisely because they are generally so cynical about, and dismissive of, politics and politicians. Indirect evidence for this cynicism can be gleaned from Gallup's long-running time-series on voters' 'approval of the government's record'. These data show that, whichever party is in power, the vast majority of voters most of the time disapprove of what the government of the day has done.[3] In these circumstances of general cynicism, it is possible that positive news about a political party – any political party – represents more of a challenge to voters' existing mind-sets, thereby invoking more of a reaction in terms of changes in their party-support perceptions. Negative news images, on the other hand, since they conform with and confirm voters' prior predispositions, perhaps produce less of a response.

A third possible explanation for the asymmetrical effects of positive and negative news is that the images to which our respondents were exposed varied in intensity: the positive news stories included in our experiments were somehow more powerful than the negative ones. In compiling our videos, we obviously sought to ensure that such imbalances did not occur. Equally, however, we cannot be sure that we eliminated them altogether. To some degree, readers can judge these matters for themselves by examining the summaries of the videos' contents which are provided in the Appendix. We can only assert that, in our view, there were no obvious differences in intensity between the positive and negative news videos that we employed. We are confident that our respondents genuinely reacted differently to positive as opposed to negative news items about the major political parties.

The Effects of Stop-watch Imbalance

Table 9.4 provides a preliminary test of our second main hypothesis. It compares the mean size and direction of changes in party preferences caused by exposure to the stop-watch video stimuli compared with the control group who were shown a 'balanced' (5:5:4) news broadcast. The results show a mixed pattern. Those who watched the *Conservative* news bulletin (CON20) experienced a noticeable (but statistically insignificant) increase in Conservative support, as predicted by Hypothesis 2. However, there was also a significant and stronger increase in Liberal Democrat support among these participants. Viewers who watched the *Labour* video (LAB20) also modestly increased their support for Labour and for the Liberal Democrats, although these changes did not achieve statistical significance. Exposure to the *Liberal Democrat* bulletin (LIB20) also proved to have no significant impact on LibDem support.

A set of multivariate tests of the stop-watch hypothesis are shown in Table 9.5. The table shows the results of applying statistical controls for socio-demographics, political knowledge and interest, television-watching habits, and prior partisanship. When these controls are applied, the consequences of exposure to our stop-watch videos appear to become even more ambiguous: exposure to the Conservative video continues to increase Liberal Democrat support (see the significant positive coefficient

Table 9.4: Mean Changes in Party Preferences by Stop-Watch Balance

Video	Change in Party Preferences					
	Conservative		Labour		LibDem	
Control	+.10	(846)	+.01	(891)	+.08	(794)
Conservative (CON20)	+.23	(70)	+.05	(78)	+.43**	(65)
Labour (LAB20)	−.01	(76)	+.17	(76)	+.17	(71)
Liberal Democrat (LIB20)	+.12	(56)	−.28*	(61)	−.11	(50)

Note: Figures in parentheses indicate the number of cases in the mean calculation. *denotes ANOVA difference of means test significant at p<.05; ** denotes p<.01. CON20 = Conservative 20 minutes. LAB20 = Labour 20 minutes. LIB20 = Liberal Democrat 20 minutes.

Source: Experimental Study of Television News, 1997.

TABLE 9.5:   Direct Effects of Stop-Watch News on Party Preferences

| | Change in Party Preferences | | | | | |
| | Conservative | | Labour | | LibDem | |
	b	se	b	se	b	se
Exposure to CON20 coverage	.09	.11	.04	.12	.31*	.15
Exposure to LAB20 coverage	−.11	.11	.14	.13	.07	.14
Exposure to LIB20 coverage	.01	.13	−.36**	.14	−.23	.17
Corrected. R^2	.01		.04		.05	
N	900		947		843	
Standard error of estimate	.91		1.05		1.11	

Note: Estimation is by OLS. The following control variables (parameters not reported) were included in the estimation: gender, age, ethnicity, graduate/not, home-owner/not, unemployed/not, political interest, interest in political news, political knowledge, television-watching habits, pre-test party support score. * denotes coefficient significant at $p<.05$; **$p<.01$; ***$p<.001$

Source: Experimental Study of Television News, 1997.

for CON20 in column 5); but exposure to LIB20 now significantly reduces Labour support (see the significant negative coefficient for LIB20 in column 3). The results, in short, suggest no direct time-imbalance effects of the sort originally envisaged in H2, but two sorts of 'collateral' exposure effect: greater Liberal Democrat exposure damages Labour, even though it does not benefit the Liberal Democrats themselves; and greater Conservative exposure assists the Liberal Democrats but not the Conservatives. Yet as we show below, both of these results are insufficiently robust to withstand further, more stringent, empirical tests. Before we present these tests, however, we briefly outline the experimental findings relating to our third main hypothesis: the effects of agenda-balance.

The Effects of Agenda-balance

Put simply, we found no experimental evidence to support the notion that party preferences are affected by exposure to issues that might be presumed to benefit one party rather than another. As Table 9.6 indicates, there were no significant differences, in terms of changing party-support patterns, between the groups that were exposed to specific issue videos and those that were shown the 'control' videos. For example, respondents who were shown the 'health' video – clearly involving an issue on which most voters strongly preferred Labour – were no more likely to increase their support for Labour than voters who were not exposed. Similarly, respondents shown the 'Europe' video – invoking an issue which consistently proved divisive for the Conservatives – were no more likely to reduce their support for the Conservatives than respondents in the control group. Based on Chapter 8 we concluded that certain issues could potentially rise in importance for viewers if aired on the news, notably foreign policy issues which started as low salience concerns. Nevertheless it would seem from the results in this chapter that parties do *not* necessarily benefit

TABLE 9.6:   *Mean Changes in Party Preferences by Agenda-Setting News*

Video	Change in Party Preferences					
	Conservative		Labour		Lib Dem	
Control	+.11	(854)	+.02	(902)	+.10	(801)
Taxation	+.11	(62)	−.03	(67)	+.07	(58)
Unemployment	−.05	(53)	−.04	(59)	−.02	(48)
Health	+.08	(61)	+.07	(62)	+.07	(59)
Pensions	+.23	(52)	+.01	(60)	+.10	(48)
Europe	−.07	(44)	−.15	(44)	−.10	(44)
Overseas aid	+.20	(67)	+.13	(74)	+.00	(67)

Note: Figures in parentheses indicate the number of cases in the mean calculation.
*denotes ANOVA difference of means test significant at $p<.05$; ** denotes $p<.01$.

Source: Experimental Study of Television News, 1997.

– or suffer – if 'their' issues (or their *bêtes noires*) are given disproportionate prominence in television news broadcasts. Any agenda-setting effects do not therefore translate into changes in voting choice.

Summarizing the Experimental Effects

Table 9.7 provides a summary model of the effects of exposure to different sorts of television news on voters' electoral preferences. The model estimates the effects of all our video exposures simultaneously and also applies the battery of controls shown earlier in Tables 9.3 and 9.5. The results are very clear. Indeed, they remove the limited number of anomalies that we observed in our discussion of time-imbalance effects. In Table 9.7, the only significant television news exposure effects are those relating to (both Labour and Conservative) Positive news. When appropriate controls are applied, none of the other exposure-types exerts a significant effect on voter preferences: the Negative news, time-imbalance and issue-focus terms all yield non-significant coefficients, implying that these types of news exert no direct effect on voters' preferences. In terms of our three original hypotheses, therefore, we find no experimental support for either H2 (time-imbalance effects) or H3 (issue-agenda effects) and only partial, asymmetric, support for H1 (directional effects).

Evidence from Public Opinion in the Campaign

The experimental evidence shows that voters can *potentially* be influenced by television news, and in particular by 'positive' news about a particular party. But did this actually happen in the real world? The obvious question which arises is what effects, if any, actual TV news had on the electoral fortunes of the major parties during the 1997 campaign. Clearly, if the tone of television coverage does affect party support in the real world, then we would expect to find that significant shifts in public opinion during the campaign are linked to variations in the character of the coverage

TABLE 9.7: *Summary Model of the Effects of News Videos on Party Preferences*

Video Exposure	Change in Party Preferences					
	Conservative		Labour		LibDem	
	b	se	b	se	b	se
Positive Conservative coverage	.46***	.14	–.17	.17	.00	.18
Negative Conservative coverage	.19	.14	.24	.17	.11	.18
Positive Labour coverage	.23	.14	.53***	.17	.05	.18
Negative Labour coverage	.20	.16	.04	.17	.14	.20
CON20 coverage	.23	.13	.13	.15	.28	.17
LAB20 coverage	.03	.13	.23	.15	.03	.16
LIB20 coverage	.15	.14	–.27	.16	–.26	.18
Taxation coverage	.13	.14	.05	.15	–.03	.18
Unemployment coverage	.04	.15	–.01	.16	–.16	.19
Health coverage	.10	.14	.14	.16	-.10	.17
Pensions coverage	.27	.15	.10	.16	.03	.19
Europe coverage	–.06	.15	-.09	.18	-.31	.19
Overseas aid coverage	.23	.14	.19	.15	.10	.17
Corrected. R^2	.01		.05		.05	
N	900		947		843	
Standard error of estimate	.90		1.04		1.11	

Note: Estimation is by OLS. The following control variables (parameters not reported) were included in the estimation: gender, age, ethnicity, graduate/not, home-owner/not, unemployed/not, political interest, interest in political news, political knowledge, television-watching habits, pre-test party support score. * denotes coefficient significant at p<.05; **p<.01; ***p<.001

accorded to the different parties during the course of the campaign.

Figures 9.1 and 9.2 provide two competing accounts of the day-by-day variations in support experienced by the three major parties during the official campaign in April 1997. Figure 9.1 reports the support levels measured by the BES's rolling campaign panel, which interviewed 100–150 respondents on each day of the campaign. Figure 9.2 shows the average support levels recorded by the main commercial opinion polls – the 'poll of polls' – over the same period.[4] Unfortunately, there is a clear mismatch between the two figures. The day-to-day shifts in the Conservative and Labour graphs in Figure 9.1 clearly bear no relation to their counterparts in Figure 9.2. Indeed, the correlation between the Conservative graphs in Figures 9.1 and 9.2 is r = –.24; the equivalent for Labour is +.01. Although the correlation between the two Liberal Democrat graphs is stronger (+.59), this reflects the rising trend of Liberal Democrat support which is displayed in both figures rather than a consistent pattern of day-to-day co-variation.

The strict conclusion that must be drawn from the disparities shown in these figures, however, is that one of the measures – and perhaps both – fail(s) to capture the 'true' variation in party support patterns during the 1997 campaign. Indeed, one interpretation is that the graphs – particularly those for Labour and the Conservatives – reflect random sampling fluctuations rather than clearly measured changes in party support levels.[5] Such

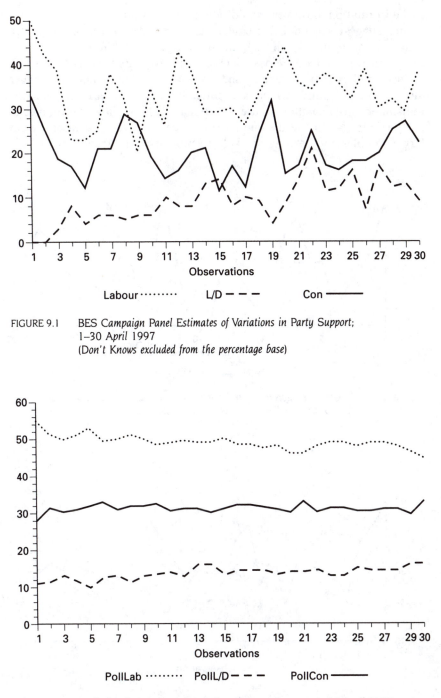

FIGURE 9.1   BES *Campaign Panel Estimates of Variations in Party Support;*
1–30 *April* 1997
(*Don't Knows excluded from the percentage base*)

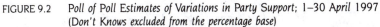

FIGURE 9.2   *Poll of Poll Estimates of Variations in Party Support;* 1–30 *April* 1997
(*Don't Knows excluded from the percentage base*)

an interpretation, however, would be unduly cautious. The fact that both figures suggest a general increase in Liberal Democrat support (and a concomitant reduction in Labour support) during the course of the campaign represents a modest degree of measurement consistency. This in turn implies that there may indeed have been real support changes during the campaign which are reflected in our measures. For the remainder of the chapter we use the commercial poll data as estimates of party support – on the assumption that, because they are based on far larger samples, they are more likely to represent the 'true' variations in

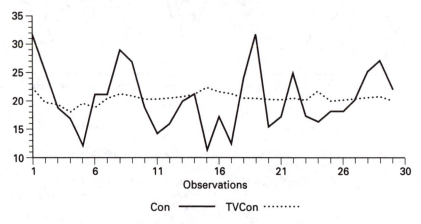

FIGURE 9.3   Conservative Support and the Balance of Conservative TV Coverage, April 1997 (Coverage scale adjusted to support metric: observed range is 3.3 to 4.5)

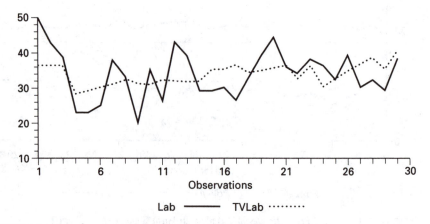

FIGURE 9.4   Labour Support and the Balance of Labour TV Coverage, April 1997 (Coverage scale adjusted to support metric: observed range is 3.3 to 4.5)

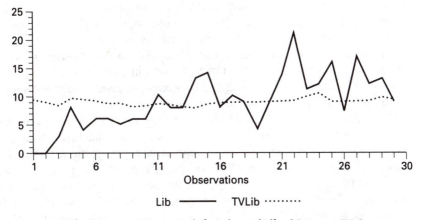

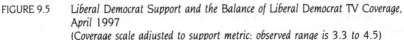

FIGURE 9.5   *Liberal Democrat Support and the Balance of Liberal Democrat TV Coverage, April 1997*
(*Coverage scale adjusted to support metric: observed range is 3.3 to 4.5*)

campaign support levels than their BES equivalents.

Figure 9.3 shows the relationship between Conservative support and variations in the overall balance of television news coverage of the Conservative party as outlined in Chapter 5. The balance measure shows the extent to which favourable references and images of the Conservative Party outnumbered unfavourable references and images for each day of the campaign. Data were not available for Saturday and Sunday news broadcasts and so the balance values were imputed for these days using standard interpolation techniques. Figures 9.4 and 9.5 show the equivalent support/coverage relationships, respectively, for Labour and for the Liberal Democrats.

It is clear from these figures that there is no consistent relationship between aggregate changes in party support and the balance of coverage accorded in news broadcasts to each of the major parties. Although there is considerable variability in the coverage measures – with the Conservatives securing favourable treatment on some days and Labour or the Liberal Democrats receiving positive coverage on others – there is little intimation that these shifts in coverage are systematically linked to changes in the parties' aggregate support levels: the pairs of graphs simply fail to match one another. This conclusion is borne out by more formal statistical methods. Although we do not report the findings in detail here, we estimated a number of time-series models which sought to test the proposition that a distinctly positive (negative) news day for a particular party would be followed by a measurable increase (fall) in that party's measured support.[6] The results of all of these models favoured the null. We simply found no evidence to indicate that there were any connections between day-to-day variations in the tone of television coverage accorded to a particular party and variations in its support ratings. Even when we looked at the incidence of exclusively 'positive' news stories about the different parties – which seemed a plausible approach given our strong experimental finding about the robust effects of positive news at the individual level – we found a similar pattern of no relationship between our measures of positive news and variations in party support patterns. Television news coverage during the campaign, in essence, did not significantly affect the overall pattern of party support.

What does all of this suggest? Our experimental evidence suggests that watching positive television news can have quite marked short-term effects. So why does the balance of television coverage during the 1997 campaign appear to have no effect on party support? There are at least four possible reasons for this apparent anomaly. The first relates to the problem of measuring variations in party support that we alluded to earlier. As we noted above, the commercial 'poll of polls', because of its larger sample, probably represents the best estimate that can be made of variations in party support levels over the campaign. However, the poll of polls' lack of fit with the BES rolling campaign poll also casts some doubt on the authenticity of both measures. In these circumstances, it could be argued that the comparisons that we make at aggregate level are inappropriate since they are based on unreliable estimates of the 'real' movements in support. The implication is not that the hypothesis linking television coverage and aggregate party support is incorrect; merely that it is inappropriately tested using the available data.

A second factor explaining why television coverage during the campaign apparently failed to influence the pattern of party support is the 'cancelling' effect of TV news. All three parties received broadly similar treatment, in terms of the balance of favourable versus unfavourable news stories, at the hands of the broadcasters (see Chapter 2). During the campaign, the average daily 'favourability score' for the Conservatives (the difference between the number of favourable and unfavourable items) was 3.8; the equivalent figures for Labour and the Liberal Democrats were 4.1 and 4.2 respectively. The minimal difference makes it extremely unlikely that one party would gain more from a typical day's coverage than either of the others. Again, therefore, the contradiction between our experimental findings and developments during the 1997 campaigning is more apparent than real. The aggregate evidence does not necessarily show that voters were unaffected by what they saw in television news broadcasts; merely that the result of many individual-level changes left overall support levels – for Labour and the Conservatives at least – broadly unchanged.

The third explanation relates to Gelman and King's (1995) notion of 'enlightened preferences'. On their account, one of the primary functions of campaigns is to provide a more informed basis for the choices that voters are already predisposed to make: campaigns confirm and mobilize existing predispositions. By the spring of 1997, when the official campaign began, British voters had already been exposed to at least two years of more or less continuous unofficial campaigning by the major parties. This in turn suggests that, in Britain in April 1997, most voters' electoral preferences were already as 'enlightened' as they were ever likely to be. In this sense, unless one party made a serious error in its campaigning strategy, it was always unlikely that the 1997 campaign would make much difference to party fortunes. At the margin, a minority of potential Liberal Democrat supporters do appear to have been influenced by the campaign – shown by the modest rise in the party's support during April 1997. Yet there is no reason to suppose that this increase in Liberal Democrat support resulted from the character of the television news coverage that it received.

Conclusions

The analysis has been divided into two distinct parts – one experimental and one based on aggregate-level changes in television coverage and party support. The experimental method we adopted is based on the simple principle that a given experimental stimulus should produce an observable test response. We wished to know if voters' attitudinal responses varied systematically at the individual level according to the types of television news coverage they were shown. The very clear answer is that they do. Our analysis provides unambiguous experimental evidence that exposure to positive news coverage of the Conservative and Labour parties can produce a clear and significant improvement in party support.

What we do not know, of course, is how enduring – or ephemeral – the changes in experimental response that we have measured might turn out to be. The short-term changes that we observed were in fact quite considerable. The mean pre-test Conservative party-image score was 3.33. Our best estimate (from Table 9.3) of the effect of ten minutes of Positive Conservative news coverage yields a coefficient of +0.36. This represents no less than a 10 per cent increase on the mean Conservative pre-test score. Remarkably, the equivalent calculation for the effects of ten minutes of Positive Labour coverage produces almost the same estimated increase on the mean Labour pre-test score.[7]

It seems highly unlikely that effects of this magnitude could last for very long. Equally, we have no way of determining, from our data, the rate at which they might discount over time. Our respondents were guaranteed confidentiality and anonymity, so we were unable to re-test them on a subsequent occasion in order to see if there might be any trace of the experimental effects that we observed. The only way of establishing the discount rates of any experimental effects would be for us to bite the 'experimental conditioning' bullet and construct a repeated-test research design. We certainly intend to do precisely this in our future work. For the moment, however, we have clear evidence that it is positive rather than negative television images that seem to best serve the electoral interests of the party concerned. As discussed further in the book's conclusion, party managers and politicians, as well as news editors, journalists and producers, should take note.

But what, if anything, does all this experimental analysis tell us about the more general effects of television news on British public opinion during the 1997 campaign? The cynical observer would almost certainly argue that, since we have 'merely' examined experimental effects, we still know precisely nothing about the effects of television news on 'real' voters 'in the real world'. Such a conclusion, however, would be both ill-advised and unfair. The value of our experiments lies in the way that they can be related to other approaches which examine similar questions from a different perspective. As we noted at the outset, aggregate correlations between television news coverage and voters' opinions have in the past been obliged to assume that exposure affects perceptions. We have been able to show that this is indeed the case. This in itself represents an important development for aggregate analysts. Indeed, the fact that we have been able to demonstrate the existence of individual-level television news coverage effects, albeit in an experimental context, provides the necessary empirical underpinning for the second – aggregate – part of our analysis.

Our aggregate results show clearly that the changes in party support during the course of the short campaign bear little relation to the pattern of positive and negative news about parties presented on television. Given what we know about individual-level effects from our experiments, this lack of an aggregate relationship may well mask a complex pattern of individual change in which floating voters were moved in different partisan directions at different times by the television news messages and images to which they were exposed. There may have been flux but not flow. Given the generally balanced coverage that the broadcasters achieved – the three major parties received broadly similar treatment in terms of favourable and unfavourable exposure over the campaign as a whole – these individual changes combined to produce only small changes at the aggregate level. The main beneficiaries of the campaign were the Liberal Democrats – though this appears to have resulted from factors other than their exposure to positive or negative television news coverage.

Finally, we should note that, although television news does not appear to have played a decisive role during the 1997 short campaign, this does not necessarily imply that its role was equally non-significant in the long campaign. While the sorts of effect that we observed in our experiments are likely to decay quite rapidly, it is also possible that each exposure leaves a trace that endures for some considerable time. The cumulative effects of multiple exposures over time, on this account, would take a long period to build up. Future research needs to address these issues.

Notes

1. In addition to these relatively straightforward tests, we also estimated a series of models which allowed for the possibility that the support patterns of strongly partisan, politically interested and/or politically informed respondents were less likely to be affected by exposure to video news than their non-partisan, uninterested and uninformed counterparts. Although we do not report the results here (details are available from the authors), we can confirm that there were no systematic differences in the response patterns of these two groups.
2. We also estimated a series of models similar to those shown in Table 9.3 (results not reported) which took explicit account of the fact that some respondents tend to be more 'unstable' in their pre-test to post-test response patterns than others. Even after this 'response instablility' had been factored into the models, the results were in all relevant respects identical to those reported here. For details, see Sanders and Norris (1998: 164–6).
3. Between January 1964 and March 1997, for example, the average 'government's record' approval rating was only 31 per cent. This is considerably lower than the average popularity of the major parties. Over the same period, the average popularity rating of the governing party was 38.4 per cent. See *Gallup Political and Economic Index*.
4. The support levels are all unweighted averages based on the fieldwork data reported by the agencies involved (Gallup, MORI, NOP, ICM). The number of polls conducted each day varied from 2 to 7. We are grateful to Ivor Crewe for supplying us with the relevant data.
5. Each of the 'point estimates' of support shown in the figures is subject to a sampling error of at least plus or minus 2 percentage points. Precise sampling errors for the commercial opinion poll data are difficult to calculate because some of the data are based on quota samples and others are based on random digit telephone polls. The conventional wisdom in the market research industry is that the sampling variance of individual commercial polls is in the region of plus or minus 3 percentage points. The BES campaign panel, with an average of only 150 respondents per daily sub-sample, has a sampling variability of over 5 points either side of the point estimate.
6. Various model specifications were explored, including models of the following form:
   (1) $P_{it} = f(B_{it-1})$
   (2) $dP_{it} = f(dB_{it-1})$
   (3) $P_{it} = f(P_{it-1}, B_{it-1})$
   where P_i is Support for Party i at time t; B_{it-1} is the Balance of Coverage for Party i at t-1; and d is the first difference operator.
7. The estimated coefficient for Positive Labour coverage in the Labour support equation is +.48 which represents 9 per cent of the mean Labour pre-test score of 5.40.

10 The Effects of Newspapers

On 17 March 1997, John Major, the incumbent Conservative Prime Minister, announced that the general election would be held on 1 May. The unusually long notice, six weeks, would he hoped give him time to improve his apparently hopeless position in the opinion polls. Yet his hopes of a morale-boosting lift-off were devastated within hours. The next morning, *The Sun*, Britain's best-selling national daily paper, announced that it was backing Labour. *The Sun*'s announcement was undoubtedly of symbolic significance. Its sharp, some would say cruel, attacks in the final days of the 1992 campaign on Neil Kinnock, the then Labour leader, were widely regarded as responsible for Labour's unexpected defeat (Linton 1995; McKee 1995; MacArthur 1992). Indeed, although it later tried to retract the headline, the newspaper itself famously proclaimed that it was '*The Sun* wot won it'. Certainly Labour's leadership took the power of the newspaper sufficiently seriously to devote considerable effort during the course of the 1992–7 Parliament to persuading the paper's staff and above all its proprietor, Rupert Murdoch, that New Labour was a party they could back.

The Sun's change of allegiance was simply the most dramatic of a number of changes of allegiance amongst Britain's newspapers in 1997. Although the *Daily Star* had not formally endorsed the Conservatives in 1992, their coverage was strongly pro-Conservative (Harrop and Scammell 1992); in 1997 the newspaper backed Labour. *The Independent* switched from being neutral in 1992 to backing Labour in 1997, albeit also calling for a tactical vote for the Liberal Democrats where appropriate. Meanwhile, instead of backing the Tories as they had done in 1992, *The Times* encouraged its readers to back Eurosceptic candidates of whatever partisan persuasion. Overall, during the 1997 campaign more than twice as many people were reading a newspaper that backed Labour as were reading one that supported the Conservatives. The traditional Tory advantage amongst the press was dramatically broken for the first time in post-war British politics.

Neither did the change in mood in Britain's newspapers come as a surprise. Large sections of the press which had backed John Major in 1992 but which were antagonistic to further European integration rapidly fell out of love with him in the wake of sterling's forced eviction from the

European Monetary Union in September 1992. In January 1994, *The Sun* itself argued 'What fools we all were for backing Major in 1992'. Large sections of the Conservative press called for John Major's defeat when he voluntarily called a leadership election in the summer of 1995 with the aim of ending the unrest within his party. Meanwhile, Tony Blair, who became Labour leader following John Smith's death in May 1994, won widespread admiration amongst Conservative journalists for pushing through the kinds of reform of the Labour Party that they had for years been calling for. In truth, what, if anything, was surprising about the behaviour of the British press in 1997 was not how many newspapers defected from the Conservative camp, but that there were not more. And, of course, the unprecedented if not surprising level of support for Labour amongst the national press was followed by the party's most successful election result ever, at least in terms of seats. For those commentators who believed that the Tories' traditional advantage in terms of press partisanship provided them with an unfair advantage at election time (see, for example, Linton 1995) the outcome of the 1997 election appears to be a clear vindication of their claims. Another simple case, it seems, of 'It was *The Sun* wot won it'. What it certainly provides is an important test case. Britain's highly partisan press (Dalton *et al.* 1998) has meant that it has always been worth asking the question, 'do newspapers influence votes?' (Curtice, 1997). But the difficulty in answering the question, as in other research on the impact of the media, is that any association between newspaper read and vote choice could reflect the outcome of one or other or both of two different social processes. One possibility is indeed that newspapers influence the way that people vote. The other, however, is that people choose to read a newspaper that chimes with their own views. Unfortunately, much previous writing on the alleged influence of the British press has failed to take sufficient account of this difficulty (see, for example, Dunleavy and Husbands 1985; Newton 1991).

The changed partisanship of the press in 1997, and not least the switch by *The Sun*, gives us, however, an unusually powerful opportunity to try and untangle the two processes. First, those who continued to read one of the papers that had changed its partisanship were no longer reading a message that they might be thought to have chosen to read. Rather they were reading a message that had been decided for them by their newspaper. So, if they then vote distinctively, their behaviour is more easily interpreted as evidence of the persuasive power of the press rather than of the influence of voters' partisanship on their purchasing decisions. Second, if the politics of a newspaper does influence purchasing decisions we should see a particularly marked change in the pattern of the readership of a newspaper that changes its politics. Those whose own politics are in line with the former politics of the newspaper should be more likely to stop reading that newspaper, to be replaced perhaps by new readers whose politics are more in tone with the paper's new partisanship. This is the opportunity that this study attempts to exploit.

We are able to do so thanks to the availability of two panel studies. The first is the 1992–97 British Election Panel Study (BEPS). This study contacted its respondents on eight occasions between 1992 and 1997. The first interview was conducted immediately after the 1992 election, the last after the 1997 election. The remaining interviews were undertaken once or twice a year in each of the four intervening years. Information on newspaper readership was acquired in five waves, including both the first and the last, while measures of actual voting behaviour or of intention were included on all of them. This means that we can relate respondents' vote choice not only to which newspaper they were reading in 1997 but also to their habits over the previous five years. We are also able to introduce some powerful controls for the possible impact of partisanship on newspaper read. The analyses in this chapter are primarily based on the data collected in the first and last waves, and are based on the weighted N. of 1,322 respondents who completed both those waves.

The BEPS panel enables us to look at the apparent influence of newspapers over the course of a whole Parliament. Yet it is during campaigns that newspapers tend to become more strident and explicit about their partisanship. It is also during campaigns that voters might be most expected to take notice of what their papers say. Certainly it is the perceived influence of newspapers during campaigns that has exercised some of their critics (Linton 1995). And it was only after the 1997 election was announced that *The Sun* explicitly announced its change of heart. To examine these arguments we need to look at how readers of different newspapers changed their minds over the course of the campaign. This we are able to do by using the BES campaign panel survey which first interviewed its respondents a year before the election in the spring of 1996, then contacted them twice during the campaign, and finally made one last call after polling day. The analyses in this chapter are based primarily on results from the first campaign wave and the post-election wave of interviewing, and are based on the 1,422 persons who responded to all four waves.

Our method builds upon the work of Curtice and Semetko (1994) and Curtice (1997). The former used panel data for the period between 1987 and 1992 to look at the relationship between newspaper reading habits and vote switching during that period. Between 1987 and 1992, however, no major newspaper changed its allegiance. The latter in contrast looked at the period between 1992 and 1995 during which time much of the traditionally pro-Conservative press was highly critical of the incumbent government. However, as no general election was held in 1995, Curtice (1997) was forced to rely on respondents' statements of how they would have voted in an election at that time. In this chapter we can examine actual behaviour at the 1997 election, behaviour that was decided after experiencing the mobilization effects of a campaign. Meanwhile we also undertake what to the best of knowledge is the first attempt in the political science literature in Britain at least to model the impact of voters' political preferences on their choice of newspaper.

Two important conclusions emerged from the two previous studies. First, we found that newspapers did apparently have some influence on individual voters. In particular we found that those who consistently read a pro-Labour or pro-Conservative newspaper over a considerable period of time were more likely to remain loyal to that paper than those who did not read a newspaper at all. Equally, those who stopped reading such a newspaper were more likely to defect. Exposure to the more critical tone of certain sections of the traditionally pro-Conservative press between 1992 and 1995 appeared to have an impact by denying the Conservatives their loyalty bonus rather than in rendering them more likely to defect than those who did not read a newspaper at all. However, in each case these effects were small – and they did not appear to be apparent at all over the few weeks of the 1992 campaign itself. Moreover, pro-Labour newspapers worked to Labour's advantage just as much as pro-Conservative newspapers appeared to generate a benefit for the Tories. As a result, there was little evidence that newspapers had much impact on the aggregate outcome of elections. Between 1987–92 and 1992–5 the net movement of voting preferences amongst the whole electorate was very similar to what happened amongst those who did not read a newspaper at all. Thus our second important conclusion from previous work has been that when it comes to the outcome of elections, the disposition of the press does not make much difference at all. We proceed to examine what new light the 1997 election can cast on this debate as follows. First we look at the degree of association between vote and kind of newspaper read in 1997, and examine how far readers' perceptions of papers that usually back the Conservatives matched the changed reality in 1997. We then look at the evidence that newspapers did influence votes in 1997, first by looking at vote switching during the campaign and then over the whole of the 1992–7 Parliament. Finally, we examine what evidence there is that readers' choice of newspaper is influenced by their politics.

Newspaper and Vote in 1997

Although the partisan tone of the press may have been unfamiliar in 1997, the partisan segmentation of the newspaper market retained much of its familiar structure. In Table 10.1 we look at the association between newspaper read and vote at the 1997 election. In so doing we classify newspapers not in terms of their position in 1997 but rather in terms of their position in most of the post-war period. We identify *The Sun* separately not because of its volte-face in 1997 but because it was the successor to the *Daily Herald*, a newspaper which had regularly backed Labour as indeed did *The Sun* itself until 1974. In short, even before 1997 it was the one newspaper in Britain which had a history of changing sides. Meanwhile we also distinguish between the allegedly more strident and certainly more down-market Conservative tabloid newspapers and their more upmarket quality counterparts.

Despite the Conservatives' record low vote, and despite the failure of *The Times* to give its explicit backing to the party, a half of those who read a quality Conservative newspaper still turned out and voted for John Major. Meanwhile no less than two in three readers of *The Mirror* and its Scottish stable-mate, the *Daily Record*, backed Labour. Indeed, despite the fact that Labour's share of the electorate was lower than what it had secured in 1964, its vote amongst *Mirror* readers was five points higher. The traditional partisan division amongst newspaper readers shows little sign of having abated in 1997. Moreover, we can also note that well over one in three readers of *The Sun* backed Labour while only just over one in five backed the Conservatives and nearly one in three stayed at home. This would seem to suggest that the paper's switch might have had some impact, not only in persuading people to back Labour, but also perhaps in discouraging Conservative supporters from voting at all. In short, on the evidence of the association between newspaper and vote in 1997 there seems every reason to believe that newspapers might well influence the way their readers vote.

Perceptions

Furthermore, it is clear that readers are not unaware of the partisanship of the newspapers they read, and that any switches of partisanship newspapers make are particularly likely to be noticed at an election campaign. True, as Table 10.2 shows, even readers of the three papers that remained faithful to the Conservatives in their editorial columns in 1997 were a little less likely to think that their paper favoured the Conservatives than was the case five years previously. This was especially so in the case of the *Mail* and *Express* readers. In so doing they reflected

TABLE 10.1: *Newspaper Partisanship and Vote in 1997*

	The Sun	Cons tabloid	Readers of: Labour tabloid	Cons quality	Other paper	None
	%	%	%	%	%	%
Did not vote	30	12	15	10	13	22
Conservative	22	43	6	51	14	18
Labour	37	28	67	22	44	40
Liberal Democrat	17	13	7	14	22	17
Other	4	5	5	3	7	4
	(365)	(433)	(332)	(227)	(232)	(1092)

Note: Conservative tabloid: the *Mail*, *The Express* and *Daily Star*
Labour tabloid: the *Mirror*, *Daily Record* (Scotland)
Conservative quality: *The Times*, *Daily Telegraph*.
Other: *The Guardian*, *The Independent*, the *Financial Times* plus all regional papers.

Source: BES 1997 cross-sectional study (electorate sample).

TABLE 10.2: *Perceived Partisanship of Newspapers, 1992–97*

| | % readers believing newspaper favoured the Conservatives | | | | |
	1992	1994	1995	1996	1997
Argued for Con vote in 1997					
The Express	89	82	78	80	70 (75)
Mail	89	76	72	65	72 (116)
Daily Telegraph	82	88	80	83	78 (82)
Did not argue for Con vote 1997					
Daily Star	49	34	28	16	15 (18)
The Sun	83	58	51	58	3 (148)
The Times	66	70	45	54	37 (26)

Note: Figures in brackets show minimum N. on which statistics in that row are based.

Source: British Election Panel Study 1992–7.

the fact that even these newspapers on balance gave the Conservatives less favourable coverage than they had done in the 1992 campaign (see Chapter 2). But perceptions of the three newspapers that backed the Conservatives in 1992 but failed to do so in 1997 changed much more markedly. Most dramatic of all was the change in perceptions of *The Sun*; only one in 33 *Sun* readers felt that their paper favoured the Conservatives in 1997 compared with over four in five in 1992. Indeed, this pattern contrasts sharply with what happened when *The Sun* originally switched its backing to the Conservatives in 1974; long after that event many of its readers still felt the paper backed Labour. But there were sharp drops also amongst readers of the *Daily Star* and *The Times* in the proportion believing that their paper backed the Conservatives even though neither set of readers had ever been as convinced of their party's support for the Conservatives as had been readers of *The Sun*. Indeed, the *Daily Star* did not formally endorse the Conservatives in its editorial column in 1992, though its coverage was in fact broadly favourable to the Conservatives (Harrop and Scammell 1992).

Perceptions of the papers which failed to back the Conservatives in 1997 did not suddenly change during the campaign. Even by 1995 when press criticism of John Major in particular was at its height, there was a 20-point drop in the proportion of *Star* and *Times* readers who felt that their paper favoured the Conservatives, while there was an even larger fall amongst *Sun* readers. But we can see that in the case of *The Sun* and *The Times* at least, the behaviour of the newspaper in the final twelve months of the Parliament had a clear impact on their readers. While we cannot be sure that this change was the result of the newspapers' campaign coverage rather than what it printed in the months immediately before the campaign, it does seems likely that *The Sun*'s dramatic announcement at the beginning of the campaign of its support for Labour was noticed by many of its readers. But the key question, of course, is whether some of them at least also followed their newspaper's advice when they entered the polling station.

Newspaper Readership and Vote Switching during the 1997 Campaign

The ideal survey for answering that question would be one that had interviewed respondents just before the campaign started and *The Sun* made its switch. Although the BES campaign panel survey did interview its respondents before polling day, that interview took place as much as twelve months before the campaign started. Any patterns that we might identify could be the product of what happened before the campaign rather than the campaign itself. The survey did, however, contact it respondents in the first fortnight of April 1997, when the campaign began to get into full swing after the Easter holiday at the beginning of the month. Respondents were asked on that occasion both which newspaper they had read the previous day and a number of questions about their vote intentions. By comparing these reports with voters' accounts in the final wave of the survey of how they actually voted we can therefore see whether those who actually reported reading *The Sun* or any other newspaper were more likely than other voters to switch towards Labour during the most intense part of the campaign. True, some of those who might have been influenced by *The Sun*'s announcement might have already switched their vote before the first interview, but our analysis covers the period when voters are most likely to be attuned to their newspaper's election coverage, encompasses the period when most newspapers formally declared their position, and the time when uncertain voters were making up their minds.

A simple summary of some of the relevant data is provided in Table 10.3. In this table we compare, for each group of newspaper readers, the level of Conservative and Labour support on polling day with the equivalent levels in early April when respondents were asked whether they had decided which way they were going to vote, and if so for whom. Two features of this comparison should be noted. First we include in the comparison both those who said they did not vote on polling day and those who said they had not decided how they had voted. Second,

TABLE 10.3: *Change in Conservative and Labour Support During 1997 Campaign by Readership*

	% Voted – % Saying Had Decided to Vote Early April		
	Con	Lab	
Paper read:			
Tory faithful	+12	+7	(221)
The Sun	+3	+2	(139)
Other ex-Tory	+3	+5	(68)
Labour faithful	+0	+8	(166)
Other	+5	+4	(64)
None	+5	+7	(723)

Note: Paper read yesterday, early April 1997.

Source: British Election Campaign Study 1997.

although many of those who said in early April that they had not decided how they would vote were, after further questioning, able to indicate the party that they thought they were most likely to vote for, no account has been taken of their answers. Our rationale for both decisions is that the impact of newspapers may lie in mobilizing voters to turn out and support a party to which they are already mildly inclined rather than in persuading them to vote for a different party. In any event the modelling we undertook in which account was taken of likely vote intentions produced largely similar results to those reported here. Our categorization of the various newspapers also demands some explanation. We have divided those who reported reading a newspaper yesterday in the first wave of the study into five groups:

- The 'Tory faithful' are readers of the three newspapers that continued to back the Conservatives in 1997: the *Mail*, the *Express*, and the *Daily Telegraph*.
- *The Sun* comprises readers of that newspaper alone.
- 'Other ex-Tory' comprises readers of either the *Daily Star* or *The Times*.
- 'The Labour faithful' are readers of the *Mirror* (*Daily Record* in Scotland) and *The Guardian*.
- 'Other' comprises readers of *The Independent*, the *Financial Times* and any other regional newspaper.

We have separated *Sun* readers simply because of the particular interest in the persuasive power of this newspaper. Meanwhile, although *The Independent* and the *Financial Times* both formally backed Labour, their news coverage was less likely to be perceived as favourable to Labour; no less than three-quarters of *Independent* readers said that their paper did not favour any party.

It should also be noted that just over a half of respondents reported not reading a newspaper yesterday. Clearly we may well have excluded from our categories of newspaper readers respondents who did in fact see one or more newspapers on a fairly regular basis during the campaign. Others might be misclassified in that the newspaper they read the day before they were interviewed was not typical of their reading during the campaign. However, despite these concerns no less than four in five respondents gave the same answer to this question when they were asked the same question in the second campaign wave a fortnight later. Moreover, this figure held true for non-readers as well as readers. Despite these caveats, there are some clear findings in Table 10.3. We should note first that both parties secured a higher share of the actual vote than they did of vote intentions a fortnight earlier even though we have included non-voters in our denominator. This reflects the fact that no less than two in five of our respondents said that they had not decided for whom they would vote when they were first interviewed during the campaign while, in contrast, only one in six said they did not vote on polling day. But it will be noted that, overall, Labour was no more successful at gathering votes during the campaign itself than were the Conservatives. Indeed, in line with the trend in the opinion polls, Labour's lead amongst those who did have a vote intention fell by four percentage points in our panel over the course of the campaign (see Chapter 11). If Labour's achievement in winning over newspapers during the campaign was meant to bring the party a bonus, in the event evidence for its appearance was strangely lacking. Of course, the difficulty with such statements is that we do not know how well or badly Labour would have done if its media coverage had been less favourable. However, if we compare what happened amongst readers of different kinds of newspaper we do have some counterfactual evidence upon which to rest claims about the influence or otherwise of newspapers. And we can see that there are some differences between the various newspaper groups in Table 10.3. Most striking is the fact that Conservative support rose by 12 points amongst readers of the Tory faithful press but not at all amongst readers of the equivalent Labour press. And while Labour was not particularly successful at winning over votes amongst *Sun* readers, such readers together with readers of other ex-Tory newspapers were not particularly likely to return to the Tory fold either.

In short, we do appear to have here some evidence that which newspaper people read did make some difference to the likelihood that they would decide during the course of the campaign to opt for one party rather than another. But there are, of course, some important limitations to this analysis. Not only have we not examined whether any of our differences are statistically significant, but we also have to bear in mind the possibility of floor and ceiling effects in our measures of changes in party support. For example, with no less than 58 per cent of readers of Labour-faithful papers having already decided to back Labour by early April, and with just 23 per cent unsure about what they would do, the scope for further increases in Labour support in this group was less than it was, for example, amongst those who were not reading a newspaper, only 30 per cent of whom backed Labour and 43 per cent of whom were undecided.

To overcome these limitations we can undertake a logistic regression of how party support developed in 1997. The results are shown in Table 10.4. Using logistic regression also enables us to use a more refined measure of changes in party support than utilized in Table 10.3. Apart from being asked whether they had decided how they would vote, and if so for whom, respondents were also asked in early April to give each party a mark out of ten to indicate the chances that they would vote for that party in the election. Instead of assuming that all voters either definitely had or had not decided to vote for a particular party at the beginning of April, we can treat them as though they are somewhere along a continuum from having definitely decided to vote for a particular party to having decided not to vote for that party at all. Thus in our logistic regression we introduce as our first independent variable the relevant mark out of ten rather than whether or not the respondent had decided to vote for that party. We undertake both an analysis of voting Conservative versus not voting Conservative (including abstention) and a parallel analysis of voting Labour versus not voting Labour. In each case the first independent variable is the mark for that particular party. Our substantive interest, however, is in our second variable, that is the newspaper group to which our respondent belonged. Note that in each case the coefficient shows the estimated difference between the behaviour of the newspaper group in question and the behaviour of those who said they did not read a newspaper yesterday. Our assumption in so doing is that the latter group was not influenced by the partisanship of any particular newspaper and thus the difference between their behaviour and that of any other newspaper group gives us an indication of the persuasive power or otherwise of that kind of newspaper. Note, however, that on occasions our discussion will also make reference to other relevant comparisons that can be made between the groups.

Our results are relatively straightforward. As we might have expected from Table 10.3, we find that readers of a Tory-faithful paper were significantly more likely to decide during the campaign to opt for the Conservatives while readers of a Labour-faithful paper were less likely to do so. Meanwhile, as we suspected might be the case once we take into account floor and ceiling effects, the rise in Labour support amongst readers of the Labour-faithful papers was rather greater than we might have anticipated. In short we once again appear to have evidence that at the margins at least newspapers can help shore up the loyalty of their readers to the party the newspaper favours. Indeed, the evidence for that being true over an election campaign rather than over the longer period of a Parliament is in fact on this evidence much stronger in the 1997 campaign than it was in 1992 (Curtice and Semetko 1994). At the same

TABLE 10.4: *Logistic Model of Vote Switching in 1997 Campaign by Readership*

	Con v. non-Con		Lab v. non-Lab	
	\multicolumn{4}{c}{Dependent Variable Vote 1997}			
Probability of voting Con	+.63	(.04)		
Probability of voting Lab			− +.51	(.03)
Newspaper read:				
Tory faithful	+.80	(.27)*	−.39	(.25)
The Sun	−.12	(.37)	−.04	(.28)
Other ex-Tory	+.09	(.48)	−.08	(.05)
Labour faithful	−1.24	(.59)*	+.86	(.25)*
Other	+.93	(.58)	−.45	(.36)

Note: Main entries are logistic parameter coefficients. In the case of newspaper read they are contrast coefficients which show the difference between the behaviour of the relevant group and those who reported not reading a newspaper. Entries in brackets are standard errors. * coefficient is significant at the 5 per cent level or less. The period is in early April 1997.

Source: British Election Campaign Study 1997.

time, however, we find little evidence that the defection of *The Sun* or any other ex-Tory newspaper had much impact on their readers, who behaved little differently from those who did not read a newspaper at all. Over the relatively short period of a campaign, at least, it seems that newspapers trumpeting a relatively new tune are unlikely to receive an echo from their readers. *The Sun*'s defection may have been of symbolic significance, but whether it was of any practical significance seems open to doubt. There is, however, one important caveat to this argument. For we might ask ourselves what might have happened amongst their readers during the campaign if *The Sun* and the other ex-Tory papers had in fact decided to continue to back the Conservatives. On the evidence of Table 10.4 it might be suggested that they would have been more likely to have switched to the Conservatives just as the readers of the Tory-faithful press did. Labour may not have gained any advantage for themselves in winning over *The Sun*, but they may well have helped neutralize what otherwise would have been a benefit for the Conservatives.

Newspaper Readership and Vote Switching between 1992 and 1997

Of course, one argument against what we have done so far is that no matter how intense an election campaign might be, in the British context at least it is simply too short a period in which to anticipate much in the way of evidence of media influence. It is not the few dramatic headlines or pictures that might be produced during a campaign that matter, but rather the constant and consistent diet of partisan-coloured news that readers might receive over months or even years. If so, no sudden switch of partisanship can be expected to make a difference. In practice, as we have already noted, none of the newspapers that failed to back the Conservatives in 1997 after having done so in 1992 underwent a sudden conversion. The tone of their coverage over much of the previous Parliament had been unfavourable to the Conservatives too. So perhaps we might see clearer evidence of newspaper influence if we look at vote switching across the whole of the 1992–7 Parliament. This we can do by looking at the evidence of the 1992–7 British Election Panel Study. This approach, however, poses its own particular analytic challenges. If we wish to examine the impact of regular and prolonged exposure to the message of a newspaper we need to be sure that those we classify as a reader of a newspaper did see the paper regularly and did not simply pick up yesterday's paper by accident. Fortunately, in BEPS respondents were asked whether they read a newspaper regularly. Meanwhile, we have to remember that over a five-year period, some people might decide to change the kind of newspaper they read, or might start or stop being regular readers. Indeed, if we classify newspapers into the same groups that we used in the previous section, then we find that no less than 38 per cent of BEPS respondents reported reading a different kind of paper in 1997 (including moving into or out of not reading a paper) than the one they were reading in 1992. We thus have to refine our categorization of newspaper readers to incorporate those who changed the kind of newspaper they read. We developed the following categories:

- **Constant Tory.** Respondents reading any of the *Mail*, the *Express*, or the *Daily Telegraph* in both 1992 and 1997.
- **Constant *Sun*.** Respondents reading *The Sun* in both 1992 and 1997.
- **Constant ex-Tory.** Respondents reading either of the *Daily Star* or *The Times* in both 1992 and 1997.
- **Constant Labour.** Respondents reading either of *The Mirror/Daily Record* or *The Guardian* in both 1992 and 1997.
- **New constant Tory.** Respondents who were reading any of the *Mail*, *The Express* or the *Daily Telegraph* in 1997 but not in 1992. (Note that some of these respondents may have been reading a pro-Tory newspaper in 1992 in the form of *The Sun*, the *Daily Star* or *The Times*.)
- **New *Sun*/ex-Tory.** Respondents who were reading any of *The Sun*, the *Daily Star* or *The Times* in 1997 and were not reading any of those papers in 1992.
- **New Labour.** Respondents who were reading *The Mirror/Daily Record* or *The Guardian* in 1997 but were not doing so in 1992.
- **Ex-any Tory.** Respondents who were reading any of the *Mail*, *The Express*, the *Daily Telegraph*, *The Sun*, the *Daily Star* or *The Times* in 1992 and who in 1997 either said they were not reading a paper regularly or else were reading one of the Other papers, that is *The Independent*, the *Financial Times* or a regional paper.
- **Ex-Labour.** Respondents who were reading either *The Mirror/Daily Record* or *The Guardian* in 1992 and who in 1997 either said they were not reading a paper regularly or else were reading one of the Other papers.
- **Constant None.** Respondents who in 1992 were either not reading a

TABLE 10.5: *Change in Conservative and Labour Support by Readership, 1992–97*

| | % voted 1997 – % voted 1992 | | |
	Con	Lab	
Readership history:			
Constant Tory	−18	+5	(206)
Constant *Sun*	−19	+11	(96)
Constant ex-Tory	−19	−4	(28)
Constant Labour	− 2	+7	(158)
New constant Tory	−14	+10	(110)
New *Sun*/ex-Tory	−13	+7	(83)
New Labour	−3	+19	(58)
Ex-any Tory	−19	+4	(102)
Ex-Labour	−7	+2	(48)
Constant None	−13	+12	(325)

Source: British Election Panel Study 1992–7.

newspaper regularly or were reading an Other paper (including here *Today* which closed in 1995; although it formally backed the Conservatives in 1992, its coverage was not particularly favourable to the party) and who in 1997 were also either not reading a newspaper regularly or were reading an Other paper.

It should be noted that this classification does not cover all possible movements, though it does include all those where there might be reason to believe that the pattern of vote switching between 1992 and 1997 could have been distinctive. In total 7 per cent of respondents are not classified. In Table 10.5 we show the change in levels of Conservative and Labour support recorded between 1992 and 1997 in each of our newspaper groups. Following our earlier logic and our practice at Table 10.3, those who did not vote are included in the denominator on which these calculations are based. Despite the fact that we are looking at a much longer time period, many of the results do not immediately suggest that the partisanship of newspapers influenced their readers. Support for the Conservatives might have dropped more amongst *Sun* readers than those consistently not exposed to a partisan newspaper, but the same is also true of those consistently reading a Tory-faithful newspaper. And support amongst the latter fell as much as it did amongst those who stopped reading a pro-Conservative newspaper. Meanwhile, Labour's gains amongst *Sun* readers are no greater than they were amongst those consistently not reading a partisan paper.

But some results are consistent with the expectations we would have if the partisanship of newspapers matters. Labour's support rose most amongst those who started to read a Labour-faithful newspaper between 1992 and 1997, while its support barely rose amongst those who stopped reading such a newspaper. *The Sun* may not have made much difference to Labour's apparent support, but *The Mirror* evidently could (see also Curtice and Semetko 1994; Curtice 1997). Equally Labour does not do well amongst those who consistently read a Tory-faithful paper. In any event, given the limitations of the sizes of some of our groups, and the possibility once more of floor and ceiling effects, we should turn once again to a logistic regression. The logic of our regression, shown in Table 10.6, is similar to that in Table 10.4. Thus we run two models, one in which the dependent variable is voted Conservative in 1997 versus did not do so, and one in which it is voted Labour in 1997 versus did not do so. In calculating coefficients for each newspaper group we show the estimated difference between the behaviour of the newspaper group in question and that of those respondents who consistently reported not reading a partisan newspaper (whom it is assumed were not directly exposed to the influence of the partisan press). On this occasion, however, we include as our other independent variables, how the respondent voted in 1992 and, separately, their feeling towards the Conservative (or in the case of the Labour equation, the Labour Party) in 1992. The first of these means that in contrast to Table 10.4 our model here is one of actual vote switching rather than of movement between intentions and switching. The second variable is measured on a five-point scale from strongly in favour to strongly opposed. Its presence helps control for the possibility that those inclined, say, both to stop voting Conservative and stop reading a Conservative newspaper were in fact already less likely to be strongly attached to that party in 1992. To simplify the table, however, the results for these two control variables are not shown.

We do indeed find here some support for the claim that newspapers influence votes. And it is a pattern that is consistent with the results we obtained in respect of the campaign itself in Table 10.4. We find that those who consistently read a Tory-faithful newspaper were both less likely to defect from the Conservatives or switch to Labour (and the term for the Constant Labour group in the Labour equation is also almost significantly positive). Meanwhile, as we anticipated from inspection of Table 10.5, those who started reading a traditionally pro-Labour newspaper were more likely to switch their support to Labour. Yet in truth the support for the proposition is also rather sparse, just as we previously found it to be over the 1992–5 period. And most importantly, we find neither significant nor consistent evidence that any of the papers that switched their support away from the Conservatives brought their readers with them. All that can be said, as we noted earlier, is that *The Sun*'s defection meant the newspaper did not help to keep its Conservative supporters loyal. The difference between the Constant Conservative and Constant *Sun* coefficients is clearly significant in both equations. But even here the same cannot be said of the *Daily Star* or *The Times* for whose constant readers

TABLE 10.6: *Logistic Regression of Party Support, 1992–97*

	Con v. non-Con		Lab v. non-Lab	
Readership history:				
Constant Tory	+.51	(.23)*	−.74	(.28)*
Constant *Sun*	−.62	(.35)	+.45	(.30)
Constant ex-Tory	+.44	(.54)	−1.16	(.61)
Constant Labour	−.31	(.48)	+.50	(.27)
New constant Tory	+.51	(.31)	−.23	(.30)
New *Sun*/ex-Tory	+.41	(.35)	−.11	(.33)
New Labour	+.16	(.52)	+.94	(.38)*
Ex-any Tory	−.01	(.30)	−.53	(.32)
Ex-Labour	+.14	(.60)	−.54	(.40)

Table header spanning: Dependent Variable / Vote 1997

Note: Main entries are logistic parameter coefficients. They show the difference between the behaviour of the relevant group and those who consistently reported not reading a paper. Model also includes controls for respondent's 1992 vote and how they felt about the Conservatives in 1992 for which results are not shown. Entries in brackets are standard errors. * coefficient is significant at the 5 per cent level or less.

Source: British Election Panel Study 1992–7.

the coefficient in Table 10.6 is similar to that for Constant Conservative readers.

Politics and Newspaper Switching 1992–1997

So, if the partisanship of newspapers has only a marginal impact on readers' voting behaviour, and cannot be held responsible for the outcome of the 1997 election, why might this be so? One possibility, of course, is that voters choose newspapers so that the political message they receive chimes in with their dispositions. True, as we have already seen, patterns of newspaper readership may be relatively stable over the short period of an election campaign, but we have also seen that in the five years between 1992 and 1997, well over one in three of the respondents to BEPS changed the newspaper they read. But what evidence is there that their politics might have influenced their decision?

One way in which we can investigate this is to model using logistic regression the kind of newspaper the respondent read in 1997 in much the same way that we analysed vote in 1997. Thus in Table 10.7 we show the results of two analyses. In the first the dependent variable is whether or not the respondent was regularly reading in 1997 a newspaper that supported the Conservatives at that election, that is any of the *Mail*, *The Express* or the *Daily Telegraph*. In the second our focus of attention is whether the respondent was reading a Labour newspaper, that is any of *The Mirror/Daily Record*, *The Guardian*, *The Sun* or the *Daily Star*. So that our analysis is one of changing reading habits, we introduce as our first dependent variable the kind of newspaper the respondent was reading in 1992. Here our categorization is the same as in Table 10.3, except that readers of the *Daily Star* are grouped with readers of *The Sun* as both papers backed Labour in 1997, leaving readers of *The Times*, which failed to back any party, in a group of their own. Also included in our model (but results not shown as the association proved to be insignificant) is a variable measuring whether the respondent's household income had risen or fallen between 1992 and 1997. This was to account for the possibility that changes in their purchasing power resulted in respondents deciding to start or stop reading a newspaper at all. Our model then includes two further variables which are the ones of central interest to us here. The first is the five-point scale on whether in 1992 respondents were in favour or against the Conservative Party (in the Conservative paper model), or the Labour Party (in the Labour model), that we first came across in Table 10.6. If people's political predispositions influence their decisions to switch newspaper, we should expect to find a significant positive coefficient for this variable. In other words, for example, we are anticipating that people who were favourably disposed towards the Conservatives in 1992 were more likely to switch to a pro-Conservative newspaper in 1997 if they did not already read one. Note that we are using here a measure obtained in 1992 before any of our respondents made any decisions to switch newspaper. We thus avoid any danger that our measure of feeling towards the parties might be a consequence of any change in their newspaper-reading habits rather than a cause. The period between 1992 and 1997 was one which saw a dramatic shift in the fortunes of the Conservative and Labour parties. We might thus anticipate that one reason why people wanted to change the kind of newspaper they read was because they were looking for a paper that was more in tune with their current political views. Indeed, it has been widely argued that one reason why *The Sun* changed its political position was to ensure that it did not lose the custom of its increasingly pro-Labour readers (Seymour-Ure 1997). We have therefore also included in our model the difference between how the respondent felt towards the Conservative (in the Labour model, Labour) Party in 1994 and how they felt in 1992. This choice of date was dictated by the fact that much of the change in party fortunes had occurred by then, while in contrast with a measure based on 1997 and 1992 it was less likely that any association we might discover was a consequence of any change in newspaper-reading habits rather than a cause.

The results partly confirm our expectations. Those who were less favourably disposed towards the Conservative Party in 1992 were less likely to switch to a Conservative paper between 1992 and 1997. Equally, those who were less favourably disposed towards Labour in 1992 were less likely to take up the habit of reading a pro-Labour paper. However, in neither model were changes in respondents' feelings towards the relevant party between 1992 and 1994 statistically significant. In short, it would seem from this evidence that voters' choice of paper may well be influenced by long-held political affinities, but not by relatively recent

TABLE 10.7: *Logistic Regression of Newspaper Buying, 1992–97*

	Con v. non-Con		Lab v. non-Lab	
	Dependent Variable Read in 1997 Paper Backing			
Newspaper read in 1992:				
Tory faithful	+3.05	(.23)*	–.46	(.33)
Sun/Star	–.40	(.39)	+3.11	(.26)*
The Times	+1.04	(.61)	–4.90	(9.02)
Labour faithful	+.30	(.32)	+2.61	(.23)*
Other	+.98	(.29)*	–.12	(.35)
Feeling towards				
Con/Lab 1992	+.33	(.08)*	+.41	(.08)*
Change in feeling towards				
Con/Lab 1992–1994	+.11	(.10)	+.11	(.12)

Notes: Main entries are logistic parameter coefficients. In the case of newspaper read in 1992 they are contrast coefficients which show the difference between the behaviour of the relevant group and those who reported not reading a newspaper. Entries in brackets are standard errors. * coefficient is significant at the 5 per cent level or less.

Source: British Election Panel Study 1992–7.

changes of attitude. This indeed can be seen very clearly if we look at the behaviour of those who changed their vote between 1992 and 1997. For example, of those who voted for the Conservatives in 1992 but not in 1997, the proportion saying that they read one of the Tory-faithful newspapers in 1997 (30 per cent) was virtually unchanged from what had been the case in 1992 (31 per cent). This calculation is based on 218 respondents. People who changed their voting preference between 1992 and 1997 largely did not change their reading habits as well. Nor, incidentally, did those who did not change their voting preferences. The proportion of those who voted Conservative in 1992 and in 1997 who were reading a Tory-faithful paper in 1997 was at 42 per cent exactly the same as it was in 1992. Evidently, for example, these voters were not particularly inclined to switch to these papers from those papers which no longer backed their party's cause. This finding suggests that there are limits to the extent to which it makes sense for a newspaper to move its political position in line with the latest tide of political opinion. Not, however, that it is the case that *The Sun*'s change of position did not have any discernible effect at all on who decided to read the newspaper. To demonstrate this we analysed separately, first, readers of the Tory-faithful press in 1992 and, second, readers of *The Sun* or the *Daily Star*, in order to establish whether there was any difference in the pattern of who continued to read the two sets of newspapers in 1997. In neither model was it the case that a variable which identified whether the respondent had or had not changed their voting behaviour was significant. But the same was not true of a variable which identified whether or not the respondent thought that the paper they read favoured the Conservatives in 1992. In the case of the Tory-faithful papers those who regarded their paper as a pro-Conservative paper were significantly more likely to be buying a Tory-faithful paper in 1997 than were those who did not regard their paper as Conservative. The same was not true of *Sun* or *Daily Star* readers. It looks likely that those readers who were expecting a Conservative read concluded that they had less reason to remain loyal to *The Sun* or the *Daily Star* than had readers of the Tory-faithful press.

Conclusion

The 1997 election provided a clear opportunity for the power of the press, and of Britain's top-selling newspaper in particular, to reveal itself. In practice on the evidence of this chapter it still tended to prefer to remain in hiding. *The Sun*'s conversion did not evidently bring the Labour Party new recruits. Equally Labour's new recruits did not prove particularly keen to switch to *The Sun*. At best we have found, in line with our previous research, that newspapers have but a limited influence on the voting behaviour of their readers. Where they can make a difference is in mobilizing their more faithful readers by playing them a familiar tune, readers who indeed may well have chosen that paper precisely because it plays a tune they have long considered an old favourite. Like social class, the partisanship of British newspapers is clearly part of the structure of British voting behaviour, but whether they can explain the flux is very much open to doubt.

11 Conclusions: The Impact of Political Communications

In this chapter we first consider the debate about the overall impact of the 1997 campaign and the evidence for electoral volatility, to see whether the result was preordained years before or whether there was the potential for political communications to influence voting behaviour. We go on to summarize the main conclusions of this book about the effects of party strategy and the impact of television and the press. In the final section we consider the implications of the results for understanding the power of the news media, for the conventions covering election broadcasting, and for parties seeking to adopt the techniques of strategic communications in a mediated democracy.

Do Campaigns Matter?

The orthodox view in the Columbia and Michigan models suggests that campaigns usually have only a minimal effect, at most, on changing party fortunes. Scholars regard most elections as routine rituals, especially where contending parties are evenly balanced and few unexpected hiccups lead voters to reconsider their preferences. In this view campaigns reinforce and consolidate, but rarely alter, voting choices, so most can be understood to function as primarily symbolic events. The counting of votes, the distribution of seats, and the outcome for government certainly matters, but the campaign proper may involve everyone going through their well-rehearsed paces. As David Butler (1989: 3) expressed this view:

> The campaign may to some extent be a ritual dance, a three-week repetition of well-aired themes, making no substantial net difference to the outcome. British elections are usually won over the long-haul. A very large proportion of people vote out of team loyalty, supporting the party that they – and their parents too – have always supported; those who change their minds are usually converted, not during the final three weeks, but over months and years because of an accumulated impression, positive or negative, of the values and the performance of rival parties.

Certainly there are exceptions to this pattern but many observers feel that the 1997 British general election ran true to form so that neither political communication during the 'long' campaign in the year before polling day, nor the six-week official election campaign, made any significant difference to changing the outcome. As Anthony King summarized this argument:

> All the evidence suggests that the campaign was largely irrelevant. . . . Labour would probably have won an election at any time from the late summer of 1994 onwards; it would certainly have won one at any time in early 1997, even if there had been no campaign at all. . . . The politicians, as they always do on these occasions, puffed, panted, and rushed about the country. They stretched every sinew and strained every nerve. They gave interviews, they gave speeches, they gave their all. . . . The public, for whose benefit all these entertainments were laid on, remained almost completely inert. Scarcely a cough or sneeze could be heard from the pit. (King 1997)

Butler and Kavanagh concurred that despite all the intense effort and resources which parties poured into electioneering, despite all the coverage in the popular press, Blair's victory was utterly predictable:

> It is doubtful whether the Conservatives could have done much in the campaign to alter the final result. . . . The 1997 campaign will be looked back upon as one that neither changed the outcome of the election nor contained any memorable events, but it will be remembered as one where the techniques of controlled electioneering took a quantum leap forward. (Butler and Kavanagh 1997: 230, 243)

All the sound and fury of electioneering, if not signifying nothing, at least seemed to signify not very much at all after the event. This suggests that if all politicians had chosen to take their 'fact-finding' trips in Tuscany and Trinidad in April, if the press had decided to focus on nothing but the younger Royals, the Teletubbies and the Spice Girls, the public would have heaved a huge sigh of relief and Blair would still have emerged triumphant in Number 10.

Yet in contrast party managers, advertising consultants and market researchers within each party believed that the campaign was a vital component in Blair's 1997 victory. Philip Gould, pollster at the heart of Millbank Tower, argued that Labour's message conveyed in the last few days of the 1997 campaign was crucial:

> Almost until the last, the voters were nervous. The strike-ridden Winter of Discontent of 1978 and fear of old Labour were still haunting them. And then it happened. On the final Sunday before polling day, a group of women said, with one voice: that is it, I have talked to my friends and they are going to vote Labour, and I am going to vote Labour too. In the last weekend, the nation decided: hope would defeat fear. (Gould 1998: 11)

Liberal Democrats thought that the campaign contributed towards their best share of seats for seventy years:

> The ability of the Liberal Democrats to stay with our agenda, or stay on message, enabled us to differentiate ourselves from other political parties. We

offered a different style, a different approach and a more relevant agenda. This was rewarded with voter confidence. (Holmes and Holmes 1998: 26)

And the Conservatives also blamed their dire failure, at least in part, on the campaign. For Danny Finkelstein, director of the Conservative Party Research Department, the Conservatives lost because they failed to communicate a more positive image: 'Rightly or wrongly, they (the voters) saw us as arrogant, smug, sleazy, weak, incompetent and divided' (Finkelstein 1998: 13). Another Conservative strategist agreed: 'We had no message, at least not one that the voters listened to, Labour did' (quoted in Butler and Kavanagh 1997: 239). Practitioners and scholars therefore seem to disagree in their view of events.

Which interpretation is correct? In discounting the effects of campaigning, scholars reflect a long theoretical tradition, outlined in the introduction to the book. But it seems puzzling in the 1997 campaign that all politicians should have been so wrongheaded, all advertising consultants, pollsters and market researchers so wasteful of their time and energies, all journalists and broadcasters so mistaken in their news values. Perhaps instead of spending £56.4 million on the national campaign the major parties should more wisely have directly donated £1 to each person in Britain.

In line with more recent studies (Gelman and King 1993; Holbrook 1996) we argue that the truth lies somewhere between exaggerated notions that political communications are either decisive or irrelevant. The journalistic view, reflecting deeply rooted news values, often over-emphasizes the importance of specific events during the official campaign. News headlines splashed about the Piers Merchant 'affair', the Bell v. Hamilton battle in Tatton, or the threat from James Goldsmith's Referendum Party, made these events appear brighter, sharper and more dramatic than they probably deserve with the benefit of hindsight. Given the size of Labour's steady lead in the opinion polls since September 1992, and the size of the eventual landslide in seats, we accept that Blair's victory did not hinge decisively on the period of either the *long* campaign, defined as the twelve months before polling day, or the *short* official campaign, defined as the period from mid-March to 1 May 1997. If we can imagine a reversed situation, with Blair fighting Major's campaign, and Major fighting Blair's, it is arguable that Labour would still have won.

Nevertheless, if scholars believe that all the intense activity surrounding political communications does not matter, then they may have been looking for the wrong sort of effects. The first issue we need to consider is whether the election result was 'cast in stone', or whether evidence suggests that there was at least the potential for campaign communications to sway voters. On this basis we can go on to summarize our findings about the role of political communications in this process.

Evidence of Electoral Change

We can start by recapping the results of the election, summarizing the total net flow of the vote from 1992 to 1997, and then consider how far the long and short election campaigns contributed towards this outcome. As shown in Table 11.1 the results were historic by most criteria, primarily in terms of the massive landslide producing the 179-seat Labour majority. The Conservatives lost one-quarter of their vote, dropping to 30.7 per cent, their worst result since early Victorian Britain. Labour boosted their share of the vote to 43.3 per cent, a substantial gain of 8.9 per cent. This was clearly a solid improvement for Labour, their best result since 1970, although lower than their usual performance in the 1950s and 1960s. And the number of Liberal Democrat MPs more than doubled, to 46, although this was because of a more efficient distribution of support since their share of the vote subsided slightly, to 16.8 per cent. Across the whole country there was a massive 10.3 per cent (Butler) swing from the Conservatives to Labour, the highest any party had experienced since 1945. Moreover, this built on a series of earlier gains in elections since 1983, when a deeply divided and left-wing Labour Party reached its nadir of support. In a series of steps, the swing towards Labour was 1.7 per cent in 1987, and 2.1 per cent in 1992. In this sense, 1997 was 'one more heave'. The Con–Lab swing in this election was far greater than that achieved by Harold Wilson when he came to power in 1964 (3.0 per cent), by Edward Heath in 1970 (4.7 per cent), or even by Margaret Thatcher in 1979 (5.2 per cent). Therefore there were few doubts about the record levels of aggregate electoral volatility from 1992 to 1997.

Changes in Voting Intentions during the Campaign

But how much did party support change during the long (twelve-month) and short (six-week) campaign? We use the 1997 BES campaign panel for respondents in all waves of the survey (ABCD), broken down by week of the official campaign, measuring voting intentions with the following item:

TABLE 11.1: *Change in the Share of the UK Vote, 1992–97*

| | Percentage UK | | | | |
	1992 UK	1997 UK	Change UK	1997 GB	St. Dev of GB Mean
Con	41.9	30.7	–11.2	31.4	12.2
Lab	34.4	43.3	8.9	44.4	17.9
Lib Dem	17.8	16.8	–1.0	17.2	10.9
SNP	1.8	2.0	.2	2.0	7.6
PC	.5	.5	.0	.5	4.2
Other	3.5	6.8	3.3	4.4	3.7
Turnout	77.7	71.5	–6.2	71.6	5.56
Butler Swing				–10.3	

Source: Evans and Norris (1999).

If you were to vote, have you decided yet which party you will vote for, or
have you not decided yet?'

(a) [If 'yes, has decided'] 'Which Party is that?'
(b) [If 'no, has not decided'] 'Which party is most likely to get your vote?'

The response to the first part of this question shows widespread uncertainty and hesitancy during the official campaign: in the first two weeks
of April 1997 (Wave B) over one-third (37 per cent) of the electorate
reported that they had not yet decided how they would cast their ballot.
This proportion fell to just over a quarter (28 per cent) in the last week
of the campaign, as voting decisions crystallized, but this still represented
many millions of self-reported uncertain voters as polling day fast
approached. At least in the minds of the electorate, this hardly seems to
represent an outcome which had been preordained for years.

Table 11.2 summarizes the overall changes in party support during the
long and short campaigns (May 1996 to May 1997) as a proportion of
decided voters. The results suggest that in terms of votes the clear winners
of the campaign were the Liberal Democrats, whose support climbed
sharply in the last week before polling day. Over the long campaign the
Liberal Democrats rose by six percentage points, from 13 to 19 per cent.
In contrast to the conventional wisdom, during the long campaign voting
support for Labour fell by eight points, from 54 per cent to 46 per cent,
with the main drop occurring during the last week. Despite all the criticism
of the Conservative campaign, their support remained fairly stable in the
year running up to polling day, as did voting intentions for other parties.
If the proof of success is judged by votes gained, in the light of these
results we need to question the conventional view that Labour ran the
most effective campaign. True, the campaign probably did not decide the
outcome, given Labour's early lead, but this evidence suggests it still
mattered for levels of party support.

Since this conclusion runs counter to popular wisdom we explored
whether this result was a product of sampling or measurement error in
the BES campaign panel or whether there were similar estimates available
in other evidence. Although the exact period of comparison is slightly

TABLE 11.2: *Changes in Voting Intentions during the Long and Short Campaigns, 1996–97*

	Wave A	Wave B Week B1	Wave B Week B2	Wave C Week C1	Wave C Week C2	Wave D	Change
	May 96	1–7 Apr	8–14 Apr	15–21 Apr	22–30 Apr	2 May 97	
Vote choice							
per cent of Decided Voters							
Con	28	32	29	29	29	29	1
Lab	54	51	50	49	46	46	–8
LDem	13	10	13	14	19	19	6
Other	5	7	8	6	6	6	1
N	1104	440	752	578	674	1163	

Note: Only those respondents included in all (ABCD) waves of the panel survey.

Source: BES Campaign Panel 1996–7.

different, the comparison of the public opinion polls published by all major companies from 17 March to 1 May 1997 (in Figure 11.1) confirms the pattern which we have observed, namely a slide in Labour support from the start to the end of the campaign, with the Liberal Democrats the main beneficiaries. As with the BES campaign panel, opinion polls demonstrate that Labour support declined by seven points (from an average of 51.4 per cent in the first two weeks of the campaign down to 44.4 per cent on polling day), Liberal Democrat support climbed four points (from 12.9 to 17.2 per cent during the campaign), while the Conservatives rose by two points (from 29.8 to 31.5 per cent) (Crewe 1997). While Labour support was probably over-inflated at the beginning of this period, if polls are believed to have their finger on the nation's pulse this swing indicates significant movement. As discussed in Chapter 9, the *daily* fluctuations in party support monitored by the BES campaign panel and the 'poll of polls' do differ, perhaps due to sampling and measurement error. Nevertheless, the striking similarity in the indicators of levels of party support provided by these two independent sources increases our confidence that this does represent a reliable estimate of changes in voting intentions during the 1997 campaign.

The Flow of the Vote 1992–97

Yet net volatility is only loosely related to gross electoral volatility, meaning the total amount of vote switching that takes place between any two points in time, measured at the individual level by panel surveys or

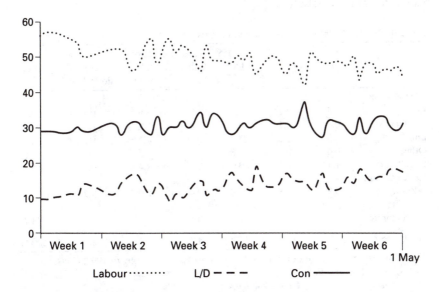

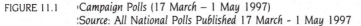

FIGURE 11.1   Campaign Polls (17 March – 1 May 1997)
Source: All National Polls Published 17 March - 1 May 1997

recalled vote. *Net* change represents the flow of the vote which produces each party's overall level of support, while *gross* change measures the electoral flux or 'churning' which occurs among voters see-sawing between parties.

We can start by estimating the flow of the vote from 1992 to 1997 based on recalled vote. This measure is often subject to certain well-known biases, in particular it tends to *under*-estimate electoral change as voters bring their recalled past vote into line with recent voting decisions. Nevertheless, the flow of the vote matrix in Table 11.3 shows that about 61 per cent of the electorate consistently supported the same party in 1992 and 1997, meaning that 39 per cent switched between general elections.[1] This level of gross electoral change is not exceptional; it is similar to the figure in the 1992 general election (62 per cent), although lower than in 1987 (69 per cent) and 1983 (64 per cent), as monitored by BES panel surveys (see Norris 1997a: Table 5.3).

In terms of the changes in party fortunes from 1992 to 1997, the loss of Conservative support came from three main sources: 3.9 per cent of the electorate were ex-Conservatives who stayed home, 3.2 per cent of the electorate were ex-Conservatives who voted Liberal Democrat, and, most remarkably, 4.4 per cent of the electorate (representing the equivalent of about 2 million voters) reported switching directly from Conservative to Labour. The centre party is usually regarded as a 'turn-around station' or 'half-way house', for temporary defectors from the major parties. To a striking degree, many more voters in this election moved directly between the major parties, or rather from the Conservatives to Labour, than is usual in British elections.

TABLE 11.3:   *Flow of the Vote Between General Elections, 1992–97*

| | 1997 General Election | | | | | | |
	Con	LibDem	Lab	Other	Didn't vote	Refused/ don't know	Total
1992 election							
Con	**17.6**	3.2	4.4	1.3	3.9	0.2	30.7
Lib Dem	0.4	**5.1**	2.3	0.4	1.2		9.4
Lab	0.5	1.8	**25.3**	0.8	4.1	0.2	32.7
Other	0.0	0.3	0.8	**2.4**	0.5		4.0
Didn't vote	1.1	1.1	3.0	0.6	**9.4**	0.1	15.2
Refused/don't know	0.3	0.8	0.8	0.4	0.9	**1.2**	
Entering electorate	0.4	0.6	1.3	0.1	1.3		3.7
Total	20.3	12.7	37.8	4.7	21.2	1.8	100 %

Note: This estimate is based on how voters in 1997 recalled voting in 1992. Constant voters are highlighted in bold.
Total constant: 17.6 + 5.1 + 25.3 + 2.4 + 9.4 + 1.2 = 61.0%.
Total change: 39.0%.

Source: 1997 cross-sectional BES survey N.3615.

As well as picking up support from ex-Conservatives, Labour was also particularly successful among those who had abstained in 1992 and among first-time voters. There was almost a straight Labour–Liberal Democrat swap: 2.3 per cent of the electorate who had voted Liberal Democrat in 1992 switched to Labour but this was counter-balanced by 1.8 per cent of the electorate who had voted Labour in 1992 and who switched to the Liberal Democrats. Overall the Liberal Democratic vote proved softest, as is common, with 5.1 per cent of the electorate staying loyal from 1992 to 1997. This pattern in the BES survey is confirmed with evidence of aggregate party support at constituency level. The change from 1992 to 1997 in the Labour and Liberal Democratic share of the vote was strongly inter-correlated (R=0.63). The sharp fall in the Conservative vote was most strongly related to the surge in Labour support (R=0.40), and more weakly correlated with the change in Liberal Democratic support (R=0.21). We can conclude that the net change in the vote saw a remarkable swing from the Conservatives to Labour from 1992 to 1997, but the overall level of vote churning or electoral flux in this period was far from exceptional.

The Flow of the Vote during the Long Campaign, May 1996–1997

If we use an equivalent voter matrix in the BES campaign panel we can examine the flow of the vote from May 1996 to May 1997, which helps us to understand the dynamics of change during the long campaign. The pattern in Table 11.4 shows that during the year the largest group of switchers (4.6 per cent of the electorate) moved from Labour to the Liberal Democrats, while in contrast far fewer (1.5 per cent) shifted from the Liberal Democrat to Labour. This net gain which the Liberal Democrats received from Labour goes a long way to explaining their overall rise in support during the election campaign which we have

TABLE 11.4: *Flow of the Vote During the Long Campaign, May 1996–97*

| | May 1997 General Election Voted | | | | | | |
	Con	LibDem	Lab	Other	Didn't vote	Refused/ don't know	Total
May 1966 Vote Intentions							
Con	**16.2**	1.8	1.1	0.4	1.7	0.6	21.9
Lib Dem	1.2	**5.8**	1.5	0.4	0.8	0.6	10.3
Lab	1.5	4.6	**29.5**	1.1	4.1	0.8	41.7
Other	0.4	0.6	0.6	**2.1**	0.1	0.0	3.7
Won't vote	2.5	1.5	3.2	0.6	**6.7**	0.2	14.6
Refused/Don't know	2.0	1.2	1.5	0.5	2.0	**0.7**	7.9
Total	23.8	15.6	37.3	5.1	15.3	3.0	100

Note: Constant voters are highlighted in bold. Only respondents in all (ABCD) waves of the panel survey are included (N.1423).
Total Constant: 16.2 + 5.8 + 29.5 + 2.1 + 6.7 + 0.7 = 61.0%.
Total Change: 39%.

already observed in Table 11.2. In contrast, with churning the Liberal Democrats gained and lost support fairly evenly across all the other categories in the matrix. The Liberal Democrat strategy, placing themselves to the left of the political spectrum on many welfare issues like education and public spending (Budge 1999), may have encouraged the switch from ex-Labour supporters. The pattern of tactical voting in key seats also played an important role here (Curtice and Steed 1997; Norris 1997d; Evans *et al.* 1998; Curtice 1999).

During the long campaign there was another important source of change for Labour, however, since many of their potential supporters failed to materialize at the ballot box. This confirms other aggregate evidence which found that electoral participation declined most sharply in safe Labour seats (Denver and Hands 1997b). The most plausible reason why potential Labour voters stayed at home was that the series of opinion polls and by-elections had pointed towards a comfortable Labour victory for many years, reducing the incentive to turn-out (Heath and Taylor 1999). This indicates that Labour's strategy in the campaign, while attracting some new voters into the fold, failed to mobilize their base.

The Timing of Voting Decisions

The evidence which we have considered from two independent sources (the BES campaign panel and the available published opinion polls) therefore suggests that, despite doubts about the importance of the campaign among scholars, there was considerable electoral volatility during the year before polling day. This produced a significant net fall in Labour's support (by eight points) as many of their potential supporters switched instead towards the Liberal Democrats, particularly late in the campaign.

But it is certainly possible that this apparent volatility could be a product of measurement error in conventional measures of voting intentions. An alternative indicator of the effect of the campaign can be estimated from the BES cross-sectional survey when people were asked:

> 'How long ago did you decide that you would definitely vote the way you did: was it . . . a long time ago, sometime last year, sometime this year, or during the election campaign?'

Overall in Table 11.5 just over half (56 per cent) said they had decided how to vote 'a long time ago', while just over one-quarter (27 per cent) decided 'during the campaign'. With the exception of 1979, this proportion was higher than any previous general election since the BES series began, and was far higher than the pattern in the early 1960s. The Liberal Democrats were particularly strong among late deciders, which is consistent with the swell in Liberal Democrat support we have already noted which occurred in the last week before polling day. In 1997, 42 per cent of all Liberal Democrats said that they decided during the election

TABLE 11.5: *Reported Timing of Voting Decision, 1964–97*

| | per cent of Voters who Decided | | |
	'...a Long Time Ago'	Over the Last Year or Two	During the Campaign
1964	78	11	12
1966	77	12	11
1970	70	18	12
1974F	64	14	23
1974O	60	18	22
1979	57	15	28
1983	60	18	22
1987	62	17	21
1992	60	16	24
1997	56	17	27

Source: BES 1964–97.

campaign, compared with only 21 per cent of Labour and 22 per cent of Conservative voters. This level is fairly consistent with the usual patterns evident in the BES series since February 1974.

Changes in Party and Leadership Image

Lastly, what of other indicators of changes in party and leadership image during the campaign? The evidence from the BES campaign panel in Table 11.6 shows that the impact of the campaign on changes in leadership ratings were very modest, at best. The main shift concerns the improved evaluations of Paddy Ashdown in terms of the best choice of party leader for Prime Minister, with a rise of 7 points during the official campaign, compared with a drop in the evaluations of both Tony Blair and John Major. There was also a similar 10-point rise during the official campaign in the proportion who believed that Paddy Ashdown would do a good job as Prime Minister. This pattern is certainly consistent with the earlier evidence for the rise in Liberal Democrat support. The other indicators of changes during the election in the images of John Major and Tony Blair are all either neutral or slightly negative.

The BES campaign panel survey also monitored changes in the image of the Labour and Conservative parties using the standard BES items to see whether they were widely perceived as united or divided, good for one class or good for all, capable of strong government and whether each party would stand up for Britain abroad. The results in Table 11.7 show a pattern of overall stability during the official campaign, even with the rows over Europe breaking out within the Conservative leadership during April. Clearly any damage done to the Conservative party image was already evident to the public well before the official campaign opened: few people regarded the Conservatives as united and the party was also seen less favourably in terms of being capable of strong government. This suggests that this image may have been reinforced, but there is no evidence here that party images were significantly altered by the campaign.

TABLE 11.6:   *Changes in Party Leadership Ratings, Official Campaign*

	Wave B Week B1 1–7 Apr	Wave B Week B2 8–14 Apr	Wave C Week C1 15–21 Apr	Wave C Week C2 22–30 Apr	Change
Major best PM	30	29	29	26	-4
Blair best PM	44	42	41	39	–5
Ashdown best PM	18	21	23	25	7
Major good job as PM	48	48	50	47	–1
Blair good job as PM	75	76	77	78	+3
Ashdown good job as PM	55	59	64	65	+10
Major strong leader	41	40	39	42	1
Major caring	71	66	67	68	–3
Major decisive	35	33	35	33	–3
Major sticks to principles	52	56	56	53	1
Blair strong leader	71	70	70	70	–1
Blair caring	80	77	80	76	–4
Blair decisive	67	64	66	65	–3
Blair sticks to principles	60	56	60	57	–4

Note: Only those included in ABCD Waves (N.1461). Excluding Don't know/Can't choose.

Source: British Election Campaign Panel 1996–7.

TABLE 11.7:   *Changes in Party Images, Official Campaign*

	Wave B Week B1 1–7 Apr	Wave B Week B2 8–14 Apr	Wave C Week C1 15–21 Apr	Wave C Week C2 22–30 Apr	Change
United/divided Con	11	15	11	13	2
United/divided Lab	61	60	70	65	3
Good one class Con	63	67	67	63	0
Good one class Lab	27	28	25	25	–3
Capable str govnt Con	35	38	38	37	2
Capable str govnt Lab	60	56	66	61	1
Stands up for GB Con	59	53	45	58	–1
Stands up for GB Lab	50	51	53	50	0

Note: Only those included in ABCD Waves (N.1461).

Source: British Election Campaign Panel 1996–7.

The Impact of Political Communications

Although some scholars believe that the results of the election were chiselled in granite for years, the indicators we have examined suggest that there was considerable electoral flux during the long campaign. In contrast to the conventional wisdom, we have found that the Liberal Democrats were the main beneficiaries of the long campaign, tripling their share of the vote in the twelve-month run up to polling day. Therefore how far is this due to the pattern of political communications during the campaign? It is difficult to assess how far any change can be attributed directly to how parties campaigned during the election, since most of the impact of this activity comes to voters through the filter of the news media. But we can review and summarize the major findings of this book in terms of two core issues. First, how far did the communications strategy of each party set the agenda for the news media during the 1997 campaign? And, in turn, how far did coverage by the news media influence voters' civic engagement, issue concerns and party preferences?

Did Party Communications Strategy Set the News Media Agenda?

We concur with the assessments of many commentators that the 1997 election was a landmark in the attempt by all British parties, but particularly by Labour, to use the techniques of professional news management, market research and election coordination to control the communications environment. Strategic communications are characterized by a coordinated set of aims and objectives, the projection and reinforcement of a consistent image and popular message, and a framework using resources to maximum advantage. All these features of modern electioneering have been widely discussed and most have assumed that as a result of these techniques Labour ran the most effective campaign. Yet we argue, based on the evidence in Chapter 4, that in terms of sticking to a coherent message which prioritized certain consistent themes across the manifesto, press releases and party political broadcasts, it was the Liberal Democrats who ran the most effective campaign, and the most positive one as well. More than any other party the Liberal Democrats stuck to arguing for their key proposals on welfare, the economy and education. The Conservatives proved the most negative and the most often deflected from their chosen battleground, as observers widely noted. And Labour fell between these two extremes, with a largely balanced campaign in terms of positive v. negative messages and a fairly consistent campaign in terms of issue agendas.

Did party strategy actually influence the news agenda? Our conclusion is that in the 1997 campaign the party and the news agendas remained worlds apart. While the news media preferred to focus on campaign strategy, devoting roughly two-thirds of their coverage to the conduct of the campaign, opinion polls and the party leaders, the parties focused on the substantive issue agenda of welfare, the economy and education. Comparing only the issue coverage, we found a weak relationship between the issues prioritized in the news and those of major concern to parties. No party was consistently more successful than any other in setting the news agenda across different media outlets. It appears as though parties are trying ever harder to set the agenda, but the rise of a more autonomous news media may have undermined the ability of politicians to get their message across. Whether this press–media dealignment is healthy for democracy, or a major cause of concern, remains a matter of interpretation.

Did Coverage by the News Media Influence Voters?

This brings us to the issue at the heart of this book, namely how far news coverage can and did influence the electorate's participation, issue concerns and party support.

Civic Engagement

Some hope that the news media can function as an effective source of information about public affairs which is critical in a democracy but others have expressed concern that the predominant values in the news media, such as the focus on government scandal and political conflict, encourages political cynicism and civic malaise. The evidence which we considered based on the campaign panel survey leads us to believe that the *short-term* impact of the news media, for good or ill, has been greatly exaggerated. We found no evidence that different patterns of media use and attention were associated with changes in how much people learnt about the electoral choices before them, or that these patterns influenced changes in political trust and efficacy, or changes in electoral participation. Nevertheless, we also established that people who were more attentive to the news were also more knowledgeable and had higher levels of civic engagement. Clearly there is an interaction effect, as people who are more interested and aware of political affairs are more likely to be drawn to news. Nevertheless, we posit that in the long term this process acts as a virtuous circle. This leads us to believe that, contrary to theories of video-malaise, the cumulative effects of watching television news and reading the press are largely positive.

Agenda-setting

The power of the press to tell us 'what to think about' has been a long-standing concern of American research. Yet there are good reasons to be sceptical about how far we can generalize from the American campaigns to the British context in this regard. In our experimental studies we did find that the priority of 'unobtrusive' issues in the television news agenda, such as the problem of overseas development, has the capacity to slightly increase the saliency of these issues for voters. Nevertheless, the agenda-setting role for television news was very modest and failed to operate for issues which were already of high concern to voters, like jobs, education and health care. Moreover, when we examined the case-study of Europe, which suddenly rose to prominence in terms of campaign headlines, we found that all the acres of newsprint which editorial writers devoted to trying to raise voters' concern had no effect whatever. In open-ended questions about the most important problem facing the country, the public continued to believe, no matter what the papers told them, that bread-and-butter issues were of far greater priority than Brussels. This healthy independence challenges some of the common assumptions about the power of the press to tell us 'what to think about'. In some cases this may be true, but we need to understand the conditionality of agenda-setting effects so that we know when the theory does, and does not, apply.

Political Persuasion

Lastly, we can draw three main conclusions from this study about the influence of the news media over party preferences. First, in this book, contrary to the findings in previous British studies, we provide powerful experimental evidence which shows that voters' party preferences can indeed be influenced by what they see on television news. In the light of our experimental findings, we conclude that voters' party preferences remain largely unaffected either by what we have termed *stop-watch balance* (the length of time that television news devotes to a particular political party) or by *agenda-balance* (the tendency of news broadcasts to concentrate on one set of issues rather than another). What we find can matter, in contrast, is the *direction* of television news coverage – whether TV news portrays a party in a *positive* (favourable) or a *negative* (unfavourable) light. Contrary to much of the American literature on political advertising, we found that the effects on preferences of exposure to positive news images are much more powerful than exposure to negative ones.

But did any party actually benefit from positive television news? Before we can jump to the conclusion that positive communications led to the rise in Liberal Democrat support, we need to stress the conditionality of the experimental results. We also demonstrated that in practice positive television coverage of particular parties had little effect in changing their overall pattern of support during the campaign as measured by daily opinion polls. We argue that this pattern probably reflects the fact that British broadcasting, operating under the conventions of balance and impartiality, means that positive news on television about one party tended to be cancelled out by positive news about its rivals. Conditional media effects in an experimental setting can tell us what *would* happen if TV news followed certain patterns of coverage (for example, if it always and only gave positive coverage to one party) but the content analysis of the media and the British Election Campaign study tell us what actually did happen in the contest.

We also examined the evidence for the powers of persuasion for newspapers, in particular whether *The Sun's* switch to Labour brought their readers with them. Here we found grounds which confirm that in the long term patterns of newspaper use are positively associated with party preferences. By reinforcing partisan preferences the steady pattern of newspaper coverage functions, like the influence of class, as a mechanism to help structure voting behaviour. Yet, as shown by the classic case of *The Sun*, the ability of the press to switch their readers' political leanings are extremely limited.

The Implications for the Press, Broadcasters and Parties

What do our findings imply for understanding the power of the press, for broadcasting policy, and for parties seeking to use strategic communications in modern campaigns?

The overall conclusions of our analysis suggest that although newspapers may wish to consciously influence the electoral process, whether by switching party allegiances with the aim of changing the political leanings of their readers (like *The Sun*), or by launching anti-European campaigns (like the *Daily Mail*), the power of the press to influence their readers is limited in the short term. Despite the avalanche of editorial opinion advising readers that Europe was the decisive issue facing them at the ballot box, we found that public opinion remained unmoved, preferring to focus on the domestic problems of our daily lives than to worry about EMU. The issue certainly mattered to some voters, particularly those who supported the anti-European parties. But we found no evidence that the outpourings of print significantly changed the public's issue concerns. Certain types of stories highlighted in the press may be able to raise public awareness, whether about the Ethiopian famine, mad cow disease or the dangers of breast cancer. But it is not apparent that the press had the power to set the public agenda in the 1997 general election.

What are the lessons for television journalists? While the press is largely unregulated, broadcasters have to follow strict guidelines under the Representation of the People Act and under the agreements which govern election coverage. At present, the notions of television balance that we have investigated in this book – directional, stop-watch and issue-agenda – are applied to varying degrees by British broadcasters during election campaigns. The BBC *Producer Guidelines* stress the strict need for political impartiality as does the Independent Television Commission's *Programme Code*.[2] The question raised by the conventions of balance is whether 'due impartiality' is achieved in practice. If the rules were radically altered, as some suggest – for example, if third parties like the Liberal Democrats were given equal airtime, if parties could advertise on television according to their financial resources, or if there were no rules governing party balance and the contents of news programmes was determined purely by news values – would this matter?

In our research the experiments systematically varied the contents of the media messages received by different respondents and closely monitored the effects. The results suggest that the principle of *stop-watch* balance, which is so pervasive in regulating coverage of election news in British broadcasting, is not grounded in the way that voters react to television news. The evidence indicates that the short-term effects of the amount of news coverage of each party, measured by the stop-watch principle, do not provide an automatic boost in that party's support, or a consistent decrease in support for other parties. We found no support for the idea that newsrooms need to be concerned unduly about *agenda balance*: the policy topic of stories which we examined had no differential effect on party preferences. A TV programme which focused heavily on coverage of health and jobs, for example, would not thereby be improving Labour support any more than one which carried many stories about tax would necessarily help the Conservatives. The assumptions of *directional* balance are that what matters is less the amount than the positive or negative contents of television news. In this view, impartiality is achieved by an even-handed approach to criticism and praise of each party. The evidence demonstrates that directional balance is important and, in particular, that positive news about a party has the capacity to provide a short-term and modest boost to its electoral fortunes. In summary, we conclude that what matters is *how* favourably parties are depicted in television news, in particular with positive coverage, rather than *how much* coverage they receive or on what topics.

These results may have important implications for the conventions which dominate British broadcasting during election campaigns. If we can generalize from the results of short-term experiments to the cumulative experience of the real world, and this is a real 'if', then it follows that all the paraphernalia of stop-watch balance which is so carefully monitored by the party managers and by news executives and producers may, at best, be irrelevant, and, at worst, may obscure any real biases in British television journalism. A more *laissez-faire* attitude to time balance, in which stories are driven by news values more than by the need to give proportional coverage to each party, irrespective of what they are actually doing during the campaign, might produce more stimulating and effective coverage. Yet since it is relatively easy and mechanical to measure the time allocated to different parties, while it is highly problematic and controversial to measure directional bias, the principle of stop-watch balance will probably continue to be observed in British broadcasting. Whether this principle continues to make sense in a more fragmented and complex news environment, as we move towards the widespread adoption of new media like the internet and a multiplicity of digital television outlets, remains a matter for debate.

Lastly, what are the lessons for parties? As well as being of intrinsic importance to debates about the effects of television news, this focus on positive and negative news has more than passing relevance for the kinds of campaigning that political parties adopt. Evidence from the United States shows not only that American journalists have become more 'negative' in the way they approach the reporting of political stories (Patterson 1993) but also that 'negative campaigning' matters for turnout in American elections (Ansolabehere and Iyengar 1995). Given the tendency for the United States to export its cultural and political habits to the UK, both negative reporting and campaigning may increase in Britain in the future. Although there are obvious differences between news and party election broadcasts, the evidence we present about the relative roles played by positive and negative television images could have important implications for the likely success of the alternative strategies available to political parties. While we do not have direct evidence, this line of reasoning is consistent with the observations that the Liberal Democrats were the main party to benefit from the 1997 campaign, they used the most consistently positive communication strategy, and on balance they received slightly more positive coverage across all television news programmes. We can conclude that campaigning has become far more complex than in the post-war era. The rise of post-modern campaigns, characterized by a more autonomous and fragmented media, more professionalized strategic communications by parties, and a more dealigned electorate, creates new challenges for effective communications between politicians and voters in a mediated democracy.

Notes

1. Confirmation of these estimates can be found in the 1997 BBC/NOP exit polls which found a similar level of gross volatility based on recalled vote in 1992 (Kellner 1997: 110).
2 See ITC *Programme Code*: http://www.itc.org.uk/regulating.

Technical Appendix

1. 1997 British Election Study, Cross-Sectional Survey
2. 1997 BES Campaign Panel
3. The 1997 Content Analysis
4. The 1997 Experimental Study of Television News

Web Resources: It should be noted that further technical details for the British Election Study, including full questionnaires, can be found at http://www.strath.ac.uk/Other/CREST/. Further details about the 1997 Experimental Study of Election News, including questionnaires, can be found at http://www.ksg.harvard.edu/people/pnorris.

1. British Election Study, 1997

The British General Election Surveys (BES) constitute the longest series of academic surveys in Britain. They have taken place immediately after every general election since 1964, giving a total of eleven to date. In addition to these post-election cross-sectional surveys, panel surveys (in which respondents to the previous election survey were reinterviewed at the subsequent election) have been conducted between every pair of elections except 1979 and 1983. There have also been two non-election year surveys (in 1963 and 1969); a postal referendum study in 1975; additional or booster Scottish studies in 1974, 1979, 1992 and 1997; an additional Welsh study in 1979; a Northern Ireland election study in 1992; campaign studies in Britain in 1987, 1992 and 1996/7; a booster sample of ethnic minority members in 1997; a qualitative study in 1997; Scottish (two) and Welsh referendum studies in 1997; a Northern Ireland referendum and election study in 1998.

The data-sets arising from these surveys, together with questionnaires and technical documentation, have been deposited at the ESRC Data Archive at the University of Essex. Summary information about the 1963 to 1987 surveys, and further references, are provided in an appendix to *Understanding Political Change* (Heath *et al.* 1991), and for the 1997 survey in the appendix to *Critical Elections* (Evans and Norris 1999).

The series originated with David Butler (Nuffield College, Oxford) and Donald Stokes (University of Michigan) in 1963, who also conducted the 1964, 1966 and 1970 surveys. The series then passed to Bo Sårlvik and Ivor

Crewe (University of Essex) who conducted the February and October 1974 surveys, joined by David Robertson for the 1979 survey. The 1983, 1987, 1992 and 1997 surveys have been directed by Anthony Heath (Jesus then Nuffield College, Oxford), Roger Jowell (Social and Community Planning Research (SCPR) London) and John Curtice (University of Liverpool then Strathclyde); in 1997 these directors were joined by Pippa Norris (Harvard University). The 1997 British Election study was conducted by the Centre for Research into Elections and Social Trends (CREST), a research centre funded by the Economic and Social Research Council (ESRC) and based jointly at SCPR and Nuffield College, Oxford, directed by Anthony Heath and Roger Jowell, with John Curtice.

The 1997 British post-election cross-sectional survey was funded by the Economic and Social Research Council (ESRC) (grant no. H552/255/003) and the Gatsby Charitable Foundation, one of the Sainsbury Family Charitable Trusts, which again allowed its core-funding of SCPR's British Social Attitudes survey series to be devoted to the BES series in election year. More detailed information about the cross-sectional survey design and fieldwork, including the SES and EMS, is presented in *The 1997 British Election Study: Technical Report* (Thomson *et al.* 1999a); both the full questionnaires and a comprehensive codebook are available from the ESRC Data Archive at the University of Essex, as are the data-files.

2. The 1997 BES Campaign Panel Study

The 1997 BES Campaign Panel was funded by the Economic and Social Research Council (ESRC) (grant no. H552/255/003) and the Gatsby Charitable Foundation, one of the Sainsbury Family Charitable Trusts, which again allowed its core-funding of SCPR's British Social Attitudes survey series to be devoted to the BGES series in election year. More detailed information about the Campaign Panel survey design and fieldwork is presented in *The British General Election Study: Campaign Panel: Technical Report* (Thomson *et al.* 1999b) and *British Social Attitudes and Northern Ireland Social Attitudes 1996 Surveys: Technical Report* (Lilley *et al.* 1998); both the full questionnaires and a comprehensive codebook are available from the ESRC Data Archive at the University of Essex, as is the data-file.

Wave A of the Campaign Panel consisted of the 1996 British Social Attitudes survey which included a special election study module of questions. This survey had a random sample drawn from the Postcode Address File. The sample was designed to be representative of adults aged 17 or above living in private households in Great Britain south of the Caledonian Canal. The age cut-off of 17 was chosen in order to include respondents who would turn 18 (and thus become eligible to vote) between the 1996 British Social Attitudes survey and the 1997 general election.

Sampling from the Postcode Address File involves a multi-stage design. First, any postal sector with fewer than 500 delivery points (DPs) was grouped with another. The list of (grouped) sectors was then sorted into 11 standard regions (treating London and the South East as two separate regions). Within each region, sectors were listed in ascending order of population density. Cut-off points were drawn at one-third and two-thirds down the ordered list of DPs so that, within each region, three roughly equal-sized bands were created. Within each of the 33 bands, sectors were listed in order of percentage owner-occupiers. Two hundred sectors were selected systematically with probability proportional to DP. Thirty addresses were selected from each sector by starting from a random point on the list of addresses, and choosing each address at a fixed interval. The Multiple-Output Indicator (MOI), available through the PAF, was used when selecting addresses. It shows the number of accommodation spaces (or 'dwelling units') sharing one address. Thus, if the MOI indicates more than one dwelling unit at a given address, the chances of a given address being selected from the list of addresses would increase so that it matched the total number of dwelling units. As would be expected, the vast majority (97 per cent) of MOIs had a value of one. The remainder were incorporated into the weighting procedures.

At each issued address, the interviewer established the number of occupied dwelling units (DUs) and, where there were several, selected one DU at random for interview (using a Kish grid and random numbers generated separately for each serial number). At each (selected) DU the interviewer established the number of adults aged 17+ normally resident there, and selected one adult at random (using the same procedure as for selecting a DU). The unequal selection probabilities arising from these procedures are taken into account by the weighting.

Fieldwork for the 1996 British Social Attitudes survey took place in April to June 1996, with a few interviews in July and August. The achieved sample size (including 17-year-olds) was 3,662 respondents. Respondents to wave A were asked (a) whether there was a telephone in their accommodation, (b) if so, what their telephone number was and, (c) regardless of their answer to the two earlier questions, whether they were prepared to take part in a short follow-up survey. (Where respondents had a telephone, the question made clear that the follow-up would be a telephone interview.) Respondents who had either refused to be re-interviewed or said they were prepared to be re-interviewed but not on the telephone, were contacted by telephone in early 1997 to persuade them to agree to take part after all. As a result, a sample of 2,931 respondents with telephone numbers was issued for wave B of the Campaign Panel, including 122 people who had been persuaded in the pre-survey conversion exercise.

At each of the subsequent waves C and D, people who were obviously unsuitable to approach again were excluded (e.g. people who had died or emigrated, those who made it very clear that they were not prepared to be re-interviewed, and those who could not be traced). Non-contacts and other (softer) refusals were, however, re-issued at each round.

Two small-scale pre-tests of questions for waves B, C and D were carried out in October and December 1996. The pilot interviewers were personally debriefed by the research team.

Waves B, C and D consisted of telephone interviews conducted by SCPR interviewers based at the SCPR office in Brentwood. The inter-viewers were personally briefed by members of the BES research team. In all, 34 interviewers worked on wave B. All interviewers working on waves C and D had previously worked on wave B.

The interview was administered using computer-assisted telephone interviewing (CATI). The average length of the interview was 12.8 minutes for wave B, 11.1 minutes for wave C and 3.9 minutes for wave D. Wave B was conducted during the period 1–16 April, wave C during the period 17–30 April and wave D during the period 2–31 May. Efforts were made at waves B and C to ensure – as far as possible – that random subsamples of respondents were interviewed on each day.

The response at each wave is given in Table A1.

TABLE A1: *Response Rate*

		N	%	N	%	N	%
Wave A	Issued	6,000					
	Out of scope	625					
	In scope	5,375	100.0				
	Interview obtained	3,662	68.1				
	Interview not obtained	1,712	31.9				
	Of which:						
	– refusal	1,402	26.1				
	– not contacted	125	2.3				
	– other	186	3.5				
Wave B	Issued			2,931			
	Out of scope			24			
	In scope			2,907	100.0		
	Interview obtained		33.5	1,800	61.9		
	Interview not obtained			1,107	38.1		
	Of which:						
	– not traced			204	7.0		
	– refusal			294	10.1		
	– not contacted			532	18.3		
	– other			77	2.6		

TABLE A1: *continued*

		N	%	N	%	N	%
Wave C	Issued					2,537	
	Out of scope					4	
	In scope					2,533	100.0
	Interview obtained		33.7		62.2	1,809	71.4
	Interview not obtained					724	28.6
	Of which;						
	– not traced					38	1.5
	– refusal					309	12.2
	– not contacted					332	13.1
	– other					45	1.8
Wave D	Issued					2,318	
	Out of scope					3	
	In scope					2,315	100.0
	Interview obtained		38.1		70.4	2,047	88.4
	Interview not obtained					268	11.6
	Of which:						
	– not traced					28	1.2
	– refusal					112	4.8
	– not contacted					117	5.1
	– other					11	0.5

Notes: Out of scope = vacant, derelict, no private dwelling, died, emigrated, not yet aged 18 by the time of the election. Refused = refusal before or after the selection procedure, 'proxy' refusals (on the selected person's behalf), broken appointments after which the respondent could not be recontacted. Non-contacts = households where no one could be contacted and those where the selected person could not be contacted. Other interview not obtained = ill or away during survey period, selected person senile or incapacitated, 'partial unproductive' (a few questions asked but interview not completed), inadequate English etc.

Questionnaire Design

For the first time on the BGES, the research team engaged in a formal consultation exercise with members of the BGES user community – an extension of the customary informal consultation procedure. This was conducted in conjunction with the Election Studies Management and Advisory Committee (ESMAC) set up by the series' principal funder, the ESRC. Members of the research team distinguished 'core' from 'non-core' survey items. BGES users were invited to submit a case for the inclusion of questions or groups of questions, and these were evaluated by subject working groups comprised of both members of the research team and members of the user community. A conference of invited users was held under the auspices of ESMAC on 4 June 1996, and the draft question-naire was discussed at a session of the 1996 annual conference of the

Elections, Public Opinion and Parties (EPOP) sub-group of the Political Studies Association (held in Sheffield 13–15 September 1996).

Validation of Turnout and Registration

As in 1987 and 1992, respondents' reports of turnout at the 1997 election were checked against the official records (Swaddle and Heath 1989). The marked-up Electoral Register held at the Lord Chancellor's Office for a year after the general election shows which electors voted, or were issued with postal votes, and is available for public inspection. Corresponding information for respondents in Scotland was obtained from the Sherriffs' Clerks. Supplementary checks of registration (but not turnout) were carried out on ordinary (that is, not marked-up) registers at the Office of National Statistics offices in Titchfield in July 1998. Figures reported in this volume use data based on the initial validation study; results from the supplementary registration study are included in the final data-file.

Weighting

A weighting scheme has been devised to take account of differential selection probabilities at wave A. In particular, the weights take account of unequal selection probabilities at the household level. (In brief, the PAF sample generated addresses with equal probability. However, since only one person was interviewed at each address, people in small households have a larger selection probability than people in large households.) The weights also take account of attrition over the life of the panel. Because of this 'non-response weighting', there are three separate sets of weights: (a) for analysis of wave A only, waves A and B or waves A and C (WTALA); (b) for analysis of waves A, B and D or waves A, C and D (WTALAD); and (c) for analysis of waves A, B, C and D (WTALABCD).

Additional weights take account of the outcome of the electoral register checks to generate a sample of registered electors (WTERA, WTERAD and WTERABCD respectively). The weighted and unweighted sample sizes (on the preliminary data-file used in this book) are given in Table A2.

TABLE A2: *Weighting Procedure*

	Unweighted	WTALA	WTALAD	WTALABCD	WTERA	WTERAD	WTERABCD
Wave A	3,662	3,662	2,047	1,422	3,341	1,895	1,321
Wave B	1,800	1,807	1,560	1,422	1,735	1,481	1,321
Wave C	1,809	1,835	1,709	1,422	1,733	1,584	1,321
Wave D	2,047	2,092	2,047	1,422	1,978	1,895	1,321

3. Content Analysis

The content analysis was based on categories developed in earlier elections (see Semetko *et al.* 1991). All television stories on BBC1's *Nine O'Clock News* and ITN's *News at Ten* were coded from 1 to 30 April 1997 as well as all stories on page 1 of the following newspapers: *The Times, The Guardian, The Independent, Daily Mail, The Sun, The Mirror.* Page 1 of the newspapers were also coded on 1 May. All stories were coded for their main subject, as well as the main actors, and a range of other variables.

The 1997 general subject categories which aggregated more specific topics were:

Conduct of campaign: all mention of the parties' campaign organization, conduct, campaign strategy and tactics, advertising and general campaign trail activity which could not be rendered specific to party leaders. It does not include opinion polls which were classified separately.

Parties: includes internal party disagreements, discussions, meetings.

Opinion polls/horse race: media polls, election results predictions and speculation.

Party leaders: refers narrowly to the leaders, their political and personal qualities and their individual (as opposed to party) campaigns.

Campaign issues: includes issues that emerged during the campaign such as sex and sleaze in the Tory Party in 1997, or rows over the Labour Party election broadcast about the NHS in 1992 which came to be known as Jennifer's Ear.

Media treatment: includes coverage of how the media reports the election, media reporting media.

Social welfare: includes NHS, private health, poverty, homelessness, housing, pensions, party policies.

Regions: includes Scotland, Wales, Northern Ireland, party policies.

Economy: includes tax, inflation, interest rates, jobs and unemployment, privatization, industrial relations, recession and recovery, the budget, party policies.

Foreign affairs: includes Europe and the European Union, relations with foreign countries, party policies.

Education and arts: includes schools, universities, crèches, arts policy, party policies.

Constitutional reform: includes the electoral system, devolution, changes to the political system, party policies.

Infrastructure: includes housing, transport, traffic, party policies.

Environment/energy: includes oil, nuclear power, environmental changes, regulations, party policies.

Defence: includes NATO, military issues, party policies.

4. The Experimental Study of Television News

Fifteen experiments were used to examine the effects of television news on viewers. To summarize the process, respondents completed a pre-test questionnaire and were then randomly assigned to separate groups. Each group was exposed to a distinctive 30-minute selection of video news and a post-test questionnaire was then administered to each respondent. The purpose of the experiments was to establish the extent to which any changes between pre- and post-test responses varied according to the type of video footage that had been seen.

Fieldwork and the Selection of Respondents

The experiments were conducted in a central London location (Regent Street). In total 1,125 respondents were included, more than most experimental designs. Participants were drawn primarily from Greater London and south-east England. Respondents were not selected explicitly as a random sample of the British electorate, but they did generally reflect the Greater London population in terms of their social background and party preferences. The location was selected to provide a diverse group of Londoners including managers, office-workers and casual shoppers. The generalizability of the results rests not on the selection of a random sample of participants, as in a survey design, but on the way that subjects were assigned at random to different experimental groups. Any difference in the response of groups should therefore reflect the stimuli they were given rather than their social backgrounds or prior political attitudes.

Participants completed a short (15-minute) pre-test questionnaire about their media habits, political interests and opinions and personal background. They were then assigned at random to groups of 5–15 to watch a 30-minute video compilation of television news. Respondents subsequently completed a short (15-minute) post-test questionnaire. The experiments were carried out in April 1997 during the middle of the official general election campaign.

The Construction of Video Stimuli

The video compilations of news stories were chosen to represent a 'typical' evening news programme during the campaign. We drew on stories recorded from all the main news programmes on the terrestrial channels[1] from mid-February until early to mid-April 1997. The videos all had the same format. They consisted of a 'sandwich', with identical, standard footage at the top and bottom of each programme and one of fifteen different experimental video stimuli in the middle 'core'. Respondents were not told which video was being shown to which group or even that different videos were being watched by different groups of respondents. The video news compilations for the experiments are listed in Table A3.

Compilations of Video News: Standard Core

All video compilations had the same beginning and end segments consisting of:

Beginning

1. Report on the opening day of the official campaign. Commentary by Robin Oakley. Statements by Major, Blair and Ashdown. Discussion by Oakley of the four main issues of the campaign: the economy, Europe, constitutional reform and leadership. [5 minutes]
2. Continuation of news on the opening day of the campaign. Description of Major's, Blair's and Ashdown's activities during the day. Description of the timetable for the election and the timing of the next Queen's Speech. Discussion by John Pinnaar on the failure of the 'feelgood factor' to re-kindle Conservative fortunes thus far. [5 minutes]

Video stimuli

1. Description of a runaway horse incident at a racecourse. [2 minutes]
2. Discussion of motorway traffic congestion. [1.5 minutes]
3. Incident of two bombs left beneath flyover on the M6. [1.5 minutes]
4. Discussion of the introduction of self-assessment tax forms. [1.5 minutes]
5. Discussion of freemasonry in public life. [1.5 minutes]
6. Results of the Oscar award ceremony in United States. [2 minutes]

End

Examples of Stories in Positive and Negative News Experiments

Positive Conservative video

1. Feature on recent fall in inflation figures: good news on the economy for the Conservatives. [2 minutes]

TABLE A3: *Timing of 30-Minute Video Experimental Stimuli*

Experiment	Start	Core	End
Stopwatch balance			
Control	10 neutral	4 Con: 4 Lab: 3 LibDem	10 minute neutral
Conservative balance	5 neutral	20 minute Con neutral	5 minute neutral
Labour balance	5 neutral	20 minute Lab neutral	5 minute neutral
Liberal Democrat	5 neutral	20 minute LibDem neutral	5 minute neutral
Directional balance			
Con positive	10 neutral	10 Con positive	10 neutral
Con negative	10 neutral	10 Con negative	10 neutral
Lab positive	10 neutral	10 Lab positive	10 neutral
Lab negative	10 neutral	10 Lab negative	10 neutral
Agenda balance			
Tax	10 neutral	10 tax neutral	10 neutral
Jobs	10 neutral	10 jobs neutral	10 neutral
Health	10 neutral	10 health neutral	10 neutral
Pensions	10 neutral	10 pensions neutral	10 neutral
Europe	10 neutral	10 Europe neutral	10 neutral
Overseas aid	10 neutral	10 overseas aid	10 neutral
Issue control	10 neutral	10 mixed issues	10 neutral

2. 'Soft focus' portrait of Norma Major's involvement in the campaign. Recalls the victory in 1992 and states how worthwhile life has been, in public service terms, as the PM's wife. [3 minutes]
3. Feature on the release of good Balance of Payments figures. Focus on 'booming Britain'. [2 minutes]
4. Jeremy Paxman interviews Major at Number 10 for *Newsnight*. Major gives articulate, robust and assured answers to questions about: Labour's opinion poll lead; the responsibilities of government; the excellent prospects for the economy; the importance of experience in government. Major refuses to abuse Blair even though Paxman invites him to by referring to Blair as 'a phoney' and 'smarmy'. Major appears statesmanlike and generous. Major even corners Paxman over the question of Cabinet ministers jockeying for post-election position. Major appears confident and relaxed throughout. [5 minutes]

Negative Conservative video
1. Party disunity. Feature on Tebbitt attacking Heseltine in a *Spectator* review as being 'tasteless, tacky and self-centred'. Tebbit mocks Heseltine's premiership ambitions. Conservative MP criticizes Tebbit. [2 minutes].
2. Sleaze – finance. Feature on the delay in publishing the Downey Report on Neil Hamilton, Tim Smith *et al.* as a result of Major's early prorogation of Parliament, prior to the beginning of the official four-week campaign. Academic interviewed who implies that the timing has been consciously designed to prevent the report being made public before the election. Emma Nicholson MP interviewed concurring with the academic's view. Feature as a whole (a) raises Tory sleaze as an issue and (b) implies Major may be temporarily covering it up for electoral gain. [5 minutes]
3. Sleaze – morals. Feature on Piers Merchant's affair and *The Sun*'s 6-page exposure of it. More division in Tory ranks over whether this is a resignation matter. Labour and Liberal Democrat spokespeople link the affair back to issues of Tory sleaze more generally. Reporter refers to two embarrassing Tory resignations and to 'a bad week for the Tories'. [5 minutes]

Positive Labour video
1. Robin Oakley reports on Labour's economic policy. Labour spokespeople describe themselves as the party of economic competence which has broken with its own tax-and-spend past. Gordon Brown is interviewed stressing Labour's toughness on inflation. [2 minutes]
2. Mark Mardell reports on John Prescott's round-Britain bus tour, the 'Prescott Express'. Prescott is ebullient, confident, relaxed. Reporter makes very positive comments about Prescott's campaigning abilities. Film shows Prescott being populist (and clearly successful) with Old Labour supporters. Feature overall portrays Prescott as the embod-

iment of the best old Labour values – and very much part of Labour's campaigning team. [4 minutes]

3. Jeremy Paxman interviews Tony Blair. Blair, like Major, is assured and relaxed. Blair defends his socialist values and asserts his commitment to them. Stresses how Labour priorities differ from the Conservatives', even though Labour is committed to current Conservative spending levels; gives several examples. [5 minutes]

Negative Labour video

1. Steven Evans' report examines the Conservatives' critique of Labour plans for trade union reform. Thatcher is interviewed saying that Blair has 'surrendered to the unions'. Conservative spokespeople comment that if Labour win the election there will be a new era of union militancy. Reporter observes that Labour has been 'on the back foot' in this episode; implies that Labour has not thought through its policies clearly enough. [3 minutes]

2. Conflicts within Labour over the party's plans for privatization. Film of speech at last Labour Conference strongly opposing privatization of Air Traffic Control, something which Labour leadership has just said it will put into effect. Statement from Post Office Union about its opposition to plans to privatize Parcel Force. [3 minutes]

3. Divisions within the Labour Party in Scotland. Divisions over constitutional reform and taxation highlighted. Suggestion that Labour commitment to Conservative spending plans means they are no different from the Tories as far as many Scots are concerned. [2 minutes]

4. Feature on conflict within Labour over 'forced' resignations of 'Old Labour' MPs. Discussion of case of Old Labour Welsh MP being 'misled into resignation' by Shadow Welsh Secretary Ron Davies. Clear that either Davies or the MP in question (both interviewed) is lying. [4 minutes]

Note

1. The programmes sampled were *Nine O'Clock News* (BBC1), *News at Ten* (ITN), *Channel 4 News* and *Newsnight* (BBC2).

Bibliography

Ansolabehere, Stephen and Shanto Iyengar. 1995. *Going Negative: How Political Advertisements Shrink and Polarise the Electorate*. New York: Free Press.

Ansolabehere, Stephen, Roy Behr and Shanto Iyengar. 1992. *The Media Game: American Politics in the Television Age*. New York: Macmillan.

Asp, Kent. 1983 'The struggle for agenda: party agenda, media agenda and voter agenda in the 1979 Swedish election campaign.' *Communication Research*, 10(3):333–55.

Baran, Stanley and Dennis Davis. 1995. *Mass Communication Theory*. Belmont, CA: Wadsworth.

Bealey, Frank, Jean Blondel and W. P. McCain. 1965. *Constituency Politics*. London: Faber and Faber.

Bennett, W. Lance. 1996. *News: The Politics of Illusion*. New York: Longman.

Berelson, Bernard, Paul Lazarsfeld and W. N. McPhee. 1954. *Voting*. Chicago: University of Chicago Press.

Berelson, Bernard, Paul Lazarsfeld and William McPhee. 1963. *Voting*. Chicago: University of Chicago Press.

Berrington, Hugh and Roderick Hague. 1997. 'The Liberal Democrat campaign.' In *Britain Votes 1997*, eds. Pippa Norris and Neil Gavin. Oxford: Oxford University Press.

Birch, Anthony. 1959. *Small Town Politics*. Oxford: Oxford University Press.

Blackburn, Robin. 1995. *The Electoral System in Britain*. New York: St Martin's Press.

Blumler, Jay G. 1997. 'Origins of the crisis of communication for citizenship.' *Political Communication*, 14(4): 395–404.

Blumler, Jay and Michael Gurevitch. 1995. *The Crisis of Public Communication*. London: Routledge.

Blumler, Jay and Eli Katz. 1974. *The Uses of Mass Communications*. Beverly Hills, CA: Sage.

Blumler, Jay and Denis McQuail. 1968. *Television in Politics*. London: Faber.

Blumler, Jay G., Michael Gurevitch, and Thomas J. Nossiter. 1989. 'The earnest vs. the determined: election newsmaking at the BBC, 1987.' In *Political Communications: The General Election Campaign of 1987*, eds. Ivor Crewe and Martin Harrop. Cambridge: Cambridge University Press.

Brosius, H. and H. M. Kepplinger. 1990. 'The agenda-setting function of television news.' *Communications Research*. 17(2): 183–211.

Bryant, Jennings and Dolf Zillmann. 1994. *Media Effects*. Hillsdale, NJ: Lawrence Erlbaum.

Brynin, Malcolm and David Sanders. 1997. 'Party identification, political preferences and material conditions: evidence from the British Household Panel Survey, 1991–92.' *Party Politics*, 3: 53–77.

Budge, Ian. 1999. 'Party policy and ideology: reversing the 1950s?' In *Critical Elections: British Parties and Voters in Long-term Perspective*, eds. Geoffrey Evans and Pippa Norris. London: Sage.

Budge, Ian and David Farlie. 1983. *Explaining and Predicting Elections*. London: Allen & Unwin.

Butler, David. 1952. *The British General Election of 1951*. London: Macmillan.

Butler, David. 1955. *The British General Election of 1955*. London: Macmillan.

Butler, David. 1989. *British General Elections Since 1945*. Oxford: Basil Blackwell.

Butler, David and Dennis Kavanagh. 1974. *The British General Election of February 1974*. London: Macmillan.

Butler, David and Dennis Kavanagh. 1975. *The British General Election of October 1974*. London: Macmillan.

Butler, David and Dennis Kavanagh. 1980. *The British General Election of 1979*. London: Macmillan.

Butler, David and Dennis Kavanagh. 1984. *The British General Election of 1983*. London: Macmillan.

Butler, David and Dennis Kavanagh. 1988. *The British General Election of 1987*. London: Macmillan.

Butler, David and Dennis Kavanagh. 1992. *The British General Election of 1992*. New York, N.Y: St. Martin's Press.

Butler, David and Dennis Kavanagh. 1997. *The British General Election of 1997*. London: Macmillan.

Butler, David and Anthony King. 1965. *The British General Election of 1964*. London: Macmillan.

Butler, David and Anthony King. 1966. *The British General Election of 1966*. London: Macmillan.

Butler, David and Michael Pinto-Duschinsky. 1971. *The British General Election of 1970*. London: Macmillan.

Butler, David and Austin Ranney. 1992. *Electioneering*. Oxford: Clarendon Press.

Butler, David and Richard Rose. 1960. *The British General Election of 1959*. London: Macmillan.

Butler, David and Donald E. Stokes. 1974. *Political Change in Britain: the Evolution of Electoral Choice*. 2nd ed. London: Macmillan.

Campbell, Angus, Philip Converse, Warren E. Miller, and Donald E. Stokes. 1960. *The American Voter*. New York: Wiley.

Cappella, Joseph and Kathleen Hall Jamieson. 1996. 'News frames, political cynicism and media cynicism.' Media and Politics Special Edition of *The Annals of the American Academy of Political Science*, XX(X):71–84.

Cappella, Joseph N. and Kathleen H. Jamieson. 1997. *Spiral of Cynicism*. New York: Oxford University Press.

Cathcart, Brian. 1997. *Were You Still Up for Portillo?* London: Penguin.

Chaffee, Steven H. and Stacey Frank Kanihan. 1997. 'Learning politics from the mass media.' *Political Communication*, 14(4): 421–30.

Chan, Sophia. 1997. 'Effects of attention to campaign coverage on political trust.' *International Journal of Public Opinion Research*, 9(3): 286–96.

Cohen, Bernard. 1963. *The Press and Foreign Policy*. Princeton, NJ: Princeton University Press.

Crewe, Ivor. 1997. 'The opinion polls: confidence restored?' In *Britain Votes 1997*, eds. Pippa Norris and Neil Gavin. Oxford: Oxford University Press.

Crewe, Ivor and Brian Gosschalk. 1995. *Political Communications: the General Election Campaign of 1992*. Cambridge: Cambridge University Press.

Crewe, Ivor and Martin Harrop. 1989. *Political Communications: the General Election Campaign of 1987*. Cambridge: Cambridge University Press.

Crewe, Ivor, Bo Särlvik and James Alt. 1977. 'Partisan dealignment in Britain 1964–74.' *British Journal of Political Science*. 7:129–90.

Crewe, Ivor, Brian Gosschalk, and John Bartle. 1998. *Political Communications: Why Labour Won the General Election of 1997*. London: Frank Cass.

Curran, James and Jean Seaton. 1991. *Power Without Responsibility: The Press and Broadcasting in Britain.* London: Routledge.

Curtice, John. 1996. 'Do the Media Set the Agenda?' Paper presented at the ECPR Joint Sessions of Workshops, University of Oslo.

Curtice, John. 1997. 'Is the Sun shining on Tony Blair? The electoral influence of British newspapers.' *The Harvard International Journal of Press/Politics,* 2(2):9–26.

Curtice, John. 1999. 'Region: new Labour, new geography?' *In Critical Elections: British Parties and Voters in Long-term Perspective,* eds. Geoffrey Evans and Pippa Norris. London: Sage.

Curtice, John and Roger Jowell. 1995. 'The sceptical electorate.' In *British Social Attitudes, the 12th Report,* eds. Roger Jowell *et al.* Aldershot: Dartmouth. ·

Curtice, John and Roger Jowell. 1997. 'Trust in the political System.' *British Social Attitudes: the 14th Report,* eds. Roger Jowell *et al.* Aldershot: Ashgate.

Curtice, John and Holli Semetko. 1994. 'Does it matter what the papers say?' In *Labour's Last Chance?* Eds. Anthony Heath, Roger Jowell, and John Curtice. Aldershot: Dartmouth.

Curtice, John and Michael Steed. 1997. 'Appendix 2: the results analyzed.' In *The British General Election of 1997,* David Butler and Dennis Kavanagh. London: Macmillan.

Dahlgren, Peter. 1995. *Television and the Public Sphere.* London: Sage.

Dahlgren, Peter and Colin Sparks. 1997. *Communication and Citizenship.* London: Routledge.

Dalton, Russell J. 1996. *Citizen Politics: Public Opinion and Political Parties in Advanced Industrialized Democracies.* Chatham NJ: Chatham House.

Dalton, Russell, K. Kawakami, Holli Semetko, H. Suzuki, and K. Voltmer. 1998 'Partisan Cues in the Media: Cross-National Comparisons of Election Coverage.' Paper presented at the Annual Meeting of the Mid-West Political Science Association, Chicago.

Davis, Richard and Diane Owens. 1998. *New Media and American Politics.* New York: Oxford University Press.

Dearing, John W. and Everett M. Rogers. 1996. *Agenda-Setting.* London: Sage.

Della Porta, Donatella and Yves Meny. 1997. *Democracy and Corruption in Europe.* London: Pinter.

Delli Carpini, Michael and Scott Keeter. 1996. *What Americans Know About Politics and Why It Matters.* New Haven, CT: Yale University Press.

Denver, David and Gordon Hands. 1992. *Issues and Controversies in British Electoral Behaviour.* London: Harvester.

Denver, David and Gordon Hands. 1997a. *Modern Constituency Campaigning.* London: Frank Cass.

Denver, David and Gordon Hands. 1997b. 'Turnout.' In *Britain Votes 1997,* eds. Pippa Norris and Neil T. Gavin. Oxford: Oxford University Press.

Denver, David, Gordon Hands, and Simon Henig. 1998. 'A triumph of targeting? Constituency campaigning in the 1997 election.' In *British Elections and Parties Review,* eds. David Denver *et al.* London: Frank Cass.

Diez-Nicolas, Juan. and Holli A. Semetko. 1995. 'La television y las elecciones de 1993.' In *Communicacion Politica,* eds. A. Munoz-Alonso and J. Ignacio Rospir. Madrid: editorial Universitas, S.A.

Downs, Anthony. 1957. *An Economic Theory of Democracy.* New York: Harper & Row.

Draper, Derek. 1997. *Blair's Hundred Days.* London: Faber and Faber.

Dunleavy, Patrick and Christopher Husbands. 1985. *Democracy at the Crossroads.* London: Allen and Unwin.

Esaisson, Peter and Soren Holmberg. 1996. *Representation from Above.* Aldershot: Dartmouth.

Evans, Geoffrey and Pippa Norris. 1999. *Critical Elections: British Parties and Voters in Long-term Perspective*. London: Sage.

Evans, Geoffrey, John Curtice, and Pippa Norris. 1998. 'New Labour, new tactical voting?' In *British Elections and Parties Review*, eds. David Denver *et al.* London: Frank Cass.

Fallows, James. 1996. *Breaking the News: How the Media Undermine American Democracy*. New York: Pantheon.

Faucheux, R. ed. 1995. *The Road to Victory: The Complete Guide to Winning in Politics*. Washington D.C.: Campaigns and Elections.

Finkelstein, Daniel. 1998. 'Why the Conservatives lost.' In *Political Communications: Why Labour Won the General Election of 1997*, eds. Ivor Crewe, Brian Gosschalk and John Bartle. London: Frank Cass.

Flanagan, Scott C. 1996. 'Media Exposure and the Quality of Political Participation in Japan.' *Media and Politics in Japan*, Susan J. Pharr and Ellis S. Krauss. Honolulu: University Press of Hawaii.

Friedrichsen, Mike. 1996. 'Politik-Und Parteiverdruss Durch Skandalberichterstattung?' *Medien Und Politischer Prozess*, Otfried Jarren, Heribert Schatz, and Hartmut Wessler. Opladen: Westdeutscher Verlag.

Franklin, Bob. 1994. *Packaging Politics*. London: Edward Arnold.

Gadir, S. (1982) 'Media agenda-setting in Australia: the rise and fall of public issues.' *Media Information Australia*, 26: 13–23.

Garment, Suzanne. 1991. *Scandal*. New York.

Gavin, Neil. 1998. *The Economy, Media and Public Knowledge*. London: Leicester University Press.

Gavin, Neil and David Sanders. 1996. 'The impact of television news on public perceptions of the economy and government, 1993–1994.' In *British Elections and Parties Yearbook*, 1996, eds. David M. Farrell *et al.* London: Frank Cass.

Gavin, Neil and David Sanders. 1997. 'The economy and voting.' In *Britain Votes 1997*, eds. Pippa Norris and Neil Gavin. Oxford: Oxford University Press.

Geddes, Andrew and Jon Tonge, eds. 1997. *Labour's Landslide*. Manchester: Manchester University Press.

Gelman, Andrew and Gary King. 1993. 'Why are American presidential election campaign polls so variable when votes are so predictable?' *British Journal of Political Science*, 23: 409–51.

Gerbner, George. 1980. 'The mainstreaming of America.' *Journal of Communication*, 30: 10–29.

Gerbner, George, Larry Gross, Michael Morgan and Nancy Signorielli. 1994. 'Growing up with television: the cultivation perspective.' In *Media Effects*, Jennings Bryant and Dolf Zillmann. Hillsdale, NJ: Lawrence Erlbaum.

Gibson, Rachel K. and Stephen J. Ward. 1998. 'UK political parties and the internet: "politics as usual" in the new media?' *The Harvard International Journal of Press/Politics*, 3(3): 14–38.

Glasgow Media Group. 1976. *Bad News*. London: Routledge and Kegan Paul.

Glasgow Media Group. 1980. *More Bad News*. London: Routledge and Kegan Paul.

Goddard, Peter, Margaret Scammell and Holli Semetko. 1998. 'Too much of a good thing? Television in the 1997 election campaign.' In *Political Communications: Why Labour Won the General Election of 1997*, eds. Ivor Crewe, Brian Gosschalk and John Bartle. London: Frank Cass.

Gould, Philip. 1998a. 'Why Labour won.' In *Political Communications: Why Labour Won the General Election of 1997*, eds. Ivor Crewe, Brian Gosschalk and John Bartle. London: Frank Cass.

Gould, Philip. 1998b. *The Unfinished Revolution: How the Modernisers Saved the Labour Party*. London: Little Brown and Co.

Graber, Doris. 1984. *Processing the News: How People Tame the Information Tide*.

New York: Longman.

Graber, Doris. 1994. 'Why voters fail information tests: can the hurdles be overcome?' *Political Communication*, 11(4): 331–46.

Graber, Doris, Denis McQuail and Pippa Norris, eds. 1998. *The Politics of News: The News of Politics*. Washington, DC: CQ Press.

Gunter, Barrie, Jane Sancho-Aldridge, and Paul Winstone. 1994. *Television and the Public's View, 1993*. London: John Libbey.

Gunter, Barrie. 1994. 'The question of media violence.' In *Media Effects*, Jennings Bryant and Dolf Zillmann. Hillsdale, NJ: Lawrence Erlbaum.

Hachten, William A. 1998. *The Troubles of Journalism: A Critical Look at What's Right and Wrong with the Press*. Mahwah, NJ: Lawrence Erlbaum.

Harris, Richard Jackson. 1994. 'The impact of sexually explicit material.' In *Media Effects*, Jennings Bryant and Dolf Zillmann. Hillsdale, NJ: Lawrence Erlbaum.

Harrison, Martin. 1989. 'Television election news analysis: use and abuse – a reply.' *Political Studies*, XXXVII(4): 652–8.

Harrison, Martin. 1997. 'Politics on the air.' In *The British General Election of 1997*, David Butler and Dennis Kavanagh. London: Macmillan.

Harrop, Martin. 1997. 'The pendulum swings: The British election of 1997.' *Government and Opposition*, 32(3): 306–19.

Harrop, Martin and Margaret Scammell. 1992. 'A tabloid war.' In *The British General Election of 1992*, David Butler and Dennis Kavanagh. Basingstoke: Macmillan.

Hart, Roderick. 1994. *Seducing America*. Oxford: Oxford University Press.

Heath, Anthony and Bridget Taylor. 1999. 'New sources of abstention?' In *Critical Elections: British Parties and Voters in Long-term Perspective*, eds. Geoffrey Evans and Pippa Norris. London: Sage.

Heath, Anthony, Roger Jowell and John Curtice. 1985. *How Britain Votes*. London: Pergamon.

Heath, Anthony, Roger Jowell and John Curtice. 1991. *Understanding Political Change, 1964–1987*. London: Pergamon.

Heath, Anthony, Roger Jowell, and John Curtice, eds. 1994. *Labour's Last Chance? The 1992 Election and Beyond*. Aldershot, Hants: Dartmouth.

Heath, Anthony, Roger Jowell and John Curtice. 1999. *New Labour and the Future of the Left*. Oxford: Oxford University Press.

Heffernan, Richard and Mike Marqusee. 1992. *Defeat from the Jaws of Victory*. London: Verso.

Hewitt, Patricia and Philip Gould. 1993. 'Learning from success – Labour and Clinton's New Democrats.' *Renewal*, 1(1):45–51.

Holbrook, Thomas M. 1996. *Do Campaigns Matter?* Thousand Oaks: Sage.

Holmes, Richard and Alison Holmes. 1998. 'Sausages or policeman? The role of the Liberal Democrats in the 1997 general election campaign.' In *Political Communications: Why Labour Won the General Election of 1997*, eds. Ivor Crewe, Brian Gosschalk and John Bartle. London: Frank Cass.

Holtz-Bacha, C. 1990. 'Videomalaise revisited: media exposure and political alienation in West Germany.' *European Journal of Communication*, 5: 78–85.

Hovland, Carl I. 1959. 'Reconciling conflicting results from experimental and survey studies of attitude change.' *American Psychologist*,. 14: 10–23.

Hovland, Carl I., Arthur A. Lumsdaine, and Fred D. Sheffield. 1949. *Experiments on Mass Communications*. Princeton, NJ: Princeton University Press.

Hovland, Carl, Irving Janis, and Harold H. Kelley. 1953. *Communication and Persuasion*. New Haven, CT: Yale University Press.

Huckfeldt, Robert and John Sprague. 1995. *Citizens, Politics and Social Communications*. New York: Cambridge University Press.

Humphreys, Peter J. 1996. *Mass Media and Media Policy in Western Europe*.

Manchester: Manchester University Press.

Ingham, Bernard. 1994. *Kill the Messenger* London: HarperCollins.

Inglehart, Ronald. 1990. *Culture Shift in Advanced Industrial Society*. Princeton, N.J: Princeton University Press.

Inglehart, Ronald. 1997. *Modernization and Postmodernization: Cultural, Economic and Political Change in 43 Societies*. Princeton, NJ: Princeton University Press.

Iyengar, Shanto. 1990. 'Shortcuts to political knowledge. The role of selective attention and accessibility.' In *Information and Democratic Processes*, eds. John A. Ferejon and James H. Kuklinski. Chicago: University of Illinois Press.

Iyengar, Shanto. 1991. *Is Anyone Responsible? How Television Frames Political Issues*. Chicago: University of Chicago Press.

Iyengar, Shanto and Donald R. Kinder. 1987. *News That Matters: Television and American Opinion*. Chicago: University of Chicago Press.

Iyengar, Shanto and Richard Reeves. 1997. *Do the Media Govern?* Thousand Oaks: Sage.

Jamieson, Kathleen. 1992. *Dirty Politics*. Oxford: Oxford University Press.

Johnston, Richard *et al.* 1992. *Letting the People Decide*. Montreal: McGill-Queen's University Press.

Jones, Nicholas. 1995. *Soundbites and Spindoctors*. London: Cassell.

Jones, Nicholas. 1997. *Campaign 1997: How the General Election Was Won and Lost*. London: Indigo.

Just, Marion, Ann Creigler, Dean Alger, Montague Kern, West Darrell, and Timothy Cook. 1996. *Crosstalk: Citizens, Candidates and the Media in a Presidential Campaign*. Chicago: University of Chicago Press.

Just, Marion. 1998. 'Candidate strategies and the media campaign.' In *The Election of 1996*, ed. Gerald M. Pomper. Chatham, NJ: Chatham House.

Kaid, Lynda Lee and Christina Holtz-Bacha. 1995. *Political Advertising in Western Democracies*. Thousand Oaks, CA: Sage.

Kavanagh, Dennis. 1994. 'Changes in electoral behaviour and the party system.' *Parliamentary Affairs*, 47(4): 596–613.

Kavanagh, Dennis. 1995. *Election Campaigning: the New Marketing of Politics*. Oxford: Blackwell.

Kavanagh, Dennis. 1997 'The Labour campaign.' In *Britain Votes 1997*, eds. Pippa Norris and Neil Gavin. Oxford: Oxford University Press.

Kellner, Peter. 1997. 'Why the Tories were trounced.' In *Britain Votes 1997*, eds. Pippa Norris and Neil Gavin. Oxford: Oxford University Press.

Kepplinger, Hans M. 1996. 'Skandale Und Politikverdrossenheit – Ein Langzeitvergleich.' *Medien Und Politischer Prozeb*, editors Otfried Jarren *et al.* Oplanden: Westdeutscher Verlag.

King, Anthony. 1997. *New Labour Triumphs: Britain at the Polls*. Chatham, NJ: Chatham House.

Klapper, Joseph T. 1960. *The Effects of the Mass Media*. Glencoe, IL: Free Press.

Klingemann, Hans-Dieter and Dieter Fuchs. 1995. *Citizens and the State*. New York: Oxford University Press.

Klingemann, Hans-Dieter, Richard I. Hofferbert and Ian Budge. 1994. *Parties, Policies and Democracy*. Boulder, CO: Westview.

Klite, Paul, Robert M. Bardwell, and Jason Salzman. 1997. 'Local TV news: getting away with murder.' *The Harvard International Journal of Press/Politics*, 2(2):102–12.

Kohut, Andrew and Robert C. Toth. 1998. 'The central conundrum: how can people like what they distrust?' *The Harvard International Journal of Press/Politics*, 3(1):110–17.

Langer, John. 1998. *Tabloid Television*. London: Routledge.

Lasswell, Harold. 1949. 'The structure and function of communication in society.' In *Mass Communication*, ed. W. S. Schtramm. Urbana: University of Illinois Press.

Lazarsfeld, Paul F., Bernard Berelson, and Hazel Gaudet. 1944. *The People's Choice: How the Voter Makes Up His Mind in a Presidential Campaign*. New York: Columbia University Press.

Lewis-Beck, Michael S. 1988. *Economics and Elections: the Major Western Democracies*. Ann Arbor: The University of Michigan Press.

Lewis-Beck, Michael and Tim Rice. 1992. *Forecasting Elections*. Washington, DC: CQ Press.

Lilley, Sarah-Jane, Lindsay Brook, Caroline Bryson, Lindsey Jarvis, Alison Park and Katarina Thomson. 1998. *British Social Attitudes and Northern Ireland Social Attitudes 1996 Surveys: Technical Report*. London: SCPR.

Linton, Martin. 1994. *Money and Votes*. London: Institute for Public Policy Research.

Linton, Martin. 1995 *Was it The Sun wot won it?* Seventh Guardian Lecture, Nuffield College, Oxford, 30 October.

Lippmann, Walter. 1997. (1922) *Public Opinion*. New York: Free Press.

Lodge, Milton and Kathleen M. McGraw. 1995. *Political Judgment: Structure and Process*. Ann Arbor: University of Michigan Press.

Lowery, Shearon A. and Melvin L. DeFleur. 1995. *Milestones in Mass Communications Research*. New York: Longman.

Lull, James and Stephen Hinerman, eds. 1997. *Media Scandals*. Cambridge: Polity Press.

Lupia, Arthur and Matthew D. McCubbins. 1998. *The Democratic Dilemma*. Cambridge: Cambridge University Press.

Maarek, Philippe J. 1995. *Political Marketing and Communications*. London: John Libbey.

MacArthur, Brian. 1992. 'Perhaps it was *The Sun* wot won it?' *Sunday Times*, 12 April.

Markovits, Andrei S. and Mark Silverstein, eds. 1988. *The Politics of Scandal*. New York: Holmes and Meier.

McCombs, Maxwell. 1997. 'Building consensus: the news media's agenda-setting roles.' *Political Communication*, 14(4): 433–43.

McCombs, Maxwell and George Estrada. 1997. 'The news media and the pictures in our heads.' In *Do the Media Govern?* eds. Shanto Iyengar and Richard Reeves. Thousand Oaks, CA: Sage.

McCombs, Maxwell and D. L. Shaw. 1972. 'The agenda-setting function of the mass media.' *Public Opinion Quarterly*, 36: 176–87.

McCullum, R. B. and Alison Readman. 1964. *The British General Election of 1945*. 2nd ed. London: Frank Cass.

McKee, David. 1995. 'Fact is free but comment is sacred; or was it *The Sun* wot won it?' In *Political Communications: The General Election Campaign of 1992*, eds. Ivor Crewe and Brian Gosschalk. Cambridge: Cambridge University Press.

McKie, David. 1998. 'Swingers, clingers, waverers and quaverers: the tabloid press in the 1997 election.' In *Political Communications: Why Labour Won the General Election of 1997*, eds. Ivor Crewe, Brian Gosschalk and John Bartle. London: Frank Cass.

McNair, Brian. 1994. *News and Journalism in the UK*. London: Routledge.

McNair, Brian. 1995. *An Introduction to Political Communication*. London: Routledge.

McQuail, Denis. 1992. *Media Performance*. London: Sage.

McQuail, Denis. 1994. *Mass Communication Theory*. London: Sage.

McQuail, Denis. 1997. *Audience Analysis*. London: Sage.

McQuail, Denis and Sven Windahl. 1993. *Communication Models*. London: Longman.

Mendelsohn, Paul F. and Garrett J. O'Keefe. 1976. *The People Choose a President*. New York: Praeger.

Milbrath, L. W. 1965. *Political Participation*.

Miller, Arthur, Edie Goldenberg, and Erbring Lutz. 1979. 'Set type politics: impact of newspapers on public confidence.' *American Political Science Review*, 73: 67–84.

Miller, Warren and Merrill Shanks. 1996. *The Changing American Voter*. Ann Arbor: University of Michigan Press.

Miller, William Lockley. 1990. *How Voters Change: the 1987 British Election Campaign in Perspective*. Oxford: Oxford Univesity Press.

Miller, William L. 1991. *Media and Voters: the Audience, Content, and Influence of Press and Television at the 1987 General Election*. Oxford: Clarendon Press.

Miller, William L., Neil Sonntag and David Broughton. 1989. 'Television in the 1987 British election campaign: its content and influence.' *Political Studies*, XXXVII (4): 626–51.

Milne, R. S. and H. C. Mackenzie. 1954. *Straight Fight*. London: Hansard Society.

Milne, R. S. and H. C. MacKenzie. 1958. *Marginal Seat*. London: Hansard Society for Parliamentary Government.

Mitchell, Austin. 1995. *Election '45*. London: Fabian Society.

Mughan, Tony. 1996. 'Television can matter: bias in the 1992 general election.' In *British Elections and Parties Yearbook, 1996*, eds. David M. Farrell *et al*. London: Frank Cass.

Negrine, Ralph. 1994. *Politics and the Mass Media in Britain*. London: Routledge.

Neill Report. 1998. *5th Report of the Committee on Standards in Public Life: The Funding of Political Parties in the United Kingdom*. Chaired by Lord Neill of Blayden. Cm 4057-I. London: The Stationery Office.

Neuman, W. Russell, Marion R. Just and Ann N. Crigler. 1992. *Common Knowledge*. Chicago: University of Chicago Press.

Newton, Kenneth. 1991. 'Do people believe everything they read in the papers? Newspapers and voters in the 1983 and 1987 elections.' In *British Elections and Parties Handbook 1991*, eds. Ivor Crewe, Pippa Norris, David Denver, and David Broughton. Hemel Hempstead: Harvester Wheatsheaf.

Newton, Kenneth. 1997. 'Politics and the news media: mobilisation or videomalaise?' In *British Social Attitudes: the 14th Report*, 1997/8, eds. Roger Jowell, John Curtice, Alison Park, Katarina Thomson and Lindsay Brook. Aldershot: Ashgate.

Newton, Kenneth. 1999. *Mass Media Effects: Political Mobilisation, Mediamalaise, and Social Capital*.

Norpoth, Helmut, Michael S. Lewis-Beck, and Jean-Dominique Lafay. 1991. *Economics and Politics: the Calculus of Support*. Ann Arbor: University of Michigan Press.

Norris, Pippa. 1996. 'Does television erode social capital? A reply to Putnam.' *P.S.: Political Science and Politics* XXIX(3).

Norris, Pippa. 1997a. *Electoral Change Since 1945*. Oxford: Blackwell.

Norris, Pippa. 1997b. 'Political communications.' In *Developments in British Politics 5*, eds. Patrick Dunleavy, Andrew Gamble, Ian Holliday and Gillian Peele. London: Macmillan.

Norris, Pippa. 1997c. *Politics and the Press: The News Media and Their Influences*. Boulder, CO: Lynne Reinner.

Norris, Pippa, 1997d. 'Anatomy of a Labour landslide.' In *Britain Votes 1997*, eds. Pippa Norris and Neil Gavin. Oxford: Oxford University Press.

Norris, Pippa. 1998a. 'The battle for the campaign agenda.' In *New Labour Triumphs: Britain at the Polls*, ed. Anthony King. Chatham, NJ: Chatham House.

Norris, Pippa. 1998b. 'Who surfs? New technology, old voters and virtual democracy in America.' Paper for the John F. Kennedy Conference on Visions of Governance for the 21st Century, Bretton Woods.

Norris, Pippa. ed. 1999a. *Critical Citizens: Global Support for Democratic Government.* Oxford: Oxford University Press.

Norris, Pippa. 2000. 'Television and civic malaise.' In *What's Troubling the Trilateral Democracies*, eds. Susan J. Pharr and Robert D. Putnam. Princeton, NJ: Princeton University Press.

Norris, Pippa and Geoffrey Evans. 1999. 'Was 1997 a critical election?' In *Critical Elections: British Parties and Voters in Long-term Perspective*, eds. Geoffrey Evans and Pippa Norris. London: Sage.

Norris, Pippa and Neil Gavin, eds. 1997. *Britain Votes 1997*. Oxford, Oxford University Press.

Norris, Pippa and David Jones. 1998. 'Virtual Democracy.' *The Harvard International Journal of Press/Politics*. 3(3): 1–4.

Nossiter, Tom, Margaret Scammell and Holli A. Semetko. 1995. 'Old values versus news values.' In *Political Communications and the 1992 General Election*, eds. Ivor Crewe and Brian Gosschalk. Cambridge: Cambridge University Press.

Nye, Joseph S. Jr., Philip D. Zelikow, and David C. King. 1997. *Why People Don't Trust Government*. Cambridge, MA.: Harvard University Press.

Ostergaard, Vernt Stubbe, ed. 1997. *The Media in Western Europe*. London: Sage.

Parry, Geraint, George Moser and Neil Day. 1992. *Political Participation and Democracy in Britain*. Cambridge: Cambridge University Press.

Patterson, Thomas. 1980. *The Mass Media Election: How Americans Choose Their President*. New York: Praeger.

Patterson, Thomas E. 1993. *Out of Order*. New York: A. Knopf.

Patterson, Thomas E. 1998. 'Political roles of the journalist.' In *The Politics of News: the News of Politics*, eds. Doris Graber, Denis McQuail and Pippa Norris. Washington DC: CQ Press.

Patterson, Thomas and Wolfgang Donsbach. 1996. 'News decisions: journalists as partisan actors.' *Political Communication*, 13(4): 455–68.

Patterson, Thomas and R.D. McClure, 1976. *The Unseeing Eye: The Myth of Television Power in National Elections*. New York: Putnam.

Peston, Robert. 1994. 'Tories need killer facts to stop electoral death.' *Financial Times*, 21 November.

Pharr, Susan J. 1997. 'Japanese videocracy.' *The Harvard International Journal of Press/Politics*, 2(1): 130–8.

Pharr, Susan J. and Ellis S. Krauss. 1996. *Media and Politics in Japan*. Honolulu: University Press of Hawaii.

Popkin, Samuel. 1994. *The Reasoning Voter*. Chicago: University of Chicago Press.

Postman, Neil. 1985. *Amusing Ourselves to Death*. London: Methuen.

Price, Vincent and John Zaller. 1993. 'Who gets the news? Alternative measures of news reception and their implications for research.' *Public Opinion Quarterly*, 57: 133–64.

Protess, David L. and Maxwell McCombs. 1991. *Agenda-Setting: Readings on Media, Public Opinion and Policymaking*. Hillsdale, NJ: Erlbaum.

Putnam, Robert. 1995. 'Tuning in, tuning out: the strange disappearance of social capital in America.' *P.S.: Political Science and Politics*, XXVIII(4): 664–83.

Putnam, Robert. 1996. 'The strange disappearance of civic America.' *The American Prospect*, 24.

Robinson, Michael. 1976. 'Public affairs television and the growth of political malaise: the case of "the selling of the Pentagon".' *American Political Science Review*, 70: 409–32.

Rose, Richard. 1997. 'The New Labour government: on the crest of a wave.' In

Britain Votes 1997, eds. Pippa Norris and Neil Gavin. Oxford: Oxford University Press.

Rose, Richard and Ian McAllister. 1986. *Voters Begin to Choose: From Closed Class to Open Elections in Britain*. London: Sage.

Rose, Richard and Ian McAllister. 1990. *The Loyalties of Voters*. London: Sage.

Rosenbaum, Martin. 1997. *From Soapbox to Soundbite*. London: Macmillan.

Rosenstone, Steven. 1983. *Forecasting Presidential Elections*. New Haven, CT: Yale University Press.

Saatchi, Maurice. 1997. *Spectator*.

Sabato, Larry. 1991. *Feeding Frenzy: How Attack Journalism Has Transformed American Politics*. New York: Free Press.

Sanders, David. 1991. 'Government popularity and the next general election.' *Political Quarterly*, 62: 235–61.

Sanders, David. 1993. 'Modelling government popularity in postwar Britain.' *American Journal of Political Science*, 37: 317–34.

Sanders, David. 1996. 'Economic performance, management competence and the outcome of the next general election.' *Political Studies*, 64: 203–31.

Sanders, David. 1997a, September. 'Conservative Incompetence, Labour Responsibility and the Feel-good Factor.' EPOP Conference, University of Essex, Essex.

Sanders, David. 1997b. 'Voting and the electorate'. In *Developments in British Politics 5*, eds. Patrick Dunleavy, Andrew Gamble, Ian Holliday and Gillian Peele. London: Macmillan.

Sanders, David and Pippa Norris. 1998. 'Does negative news matter? The effects of television news on party images in the 1997 British general election.' *British Elections and Parties Yearbook*, 1998 eds. Charles Pattie *et al*. London: Frank Cass.

Sanders, David and Simon Price. 1994. 'Party support and economic perceptions in the UK, 1979–87. In *British Elections and Parties Yearbook, 1994*, eds. David Broughton *et al*. London: Frank Cass.

Särlvik, Bo and Ivor Crewe. 1983. *Decade of Dealignment: The Conservative Victory of 1979 and Electoral Trends in the 1970s*. Cambridge: Cambridge University Press.

Sawicki, Frederic and Chris M. Leland. 1991. 'The formation of the electoral agenda: a case study in social welfare issues in the United States and France.' In *Mediated Politics in Two Cultures*, eds. Lynda Lee Kaid, Jacques Gerstle and Keith R. Sanders. New York: Praeger.

Scammell, Margaret. 1995. *Designer Politics: How Elections Are Won*. Houndmills, Basingstoke, Hampshire: Macmillan.

Scammell, Margaret and Martin Harrop. 1997. 'The press: Labour's finest hour.' In *The British General Election of 1997*, David Butler and Dennis Kavanagh. London: Macmillan

Scammell, Margaret and Holli Semetko. 1995. 'Political advertising on television: the British experience.' In *Political Advertising in Western Democracies: Parties and Candidates on TV*, eds. Lynda Lee Kaid and Christina Holz-Bacha. London: Sage.

Schoenbach, Klaus and Holli A. Semetko. 1992. 'Agenda-setting, agenda-reinforcing or agenda-deflating? A study of the 1990 German national election.' *Journalism Quarterly*, 69(4): 837–46.

Schudson, Michael. 1995. *The Power of News*. Cambridge, Mass: Harvard University Press.

Shoemaker, Pamela J. and Stephen D. Reese. 1996. *Mediating the Message*. New York: Longman.

Semetko, Holli A. 1996a. 'The media.' In *Comparing Democracies*, eds. Lawrence LeDuc, Richard Neimi, and Pippa Norris. Thousand Oaks, CA: Sage.

Semetko, Holli. 1996b. 'Political balance on television: campaigns in the United States, Britain and Germany.' *The Harvard International Journal of Press/Politics*, 1(1): 51–71.

Semetko, Holli A. and Klaus Schoenbach. 1994. *Germany's 'Unity' Election: Voters and the Media*. Cresskill, NJ: Hampton Press.

Semetko, Holli A., Jay G. Blumler, Michael Gurevitch, and David H. Weaver. 1991. *The Formation of Campaign Agendas: A Comparative Analysis of Party and Media Roles in Recent American and British Elections*. Hillsdale, NJ: Lawrence Erlbaum.

Semetko, Holli A., Margaret Scammell, and T. J. Nossiter. 1994. 'Media coverage of the 1992 British general election campaign.' In *Labour's Last Chance? The 1992 Election and Beyond*, eds. Anthony Heath, Roger Jowell and John Curtice. Aldershot: Dartmouth.

Semetko, Holli, Margaret Scammell, and Peter Goddard. 1997. 'Television.' In *Britain Votes 1997*, eds. Pippa Norris and Neil Gavin. Oxford: Oxford University Press.

Seymour-Ure, Colin. 1974. *The Political Impact of the Mass Media*. Beverly Hills, CA: Sage.

Seymour-Ure, Colin. 1995. 'Characters and assassinations.' In *Political Communication: the General Election Campaign of 1992*, eds. Ivor Crewe and Brian Gosschalk. Cambridge: Cambridge University Press

Seymour-Ure, Colin. 1996. *The British Press and Broadcasting Since 1945*. Oxford: Blackwell.

Seymour-Ure, Colin. 1997. 'Editorial opinion in the national press.' In *Britain Votes 1997*, eds. Pippa Norris and Neil Gavin. Oxford: Oxford University Press.

Smith, Eric. 1989. *The Unchanging American Voter*. Berkeley, CA: The University of California Press.

Swaddle, Kevin and Anthony Heath. 1989. 'Official and reported turnout in the British general election of 1987.' *British Journal of Political Science*, 19: 537–70.

Swanson, David L. and Paolo. Mancini. 1996. *Politics, Media, and Modern Democracy: an International Study of Innovations in Electoral Campaigning and Their Consequences*. Westport, Conn: Praeger.

Tait, Richard. 1995. 'The parties and television.' In *Political Communications: The General Election Campaign of 1992*, eds. Ivor Crewe and Brian Gosschalk. Cambridge: Cambridge University Press.

Takeshita, Toshio. 1993. 'Agenda-setting Effects of the press in a Japanese local election.' *Studies of Broadcasting*, 29: 194–216.

Takeshita, Toshio and Shunji Mikami. 1995. 'How did mass media influence the voters' choice in the 1993 general election in Japan? A study of agenda-setting.' *Keio Communication Review*, 17: 27–41.

Thomson, Katarina *et al.* 1999a. *British General Election Study 1997: Cross-section Survey, Scottish Election Study and Ethnic Minority Study: Technical Report*. London: SCPR.

Thomson, Katarina *et al.* 1999b. *British General Election Study 1997: Campaign Panel: Technical Report*. London: SCPR.

Thurber, James and C. Nelson. 1995. *Campaigns and Elections American Style*.

Trenaman, Joseph and Dennis McQuail. 1961. *Television and the Political Image*. London: Methuen.

Vallely, Paul, Christian Wolmar, Colin Brown, Steve Boggan and Barrie Clement. 1998. 'Blair's long trek to victory.' *The Independent*, 3 May: 17–18.

Verba, Sidney and Norman H. Nie. 1972. *Participation in America*. New York: Harper and Row.

Verba, Sidney, Kay Lehman Schlozman, and Henry E. Brady. 1995. *Voice and Equality: Civic Voluntarism in American Politics*. Cambridge, Mass: Harvard University Press.

Wald, Kenneth D. 1983. *Crosses on the Ballot: Patterns of British Voter Alignment Since 1885*. Princeton, NJ: Princeton University Press.

Ward, Stephen and Rachel Gibson. 1998. 'The first internet election.' In *Political Communications: Why Labour Won the General Election of 1997*, eds. Ivor Crewe, Brian Gosschalk and John Bartle. London: Frank Cass.

Watts, Duncan. 1997. *Political Communications Today*. Manchester: Manchester University Press.

Weaver, David, Doris Graber, Maxwell McCombs, and C. H. Eyal. 1981. *Media Agenda-Setting in Presidential Elections: Issues, Images and Interests*. New York: Praeger.

Webber, Richard. 1993. 'The 1992 general election: constituency results and local patterns of national newspaper readership.' In *British Elections and Parties Yearbook, 1993*, eds. David Denver *et al*. Herts: Harvester Wheatsheaf.

Westerstahl, Jorgen and Folke Johansson. 1986. 'News ideologies as moulders of domestic news.' *European Journal of Communication*, 1: 133–49.

Weymouth, Tony and Bernard Lamizet. 1996. *Markets and Myth: Forces for Change in the European Media*. London: Longman.

Wheeler, Mark. 1997. *Politics and the Mass Media*. Oxford: Blackwell.

Whiteley, Paul. 1997 'The Conservative campaign.' In *Britain Votes 1997*, eds. Pippa Norris and Neil Gavin. Oxford: Oxford University Press.

Worcester, Robert M. 1998. 'The media and the polls.' In *Political Communications: Why Labour Won the General Election of 1997*, eds. Ivor Crewe, Brian Gosschalk and John Bartle. London: Frank Cass.

Wring, Dominic. 1996. 'From mass propaganda to political marketing: the transformation of Labour Party election campaigning.' In *British Parties and Elections Yearbook, 1995*, eds. Colin Rallings *et al*. London: Frank Cass.

Zaller, John. 1993. *The Nature and Origins of Mass Opinion*. New York: Cambridge University Press.

Zaller, John. 1998. 'Monica Lewinsky's contribution to political science.' *PS: Political Science and Politics*, XXXI(2): 182–9.

Zucker, Harold. 1978. 'The variable nature of news influence.' In *Communication Yearbook 2*, ed. Brent D. Ruben. New Brunswick, NJ: Transaction Books.

Name Index

Alger, Dean 14, 55
Ansolabehere, Stephen 16, 50, 55, 98, 186
Asp, Kent 114

Bardwell, Robert M. 98
Baran, Stanley 43
Bartle, John 171, 172
Bealey, Frank 47
Bennett, W. Lance 70
Berelson, Bernard 4, 5, 14, 85, 100, 132
Berrington, Hugh 61
Birch, Anthony 47
Blackburn, Robin 30
Blondel, Jean 47
Blumler, Jay 5, 7, 29, 31, 44, 47, 48, 54, 82, 84, 85, 97, 98, 99, 130, 192
Boggan, Steve 11
Brady, Henry E. 90
Brosius, H. 114
Broughton, David 131
Brown, Colin 11
Bryant, Jennings 12, 43
Brynin, Malcolm 136
Budge, Ian 17, 44, 60, 81, 82, 131, 178
Butler, David 6, 9, 10, 16, 41, 48, 53, 56, 57, 58, 59, 60, 62, 85, 100, 136, 170, 171, 172

Campbell, Angus 6
Cappella, Joseph N. 3, 50, 55, 98
Cathcart, Brian 88
Chaffee, Steven H. 102, 104
Chan, Sophia 98
Clement, Barrie 11
Cohen, Bernard 119
Converse, Philip 6
Cook, Timothy 14, 55
Creigler, Ann 14, 55
Crewe, Ivor 10, 38, 73, 83, 136, 171, 172, 175, 188
Crigler, Ann N. 14
Curtice, John 6, 18, 55, 58, 100, 108, 115, 129, 136, 153, 154, 161, 164, 178, 187

Dahlgren, Peter 98
Dalton, Russell J. 99, 153
Darrell, West 14, 55
Davis, Dennis 43

Day, Neil 90
Dearing, John W. 16, 69, 70, 71, 114
DeFleur, Melvin L. 4, 43
Delli Carpini, Michael 14, 103
Denver, David 11, 23, 35, 99, 178
Diez-Nicolas, Juan 44
Donsbach, Wolfgang 98
Downs, Anthony 14
Dunleavy, Patrick 153

Esaisson, Peter 114
Estrada, George 69
Evans, Geoffrey 3, 7, 19, 37, 173, 178, 187

Fallows, James 3, 15, 84, 98
Farlie, David 17, 44, 81, 82, 131
Faucheux, R. 53
Finkelstein, Daniel 172
Franklin, Bob 2, 41
Friedrichsen, Mike 46, 99

Gadir, S. 114
Gaudet, Hazel 4, 5, 14, 85, 100, 132
Gavin, Neil 8, 10, 18, 35, 46
Geddes, Andrew 10
Gelman, Andrew 3, 8, 148, 172
Gerbner, George 16, 46, 98
Gibson, Rachel K. 12, 34
Glasgow Media Group 45
Goddard, Peter 41
Goldenberg, Edie 98
Gosschalk, Brian 10, 171, 172
Gould, Philip 37, 58, 59, 171
Graber, Doris 14, 107
Gunter, Barrie 31, 90, 101
Gurevitch, Michael 29, 31, 44, 54, 82, 84, 97, 130, 192

Hague, Roderick 61
Hands, Gordon 11, 23, 35, 99, 178
Harrison, Martin 30, 33, 45, 72, 74, 87, 99, 131
Harrop, Martin 7, 10, 25, 33, 53, 55, 67, 75, 78, 99, 152, 157
Heath, Anthony 6, 58, 99, 129, 136, 178, 187
Heffernan, Richard 58
Henig, Simon 23

Hewitt, Patricia 58, 59
Hinerman, Stephen 98
Hofferbert, Richard I. 44
Holbrook, Thomas M. 172
Holmberg, Soren 114
Holmes, Alison 172
Holmes, Richard 172
Holtz-Bacha, Christina 30
Hovland, Carl I. 4, 14, 50
Huckfeldt, Robert 11
Humphreys, Peter J. 97
Husbands, Christopher 153

Ingham, Bernard 24
Inglehart, Ronald 99
Irving, Janis 4, 50
Iyengar, Shanto 16, 50, 55, 98, 118, 132, 186

Jamieson, Kathleen H. 3, 50, 55, 67, 98
Johansson, Folke 46, 99
Johnston, Richard 114
Jones, David 12
Jones, Nicholas 2, 10, 18, 62
Jowell, Roger 6, 58, 108, 129, 136, 187
Just, Marion 14, 55

Kaid, Lynda Lee 30
Kanihan, Stacey Frank 102, 104
Katz, Eli 48
Kavanagh, Dennis 2, 9, 10, 18, 35, 37, 41, 53, 56, 57, 58, 59, 60, 62, 130, 171, 172
Kawakami, K. 153
Keeter, Scott 14, 103
Kelley, Harold H. 4, 50
Kellner, Peter 60, 186
Kepplinger, Hans M. 46, 114
Kern, Montague 14, 55
Kinder, Donald R. 50, 118, 132
King, Anthony 10, 35, 58, 171
King, David C. 108
King, Gary 3, 8, 148, 172
Klapper, Joseph T. 5
Klingemann, Hans-Dieter 44
Klite, Paul 98

Lafay, Jean-Dominique 8
Langer, John 98
Lasswell, Harold 9
Lazarsfeld, Paul F. 4, 5, 14, 85, 100, 132
Lehman Schlozman, Kay 90
Leland, Chris M. 114
Lewis-Beck, Michael S. 8
Linton, Martin 55, 60, 152, 153, 154
Lippmann, Walter 4, 16, 69

Lowery, Shearon A. 4, 43
Lull, James 98
Lumsdaine, Arthur A. 4, 50
Lupia, Arthur 3, 14
Lutz, Erbring 98

MacArthur, Brian 152
McCain, W. P. 47
McClure, R.D. 5
McCombs, Maxwell 16, 54, 69, 114
McCubbins, Matthew D. 3, 14
McKee, David 152
Mackenzie, H.C. 47, 85, 90, 100
McKie, David 9
McNair, Brian 28
McPhee, W.N. 4, 85, 100
McQuail, Denis 4, 5, 7, 43, 47, 85, 90, 100, 115
Mancini, Paulo 2, 22, 29, 79
Marquesee, Mike 58
Mendelsohn, Paul F. 5
Mikami, Shunji 114
Milbrath 90
Miller, Arthur 98
Miller, Warren E. 6
Miller, William L. 7, 17, 18, 55, 70, 71, 83, 90, 100, 101, 115, 128, 131
Milne, R.S. 47, 85, 90, 100
Moser, George 90
Mughan, Tony 48

Neill, Report 17, 32, 39, 40, 88
Nelson, C. 53
Neuman, W. Russell 14
Newton, Kenneth 16, 18, 48, 99, 100, 104, 153
Norputh, Helmut 8
Norris, Pippa 3, 7, 10, 12, 16, 17, 19, 22, 31, 34, 35, 37, 48, 74, 99, 104, 108, 109, 111, 115, 136, 151, 173, 176, 178, 187
Nossiter, Tom 73, 129
Nye, Joseph S. Jr. 108

O'Keefe, Garrett J. 5

Parry, Geraint 90
Patterson, Thomas E. 3, 5, 15, 46, 84, 98, 130, 186
Peston, Robert 57
Popkin, Samuel 14
Postman, Neil 98
Price, Simon 8
Price, Vincent 102
Protess, David L. 16, 114
Putnam, Robert 3, 15, 47, 98

Ranney, Austin 41
Robinson, Michael 15, 98
Rogers, Everett M. 16, 69, 70, 71, 114

Saatchi, Maurice 63
Salzman, Jason 98
Sancho-Aldridge, Jane 31, 90, 101
Sanders, David 7, 8, 18, 46, 53, 56, 136, 151
Sårlvik, Bo 136, 187
Sawicki, Frederic 114
Scammell, Margaret 2, 10, 18, 25, 27, 28, 30,
 31, 32, 33, 35, 41, 53, 55, 56, 60, 62, 63, 64,
 65, 66, 67, 73, 75, 76, 77, 78, 81, 82, 87, 99,
 129, 152, 157
Schoenbach, Klaus 44, 114
Schudson, Michael 98
Semetko, Holli A. 18, 27, 28, 30, 31, 32, 41,
 44, 54, 55, 62, 63, 64, 65, 66, 73, 76, 77, 78,
 81, 82, 84, 87, 100, 114, 129, 130, 153, 154,
 161, 164, 192
Seymour-Ure, Colin 23, 24, 25, 55, 92, 99,
 126, 167
Shaw, D.L. 16, 54, 69, 114
Sheffield, Fred D. 4, 50
Sonntag, Neil 131
Sparks, Colin 98
Sprague, John 11
Steed, Michael 178

Stokes, Donald E. 6, 16, 48, 85, 100, 136, 187
Suzuki, H. 153
Swanson, David L. 2, 22, 29, 79

Tait, Richard 31
Takeshita, Toshio 114
Taylor, Bridget 99, 178
Thomson, Katarina 188
Thurber, James 53
Tonge, Jon 10
Trenaman, Joseph 5, 47, 85, 100, 115

Vallely, Paul 11
Verba, Sidney 90
Voltmer, K. 153

Ward, Stephen 12, 34
Weaver, David H. 44, 54, 82, 84, 189
Webber, Richard 18
Westerstahl, Jorgen 46, 99
Whiteley, Paul 7, 53
Winstone, Paul 31, 90, 101
Wolmar, Christine 11

Zaller, John 14, 102, 103, 129
Zelikow, Philip D. 108
Zillmann, Dolf 12, 43
Zucker, Harold 123

Subject Index

age, media use 91–2
agenda balance
    effects of 142–3
    hypothesis 132
    television news 131
agenda-setting
    media influence 182–3
    process of 69–71
    theory of 9, 16–17
    video experiments 116–18
agendas, campaign communications 62–6
aggregate trends, opinion polls 46–7
attentive public 5, 92–3, 95
attitudes, media use 47–9
audiences, television news
    profile of 90–3
    size of 33f, 86–9
autonomy, national press 23–9

BBC *Producer Guidelines* 29, 73, 184
Bell, Tim 35
biases, news coverage 45
Black Wednesday 7, 35–6, 61
Blair, Tony 1, 36, 37, 38, 40, 57, 58, 59, 60, 153
Breakfast News 33
British Election Study (1997)
    campaign panel survey 49–50, 154, 158, 188–92
    cross-sectional survey 47–9, 154, 187–8
broadcasting
    conventions 29–31, 185
    impartiality 29, 31
Brown, Gordon 36, 59

cable television 34
campaign communications
    battle of the agendas 62–6
    dealignment of press 24
    party strategy 54–5
    process of 10–12
campaign news
    exposure to 90–3
    public reaction to 93–5
campaign panel survey (1997), BES 49–50
campaigns
    Conservative 38–40, 56–7

effects of 170–3
electoral change 173–80
evolution of 22–3
expenditure 40t
importance placed on 17
Labour 35–8, 58–61
mobilization function 15
see also Labour Listens campaign;
    presidential campaigns
Campbell, Alastair 36
cancelling effect, television news 148
candidates, knowledge of 107
CARMA 124
Channel 4 News 52, 86
circulation, national press 23–4, 25t
civic apathy 16
civic engagement 14–16
    media impact 97–113
    media influence 182
    party communications 66–5
civics, knowledge of 105–6
Clarke, Ken 38
class, news audiences 92
class voting 7
Clause Four debate 59
Clinton, Bill 11, 40, 58, 59
cognitive effects
    campaigns and elections 14–15
    debate about 97–9
    theory of 9
Columbia studies 85
communications see campaign communications; party communications; political communications
components, agenda-setting 71
Con–Lab swing, 1997 election 173
conditional effects, news media 13–14
conduct of campaign
    newspaper coverage 79
    television coverage 74, 75
Conservatives
    campaign effect 172
    campaign strategy 38–40
    party strategy 56–7
    support for, changes in
        1997 campaign 158t
        (1992–97) 163t

Conservatives cont.
    effects, television news 145f, 146f
consistency, party campaigns 65–6
constituency campaigns 37
content analysis 189–90
    national press 124–6
    news media 71–2
    news and party messages 43–5
conventions, broadcasting 29–31, 185
cross-sectional survey (1997), BES 47–9
cultivation analysis studies 46
cumulative media effects 12–13, 101, 113
current affairs programmes, audience size
    87
Currie, Edwina 38
cynicism, voters 140

Daily Express 25, 26, 126, 156, 159, 166
Daily Herald 24, 155
Daily Mail 25, 26, 27, 28t, 38, 44, 67, 71, 76,
    77, 78, 79, 84, 126, 156, 159, 166, 184
Daily Record 156, 159
Daily Star 25t, 28, 84, 126, 152, 157, 159,
    166, 168
Daily Telegraph 25, 26, 34, 126, 159, 166
dealignment, national press 23–9
direct mail, expenditure on 40
directional coverage
    hypothesis 131–2
    positive and negative news 137–41
    television news 130
divisions, Conservative campaign 38
Downsian theory, rational choice 14
due impartiality 29, 31
duopoly, BBC/ITV 29, 32

Early Evening News 86
economic policy
    media influence 119, 120, 123t
    public's agenda 126–8
economy
    newspaper coverage 77
    see also political economy
elderly, media use 91–2
election broadcasts, ratio of (1964–1997) 30t
Election Call 87
election news, ratio of (1964–1997) 30t
election night audience 88, 90t
electoral change, campaigns 173–80
electoral volatility 17, 173
electronic media, fragmentation of 29–34
enlightened preferences 3, 148–9
Erie County study 4
ERM debacle 7, 36
Essex forecast model 8

Europe
    impact on public concerns 122–6
    newspaper coverage 76–7
    party manifestos 63–5
    television coverage 75
evening news, audiences 86–7
expenditure, election campaigns 17, 39–40
experimental studies
    media effects 50–2
    television news 190–3
experts, political marketing 35
exposure
    measures of, television news 134–5
    to campaign news 90–3

Fair Votes 61
favourability
    press
        1992 campaign 28t
        1997 campaign 27t
    television, 1997 campaign 31, 32t
feedback loops, public opinion 18–19
fieldwork, experimental study 190
Financial Times 25t, 67, 159
Finkelstein, Danny 38, 172
flow of the vote
    (1992–97) 175–7
    (1996–97) 177–8
forecasting models 8
foreign affairs, television coverage 75
foreign policy
    media influence 119, 120, 123t
    public's agenda 126–8
front-page stories 76–9

gender, media use 92
general elections
    cognitive effects 15
    expenditure (1983–97) 39t
Gould, Philip 36, 37, 58, 60, 171
Guardian 25t, 26, 27, 28t, 38, 44, 67, 71, 76,
    78, 79, 159, 166

headlines
    online 34
    public concerns 16
Heath, Edward 38
Herald 104
Heseltine, Michael 38
hope versus fear theme 60
Horam, John 125
Hunter, Anji 36
hypotheses, media agenda-setting 117–18

impartiality, broadcasting 29, 31

Independent 11, 25t, 26, 27, 28t, 44, 71, 76, 78, 79, 125, 152, 159
internal coherence, party campaigns 65
internet 11–12
    impact of 41
    transformation of news habits 34
Irvine, Lord 36
issue agenda
    correlation, party and media agendas 79–82
    measuring 135
    newspapers 76–7
    television 71, 74–6
issue ownership 16–17, 82–3
issue salience, video experiments 116–26
issues
    media influence 119–20
    party manifestos 63t
ITC *Programme Code* 29, 184

Jenkins, Lord 35

Kinnock, Neil 1, 58, 59, 152
knowledge *see* political knowledge
knowledge scales 102

Labour
    campaign effect 171
    campaign strategy 11, 35–8
    party strategy 58–61
    press endorsements 77–8
    support for, changes in
        1997 campaign 158t
        (1992–97) 163t
        effects, television news 145f, 146f
Labour Listens campaign 18–19
leadership image, changes in 179, 180t
learning, general elections 15
Liberal Democrats
    campaign consistency 65–6, 67
    campaign effect 171–2
    party agenda 65
    party strategy 61–2
    support, effects, television coverage 145f, 147f
Linton, Martin 60
logistic model
    newspaper buying 167t
    party support (1992–97) 165t
    vote switching 161t
long campaigns 23
long-term media effects 12–13, 101, 113

McMenamin, Adrian 37
Major, John 38, 55, 63, 68, 126, 137, 152, 153

Mawhinney, Brian 38, 57
Mandelson, Peter 1, 9, 36, 58
manifestos 44
    agendas 62, 63t
    comparison of 64t
mass communications, early accounts of 4
Mattinson, Deborah 37
media
    influence on voters 182–4
    management, Labour campaign 36–7
    news coverage, criticisms of 41–2
    rise in power and influence of 2–3
    see also electronic media; news media; television; television news
media agendas 70
    correlation, party agendas 79–82
media effects 12–14
    civic engagement 97–113, 182
    public's agenda 114–29
    understanding 43–52
media use
    attitudes and behaviour 47–9
    dynamics of 111–13
meet the public sessions 40
Midnight Special 87
Millbank Tower 11, 36–7, 67
minimal effect theories 5, 100
Mirror 25t, 26, 27, 28t, 44, 71, 76, 78, 84, 92, 156, 159, 164
mobilization
    campaign function 15
    social-psychological theories 16
    theories 99–100
models, election outcomes 8
modern campaigns 23
modernization, Labour party 58–9
multivariate controls, news agenda and public concerns 120–1
My Vote 61

national press
    autonomy and dealignment of 23–9
    content analysis 124–6
    see also newspapers
negative campaigning 67, 186
negative news 28–9, 131, 137–41, 185–6
negative videos 134–5, 192–3
Netherlands, political coverage 29
New Labour: Because Britain Deserves Better 37
New Labour, creation of 1
New Labour, New Danger 57
Newby, Richard 61, 62
news, content analysis 43–5

news agenda
  impact on public concerns 118–22
  party strategy 181–3
News at Ten 29, 44, 71, 72, 86
news coverage
  biases 45
  consequences of 41–2
  influence on voters 182–4
  political participation 109–10
  press 76–9
  television 72–6
  United States, public priorities 114
news media 11–12
  content analysis 71–2
News of the World 26, 28
Newsnight 32, 33, 52, 125
newspapers
  changing allegiances 152–3
  influence of 154–5, 184
  news coverage 76–9
  partisanship 6
  perceptions of partisanship 156–7
  persuasive effects 18
  switching (1992–97) 166–8
  vote switching
    1997 campaign 158–62
    (1992–1997) 162–6
  and votes 155–6
  see also headlines; national press
Nine O'clock News 29, 31, 32, 41, 44, 52, 71, 72, 86, 88, 137

On the Record 87
one last heave strategy 58
online headlines 34
operational measures, media influence on
  voter preferences 134–6
opinion polls
  aggregate trends 46–7
  feedback loops 18–19
  Labour campaign 37
  newspaper coverage 78–9
  television coverage 72–4
over-simplification, American news 98
ownership, national press 25t

Paice, James 125
Panorama 32, 48, 49, 87
parties
  as communicators 10–11
  links with press 24
  popularity (1992–97) 36f
partisan reinforcement, theories of 4–5
partisanship
  measures 135–6

media influence 133
news audience 93
newspapers 25t, 156–7
party affiliation, editorial endorsements 24f
party agendas 70
  comparison of 64t
  correlation with news agenda 79–82
party alignments 6–7
party communications
  civic engagement 66–5
  permanent campaigns 34–40
party election broadcasts (PEBs)
  agendas 62
  audiences 87–8, 89t, 93t
  comparison of 64t
  Europe in 63–5
  proposed abolition 32
  time allocation 30, 44–5
  tone of 66–7
party identification, weakening of 7
party image, changes in 179, 180t
party loyalties, socialization theory 6
party messages
  content analysis 43–5
  feedback loop 18–19
party political broadcasts (PPBs)
  expenditure on 40
  time allocation 30
party preferences, television news 130–50
party strategy 53–4
  campaign communications 54–5
  civic dimension 55–6
  Conservatives 56–7
  Labour 58–61
  Liberal Democrats 61–2
  news agenda 181–3
party support
  logistic model 165t
  measures of changes in 134
  media influence 143–9
Payne Fund Studies 4
People's Choice, The 4
People's Election 87
perceptions
  issue ownership 82–3
  newspaper partisanship 156–7
permanent campaigns, party communications 34–40
persuasion
  arts of 4
  media influence 183–4
  theory of 9, 17–18
play-safe strategy 35
pledges, Labour manifesto 37
pocket-book voting 7–8

policies
changes in knowledge 103–4
television coverage 74
see also economic policy; foreign
policy; social policy
policy agenda 70
political characteristics, news audience 92–3
political communications
impact of 170–86
theories of 1–19
political economy, electoral behaviour 7–8
political efficacy, media impact 108–9
political interest, measures of 135–6
political knowledge
from media 14
measures of 135–6
media impact 102–7
political marketing 35
political participation, news coverage
109–10
politics, newspaper switching (1992–97)
166–8
popularity, parties (1992–97) 36f
positive news 131, 132, 137–41, 185–6
positive videos 134–5, 192, 193
post-modern campaigns 23, 32, 34–5, 41
poster wars 39–40
Powell, Jonathan 36
pre-modern campaigns 22
Prescott, John 38
presidential campaigns, cognitive effects
14–15
press *see* national press; newspapers
press endorsements, Labour 77–8
press releases
comparison of 64t
and news agendas 81t, 82t, 83t
tone of 66–7
press statement agendas 62
professionalization, party communications
35
propaganda
challenges to theories of 4–5
effect on voters 85
theories of 3–4
public, reaction to campaign coverage 85–96
public concerns
impact of Europe 122–6
impact of news agenda 118–22
news headlines 16
public evaluation
standards of television news 95t
television coverage 94t
Public Opinion 4, 16, 69
public's agenda 70

influences on 71
media effects 114–29

Question Time 87

rational choice 14
Reece, Gordon 35, 54
reinforcement
partisan newspapers 6
of voting choice 4–5
Reith, Lord 97
Representation of the People Act 75, 116
respondents, experimental study 190

Saatchi, Maurice 35, 38
Saatchi and Saatchi 54
satellite services 33–4
schematic model, political communications
9, 10f
Scotsman 104
secular dealignment 7
selective attention 5
sensationalism
American news 41, 98
British newspapers 28
Seven O'clock News 32, 33, 48, 95
short campaigns 23
short-term media effects 13, 101, 113, 148
Six O'clock News 32, 86–7
sleaze
newspaper coverage 28–9
television coverage 74–5
Smith, John 1, 36, 58
social alignments 6–7
social characteristics, news audiences 91–2
social policy
media influence 119, 120, 123t
public's agenda 126–8
social psychological theories, electoral
behaviour 6–7
Social Trends 24, 91
social welfare
Conservative emphasis on 63
party agendas 65
television coverage 75
social-psychological theories, mobilization
16
socialization theory, party loyalties 6
socio-demographic variables, voter
preferences 133, 136
socioeconomic biases, attentive public 5
standards, television news, public evaluation
95t
stop-watch balance
broadcasting 30–1, 130–1

stop-watch balance cont.
    effects of 141–3, 185
    hypothesis 132
    measuring effects of 135
strategic communications
    adoption of 1–2
    Labour victory 9
strategy meetings, Labour campaign 37
Sun 1, 24, 25, 26, 27, 28, 43, 44, 71, 76, 77,
    78, 79, 82, 84, 92, 126, 152, 153, 154, 155,
    156, 157, 164, 166, 168, 183, 184
Sunday Sport 28
Sunday Times 25

tabloidization 98
tactical agendas 62
taxation video, effects of exposure to 121t
technical appendix 187–93
television
    agenda-setting 17
    civic apathy 16
    early studies of 5
    influence of 184
    issue agenda 71
    news coverage 72–6
    persuasive effects 18
    public's agenda 115–16
television news
    audiences, size of 86–9
    experimental study of 190–3
    party preferences
        core hypotheses 131–2
        evidence from public opinion 143–9
        impact of 136–41
        mediating variables 132–4
        operational measures 134–6
        stop-watch balance, effects of 141–3
    public evaluation 94t
    standards of, public evaluation 95t

viewers, profile of 90–3
Thatcher, Margaret 24
time allocation, party broadcasts 30, 44–5
Times 24, 25, 26, 27, 28t, 34, 44, 71, 76, 77,
    78, 79, 126, 152, 156, 157, 159, 166
timing, voting decisions 178, 179t
trivial infotainment 98
trust, media impact on 108–9

United States
    media impact 98
    news coverage, public priorities 114
uses and gratifications approach 48

video experiments, agenda setting 116–18
video-malaise theories 15–16, 97–9, 112
videos, experimental study 190–3
vote switching, newspaper readership
    158–62
voters
    cynicism 140
    media influence 134–6, 182–4
votes
    newspaper readership 155–6
    see also flow of the vote
voting
    behaviour, academic surveys 47–9
    decisions, timing of 178, 179t
    intentions, changes during campaigns
        173–5
    social alignments 6–7

waverers
    campaign process 17
    media influence 132
    minimal effects theory 100
    party propaganda 85
Week in Politics, A 32, 49, 87